INDIAN CASES IN HARVARD GRAMMAR

MANAGEMENT CASES WITH INTERNATIONAL ACCOLADES

PROF DR AJIT PATIL

This book is dedicated to a Phoenix that rose from ashes. A lady who is just like a 'Next Door girl' but also a role model. Rose to the level of Managing Director of a leading bank in Mumbai from clerical grade while being a perfect home-maker. She demonstrates the power of talent, hard work, loyalty, integrity, and faith. A lady who is successful at work and also at home. An ideal daughter, wife, and mother who secured prizes as the best employee and team leader several times. She is an icon who sings while on the job, and her song is genuine and inspiring.

She was always a topper in her school with at least the lead of 10% over the number two of the class. She secured 90%+ in the 10th board exam missing the rank in the Maharashtra board by just 2 marks. She wanted to be a Charter Accountant. But there was closure in the company where her father worked as a Materials Manager. She decided to work. She was barely 18. She appeared for the bank clerk exam. The eligibility was 12th grade but the bank would recruit only graduates. She was just a 12th-grade pass then. But she stood the first rank in the qualifying written test among 5000 applicants. She got selected for the junior most grade. She got admitted to the prestigious Mumbai college for B Com. But due to her job, she could attend classes only on Mondays. Still, she secured the first rank in the college of brilliant students. (Exactly after 30 years her only daughter also secured the first rank in the same college and also secured the Gold medal with the first rank in the entire Mumbai university for B Com). She then worked with the Income Tax department and also in the Central Excise department in the early 1990s. She acquired a Cost Accountant degree alongside, a perfectly American model of earn and learn. Most of the study was done on Mumbai local trains while going and coming back from the office. Her dream was to be a leading banker. She left the Central Govt job to join a reputed bank in Mumbai, post-marriage. She told her husband that she wanted to be a responsible Indian hence restricted only to one daughter.

Her caste was notorious for dowry. She refused to marry on those nagging terms. She never disclosed her savings as a tool to attract a better marriage proposal but booked an apartment with her 8 years of hard-earned savings after a year of marriage. She has the power to mesmerize with her 'ground-to-earth talent'. She always remained a 'better half' although her husband was Engineer-MBA and Ph.D. She inspired, guided, and supported him to complete his Ph.D. while pursuing MBA herself, on weekends. She brought up her daughter as a successful homemaker and kept raising her bar in academics and in the profession.

She is my wife, Arti, a Managing Director of Saraswat Bank, Asia's number one Urban Co-operative Bank, based in Mumbai. This book is dedicated to her.....

Arti is now blessed with a leadership seat in the management of her bank with a very committed board, spearheaded by a young and dynamic Chairman, Hon. Gautam Thakur. Forbes magazine survey identified Saraswat bank as the second-best bank among all Indian banks. They are practicing all the leadership principles and practices that I preach in my classrooms, in LinkedIn articles, in my case studies, and in books. My best wishes to Gautam sir, Arti, Abhijit, board members, and the entire team of Saraswat bank.

Author and his Better-half: Mrs. Arti & Ajit Patil

Contents

Author's Profile

Prof Dr Ajit Patil

Prof Dr Ajit Patil is an accomplished management professional, erudite Management Consultant and Coach, Consummate academician, prolific writer, a celebrated professor of Marketing and Retailing, and a meticulous researcher. He is a Production Engineer with an MBA in Marketing from Sydenham Institute of Management Studies, University of Mumbai.

He is a known writer and was awarded the 'Top Voice on LinkedIn" in 2017. Case Studies written by him have won national and international awards. He has presented them at international conferences in the USA and India. Few of his case studies are published in international journals.

He has been teaching Sales/Marketing and Retailing subjects to MBA students in India and overseas for the last 18 years. He is awarded "Top-75 influential Marketing Professors in the World" in 2020.

He has published 6 books. Some of these books are textbooks for MBA/ MMS students at the University of Mumbai and Pune University.

He is awarded a PhD in Marketing Management (Retailing) by Pune University. He has been associated with the industry for over 30 years. He has worked at the senior management level in international and domestic sales and Marketing after starting his career in manufacturing.

He is actively involved in consultancy. As a Management Consultant, Adviser and Coach he provides advice on Business Strategy, Marketing Planning, and Sales Management to Small and Medium Scale companies (SMEs) and retailers.

He has conducted Management Development Programmes and In-Company training Programmes for Companies like Indian Oil Ltd, Indian Postal Services, Steel Authority of India, Padmakshi Financials, Brenntag India Ltd, Polygel Industries, etc. He regularly conducts Sales Training Programmes for the field staff, sales managers, and channel partners. He has taught in Faculty Development Programmes on Case Study teaching and writing.

He has travelled extensively in the USA, UK, Germany, France, Netherlands, Belgium, China, Fiji, Samoa and Tonga for work, research and teaching. He has done extensive proprietary post-doctoral research on the global retailers in the USA, China, Europe and Hong Kong besides the study of the Indian retail sector as a part of his Ph D.

He is a member of the American Marketing Association (AMA) and North American Case Research Association (NACRA) which are associations of marketing professionals and management professors, respectively, based in America. He stays in Thane (a Mumbai suburb) in India.

Mobile: +91 9819943643
e-mail: ajitpatilmumbai@yahoo.co.in
LinkedIn: https://www.linkedin.com/in/prof-dr-ajit-patil-mumbai-india-56281b1a/

22 August 2022

Statutory Warning For Protection Of The Intellectual Rights

Stop! Read This Page First....

Yes, I mean it. I want you to develop a context before beginning to read this book.

This book requires you to do your homework before flipping to the next pages. First of all, you must define your objective. Why are you reading it? Do you want to read it so that will be a good manager? or you are a leadership aspirant who is looking for a parachute that can drop you directly to the top? In either case, this book is useful to you.

This book is my effort to support companies and leaders in their endeavor of leadership and management development. The rationale here is to develop leadership and management by developing decision-making skills. But such efforts must follow certain steps and we can jump up the ladder.

Are Leadership and Management different?

Leadership and management are strikingly similar but distinctly different. The leader provides a purpose, sets up the mission, and takes you to a virtual world called Vision. Leader mesmerizes people and sells them mission, vision, and purpose. People want to follow the leader. They want to be with him and follow his/her footsteps. A leader is the 'head of the family' and 'the chief wage earner '. A leader faces the outside world though he is an integral part of the team. A leader is the touch point for all stakeholders and a bridge to the outside world, for his team. A leader provides resources and protects the organizational interests and its people. Hence he is a father figure. Management on the other hand resembles the mother. Management certainly has an 'inward-looking out' view but the primary focus is on internal affairs. It is because a leader takes care of public relations, resources, regulators, strategy, etc whereas the management looks after the daily chores of business, They may call it operations. It doesn't mean a leader and manager have clearly demarcated territories, it only means their focus is different. A leader is a part of the environment, he is answerable to all stakeholders including regulators, investors, suppliers, customers, and even his employees.

Management is answerable to the leader. It stays and works in a structure with systems. A leader makes things effective; Management supports him and adds value by making them efficient. Though management also supports the family (organization) by earning money, it also focuses on the proper utilization and investment of it for the future.

Management development can start from day one of your job, even before that. It orients you to work in the managerial role and equips you with certain skills and knowledge. Though management education can't guarantee a jerk-free ride, it can certainly make it smoother. Management development is about developing the perspective/outlook, learning and mastering managerial skills, and keeping yourself well informed on knowledge about the current (and also emerging and future) events, tools, trends, resources, etc. It is acquiring and updating, skills and knowledge on a continuous basis while nurturing the right attitudes required for successful operations.

Leadership Developmentinvolves grooming/nurturing young leadership talent and honing the experienced resources to be more effective and efficient. Leadership training helps managers to get transformed into leaders. The billion-dollar question is what comes first? The answer is, depends. Yes, it depends on where you are currently in the organization structure. what is your role? what are your prospects and aspirations? How do you are looking at yourself and how do your team and seniors look at you? Above all, are you willing to stake, prepare, contribute, and sacrifice what it takes to be the leader?

Management Development and Leadership Development have certain overlaps. The most important of them is the 'Decision-making skill'. Hence the initial focus of my book publishing is decision-making. I am sold on the method adopted by Harvard Business School for improving decision-making skills of leadership and management. This method is very scientific, rigorous, practical, effective, and efficient. But it needs coachability, diligence, grit, commitment to teamwork, and reading-listening-comprehending ability. It also needs faith in the tools, pedagogy, and commitment to the process.

This book is a case study book. It is written as per the guidelines laid down by Harvard though a few changes have been done to accommodate the Indian learning way. As suggested by Hardvard, you must read a textbook and the book of reading before dealing with the case study book.

The book on the science of decision-making is, "**Decisions: Leader's Footprints- Excellence in Decision-Making through Case Studies**". You can buy it on Amazon (India, USA, UK, Europe, or any other Amazon Global site). Alternatively, you can buy it on Flipkart India or at the Notion Publication website. This book, like a textbook of decision-making science, explains the spirit, ingredients, context, and process to be adopted. It gives a step-by-step method to solve case studies and learn scientific-decision making.

There are two more books. Those are the books of reading. They contain my 75 articles on Leadership and Management. All these articles were appreciated by LinkedIn readers globally.

They were written from the year 20015 to 2022. These books are "**Leadership Kaleidoscope**" and also "**Leadership: From Telescope to Microscope**". Reading these 3 books provides you the context and puts you in a much better position to solve the case studies given in this book. In case of any difficulty do get in touch with me at: ajitpatilmumbai@yahoo.co.in or join me at Hiranandani Estate at Thane for a cup of tea.

Please do write your comments on the Amazon, Flipkart, and Notion Publishing sites. It helps readers to choose the book, helps me to reach more readers, and above all provides live feedback so that certain topics can be added, and refurbished in the forthcoming editions. Wish you a very happy reading.

Prof Dr. Ajit Patil
B - 205 & 206 Eagleridge, Wood Street,
Hiranandani Estate, Thane (West),
India. Pin: 400607
Mobile +91 9819943643

Preface

I began teaching alongside my busy corporate career in 1997. I was barely 32 with five years of work experience in selling and marketing. Actually, it was an accidental entry into academics. Mr. Unnikrishnan was my neighbor and he was the academic administrator at ICWA, the reputed institute of Cost Accountants of India. He was heading the Mumbai chapter and West zone. We used to manage our housing society. Somehow he developed faith in me and offered me a teaching assignment for the senior ICWA class. He was required to look for faculty with engineer-MBA qualifications to teach one management accounting subject, 'Strategic Management'.

Unni convinced me to take 20 sessions of 3 hours each and handed over the syllabus. He even went to adjust my classes to suit my foreign travel as I was into International Marketing and was a heavy traveler. I conducted my sessions at Sydenham college, my alma mater, at Churchgate in South Mumbai.

My students enjoyed my classes and I enjoyed them more. Unni discovered my DNA without knowing that my father was a popular professor in my hometown, Solapur. After I was done with the first spell, Unni insisted to continue for the next semester and next to next and next to next semester. I ventured into academics to help my friend in need and discovered my passion for it. Life is serendipity. How to make God laugh? Tell him your plans..... I always realized he had much better plans for me than I could think of.

My father ran a weekly Marathi paper. I was a columnist there when I was barely 16. My readers loved my writing on socio-political and local issues in Solapur. After I got into Engineering college my writing stopped. It restarted only when I entered academics in early 2000. But my writing became regular in the year 2016-17 when I was received well by LinkedIn editors and readers. It was a gap of 30 years. The award by LinkedIn and awards for my case studies encouraged me to write more. Here I am in 2022 having written 128 articles, hundreds of posts, dozens of cases, and half a dozen books. God knew my plan but I wasn't knowing his.....

My epiphany is that the real growth of a professor is not when he gets into academic administration. In my view, that is diversification (though related). A professor's growth comes when he comes out of the class, and goes into industry. When his preaching in the class gets practiced by professionals on the field. Professor grows in his career when he hammers the thick walls of his class, removes the insights and wisdom from the cages of academics, and takes it to the masses. He has to take it to those who can not come to classes but are eager to take that knowledge. The professor becomes a writer.

The only thing I know is that I want to break the walls of my classroom and take my sharing to the masses. I don't want to be limited to my classroom. Thanks to the internet, LinkedIn, Notion Press Publication, YouTube, podcasts, and other social media, I want to go everywhere. My Gabriel told me only one thing... Recite.... Recite.... and I am going to do precisely that....

The Theme Of The Book

This book is the continuation of my earlier book, 'Decisions: Leader's Footprints - Excellence in Decision-Making Through Case Studies'. The purpose of both books is to develop excellence in leadership and management through decision-making skills. My mission is leadership development, supporting the budding and emerging leaders to get into the leadership saddle, hold on to it and win the war. Excellence in will come from developing problem-solving and decision-making skills to grow leadership wisdom. The earlier book explains what is a case study and how to solve it scientifically. This book provides additional case studies so that decision-making doesn't remain only knowledge but transforms into a skill.

> ***"Knowledge transforms into skill only after practicing and mastering its application."***

This is the objective of this book. Having understood what is a case study and how to solve it (from the earlier book, 'Decisions: Leader's Footprints'), this book provides opportunities to apply that knowledge to develop it into skill. **The skill of solving the case studies is the skill of decision-Making and the skill of decision-making is the skill of leadership.** This is how case studies get connected to leadership development. Harvard Business School founded this method 100 years back and produced thousands of corporate leaders using this method. I have, therefore, chosen this method for learning decision-making and leadership development.

A manager and leader have to be a jack of everything. The decision-making skill should help them to understand any context prevailing in any industry and company. Hence, these cases are cross-industry. They majorly cover pharmacy, automobiles - both two-wheeler and four-wheeler, consumer products, garments, software, retail, and the public sector. They relate to different domains like Marketing, branding, strategy, and operations.

The focus of this book is to develop a cluster of related skills that get synergized to form problem-solving and decision-making skills. There is a separate chapter in this book that deals with this objective by explaining which are those skills and how they supplement each other.

Prologue

CHAPTER ONE

List and Gist of Case Studies

Case Study: 1 - Fixing Fevicol – An Endeavour of Polygel

Publication: -It was published in the international referred management journal, Dimensions in the year 2012. (International Refereed Journal, Dimensions, ISSN 0976-5654 Apr 1, 2012). This case study was written based on my consultancy assignment, as a Strategic Advisor working with CEO and Managing Director.

Company and Brand: - This is a story of a wood adhesive brand, 'Kushal', launched by Polygel Industries (In May 2019 Nerolac Paints formed Joint Venture with Polygel for manufacturing and marketing adhesives, sealants, and construction chemicals).

Subject Area: - Marketing, Branding, Marketing Strategy, Brand Management

Dilemma: - The case study depicts its marketing strategy that succeeded against the might of Fevicol, though in a few niche markets.

Having succeeded in a niche market, the brand aspires for mass marketing with the support of an investment banker. The case study portrays a dilemma about marketing strategy to adopt while migrating to the mass market from the niche market. It is shown as a debate between the CEO of the company and the strategic advisor. CEO pleads to extrapolate the same marketing strategy that fetched results in niche marketing but the strategic advisor is in strong disagreement. He wants to craft a new strategy for mass marketing by radically rehauling the niche marketing strategy. The CEO had his compulsions but the strategic advisor has a strong argument.

Polygel Industries was a young and dynamic organization, manufacturing specialty chemicals. The company was the market leader in 'Telecom Cable Gel' in India. Having succeeded in the wood adhesive industry Polygel successfully snatched its targeted market share from the market leader and Mega brand, 'Fevicol' although in just a few cities, in India. The case study provides a good foundation to understand the nuisances of niche and mass marketing and how strategy crafting could be different. It also explains the strategic compulsions of the CEO who has to sell the strategy to the board of directors. The journal also published the CEO's viewpoint separately along with the case study. A solution provided by a couple of international students in my class at the University of the South Pacific, Fiji is also published in the same issue of the journal making it a truly acknowledged case study in the international arena.

Learning Lessons: - Niche Marketing, Mass Marketing, Marketing Strategy, STP, 4Ps, Unique Selling Proposition (USP), Generic Strategies, differentiation, and Focus.

Case Study 2: - Carving a Niche in a Crowded Market: e-Emphasys ERP

Publication: - The case study was selected by the international referee for the presentation and discussion, in the Marketing Track at the North American Case Research Organisation (NACRA) International Conference, **Orlando, USA**, Oct 2018

Company: - e-Emphasis was on IT consulting services for the BAAN platform, since its inception. Their head office is situated in Cary, North Carolina, USA.

Subject Area: - Marketing Management, Strategy

Dilemma: What should be Mission-2020? Should e-Emphasys remain as an IT services company or it should transform into an IT products company?

Learning Lessons: - Marketing Strategy, Need identification, Niche Marketing, Industry structure, Marketing strategy as per industry structure,

Focus, Start-up, Entrepreneurship, product development. This case is founded on strong primary research. Interviews of the directors and key employees were conducted by the case author himself. A focus group discussion was also used as a part of the research. The company issued a 'case release letter' after deep appreciation of the issues and the plot of the case.

Case Study: 3 - Follower's Dilemma – Indian Pharmacy Warfare

Publication: -This case study was selected and discussed during the North American Case Research Association (NACRA) conference, in **Boston, Massachusetts, USA**, in 2012. It was also published in the Journal of International Case studies of the University of Florida, USA, in 2014. OJICA, Florida International University, USA ISSN 1548 - 5137 · Oct 1, 2014.

Company and Brand: - Piramal Group of Companies led by Ajay Piramal. It relates to Piramal Healthcare, a pharmacy division of the group. This case study is based on my association with the group and inputs from my mentor Late C. M. Hattangadi, earlier Sales Director, Pfizer, then Managing Director, Parke Davis and finally heading the entire Piramal group, including pharma. (Breathed his last, in January 2020, at 90). He was the brain behind the Piramal Groups acquisition strategy and was one of the earliest medical representatives in India to rise to the position of Managing Director. The case study is partly fictionalised to make it interesting to read since it is a long and complex case. The views depicted are attributed to characters as a part of the fiction. The case was developed and written purely with academic intent and only to be used in my strategy class discussion. The last option of pharmacy retail wasn't part of the original discussion. Personifying the views is a part of fiction. But the facts and figures are real-life figures and part of the secondary data research.

Subject Area: - Business Strategy, Strategic Management

Dilemma: - The case discusses a dilemma to decide on the business model to be chosen in the light of the changed pharmacy regulation (patents law). Whether to maintain the status quo and continue on the path or to change over and play second fiddle to multi-national pharmacy giants by accepting the position of the contract manufacturer? The Vice-Chairman further extends the argument by proposing to look into the possibility of entering the 'organized pharmacy retailing'. The case begins with a narration about the diversification of a textile group into a pharmacy and its fast-paced advent. After reaching a point of success, a 5th position in the industry structure within just 15 years the company faces a challenge. India changes from process patents to product patents affecting the prospects of the company in the near future. The case discusses and debates all three options with equal rigor making students difficult to choose the course. It explains how a company can successfully diversify into a completely unrelated field before its business is challenged by a strong development in the macro-environment.

Learning Lessons: - Vision, Mission, Strategy Crafting; Competitive advantages; Diversification- Related, Unrelated; Legal factor and its impact on strategy crafting; Environmental scanning, Cost leadership, Differentiation.

Case Study: 4 - Ridding the Skidding Motorcycle -Bajaj Auto Ltd.

Publication: - The case study was selected by the international referee for the presentation and discussion, in the Marketing Track. It was at the North American Case Research Organisation (NACRA) International Conference held in **Chicago, USA,** in Oct 2017.

Company: - Bajaj Auto Ltd. The leading two and three-wheeler manufacturer in India

Subject Area: - Marketing Management, Marketing Strategy, Brand Management

Dilemma: Should Bajaj Autolaunch scooters in the Indian two-wheeler market or remained focused only on motorcycles?

Related Issues: - The case handles multiple issues, primary and secondary. The key issue of the case is how to respond to the poor sales performance in the domestic motorcycle market. At the same time, how to respond to the change in the macro-environmental factor which pushed scooter sales up but at the cost of over motorcycle sales. The slow response by Bajaj Auto on the major development in the market.

Learning Lessons: - Brand repositioning, umbrella brand, creative disruption/product cannibalization, Porter's generic strategies, product life cycle, etc.

Case Study: 5 - Bajaj Auto- Handling Marketing Myopia

Publication: - The case study was selected by the international referee for the presentation and discussion for International Case Study Conference, (ICSC 2017),held by IBS-Hyderabad, in Hyderabad, on 7th Oct 2017. It won the **First prize** competing with all international cases in all areas of management. The panel of the jury was those in the field of case study writing, from different parts of the world.

Company: - Bajaj Auto Ltd. The leading two and three-wheeler manufacturer in India

Subject Area: - Marketing Management, Marketing Strategy, Brand Management

Dilemma: The case focuses on solving a strong dilemma: Whether to launch an electric scooter or a petrol scooter while re-entering the Indian scooter market?

Learning Lessons: - Stick to knitting, Marketing Myopia, Company orientations toward the marketplace, Product adoption process, flanking strategy, Positioning, Point of difference, AIDA principle, new product launch

Case Study: 6 - How Can Cottonking Expand the Kingdom?

Publication: - This case was selected for the presentation during the 28th Annual Management education conference held at Ranchi, on 27 August

2016, organized by Ranchi University.
It also won the '**Gold Medal**' as the best case written in India during the Annual case study competition held by the Association of Indian Management Schools (AIMS) in 2016.

Company and Brand: - CottonKing, is a Pune-based Men's wear brand that operates through a franchise model with exclusive showrooms in Maharashtra.

Subject Area: - Marketing Management, Retailing, Brand Management

Primary Issue, Dilemma: - How to improve the profitability of Cottonking franchises? How to resolve a channel conflict? Should the margins be increased?

Related Issues: - Should the LinenKing range (new brand) be offered to them? Should the 'CottonQueen' brand be launched exclusively for women?

Learning Lessons: - Estimation of the commercial viability, Breakeven point, Crafting Marketing Strategy, STP, Marketing Mix-4Ps, 5Cs, Ansoff's Matrix

Case Study: 7. Maruti Suzuki – Marketing Plan in turbulent times

Publication: -This case was published in the international referred management journal, Dimensions, ISSN 0976-5654 in Jun 2015.

Company: - This is a case study on Maruti Suzuki, the leader in the Indian car industry with a 50% market share. A research-based case study on the secondary data.

Subject Area: - Marketing Management, Marketing Strategy, Marketing Plan

Dilemma: - Whether to stick to the core brand proposition of 'Compact Petrol Car which offers Value for Money' or explore other untapped market segments?

Related Issues: - Preparing a Marketing Plan for the Market Leader in turbulent times. In 2015 Maruti Suzuki was commanding 50% of the Indian car market. The case discusses critical success factors behind Maruti Suzuki's rise to the market leadership position, in India. It highlights their core competencies which were leveraged to achieve success. In the year 2015, Maruti Suzuki set up a mission to sell 2 million cars a year by 2020, requiring a growth rate of 50% during the next 5 years. The case discusses options available to Maruti Suzuki in the light of the prevailing business environment. It also discusses other related issues and provides data to prepare a Marketing Plan.

Learning Lessons: - Core Competency, Focus, Marketing Plan

Case Study: 8. Maruti Suzuki: Defending the Market Leadership

Publication: - This case was selected for the presentation during the 29th Annual Management education conference held at Hotel Orchid, Pune, on 23rd August 2017, organized by the Pune University Department of Management Sciences (PUMBA). It won the '**Gold Medal**' as the best case written in India during the Annual case study competition held by the Association of Indian Management Schools (AIMS) in 2017.

Company: - This is a case study on Maruti Suzuki, the leader in the Indian car industry with a 50% market share. A secondary research-based case study.

Subject Area: - Marketing Management, Marketing Strategy, Brand Management

Dilemma: The management was not sure whether to keep the old and new distribution networks as mutually complementary, as it was decided, or make them mutually competing. Both options had strong pros and cons. The decision could be defined by aligning the product strategy with the distribution strategy.

Related Issues: - How to defend the leadership position in the 3rd largest market of the world, competing against 7 global 'Fortune-500' giants with bigger muscle? The marketing strategy was required to sell premium cars to existing customers and existing cars to premium customers.

Learning Lessons: - Explains the well-crafted marketing strategy of one of the most successful market leaders by –developing a global perspective, highlights the cornerstones of the strategy, identifying strengths/ challenges, explaining the competitive position, macro, and microenvironment, How the market leader defends its strong position by - combining penetration, product development, and market development strategies. (Ansoff's Matrix), Innovations and Investments, Blocking the strong competitive moves. Covers marketing concepts like Marketing Warfare Strategies, Defensive Strategies, Industry structure, Strategies for the market leader, Market penetration strategy, SWOT analysis, Environmental Analysis, Distribution strategies, Exclusive distribution, Channel Conflict

Case Study: 9. Branding Smart City: Solapur

Publication: - The case study was selected by the international referee for the presentation and discussion, in the Marketing Track. It was at the North American Case Research Organisation (NACRA) International Conference held in **Chicago, USA**, in Oct 2017.

Company: - It relates to the Solapur Municipal Corporation is a part of a smart city project of the Govt. of India. The government of India selected Solapur in the first list of proposed 20 smart cities in India.

Subject Area: - Marketing Management, Marketing Strategy, Brand Management

Dilemma: - In 2015 India started working on the 'Smart City' project. It was a smart way of handling large-scale urbanization and improving the quality of life by meeting the increased needs and expectations of residents with the use of technology. Local bodies can use Smart City development to increase the efficiency of services offered and reduce their expenses.

Solapur was shortlisted by the Govt of India, among the 20 cities to be considered for the Smart City Development Project, in the first round. A few global cities like New York, London, and Mumbai created a versatile brand identity by developing many facets of the brand personality. Other cities like Las Vegas, Disneyland, and Rotterdam focused on just one 'Unique Selling Proposition' for the city branding. Supriya's (the protagonist in the case), the dilemma was, which model of city branding should be chosen for Solapur?

Related Issues: - How to bring back the lost glory of Solapur city, which brand identity should be chosen while branding Solapur city? To re-position Solapur city and create a brand. Branding Solapur was important to provide an identity to the ailing city and attract investments to create jobs. Such employment would bring back economic prosperity resulting from better living conditions and an increased standard of living for the citizens. Radical rethinking was required to develop the 'Brand Solapur' by re-positioning it in the light of the emerging opportunities.

Learning Lessons: - Vision, Mission, City branding, Brand repositioning, Brand identity, Brand Image, Brand essence, brand personality, brand associations, Consumer franchise, Smart city, Smart City project in India. This case is written with three objectives: First, teach concepts of 'Branding' through an illustrative example. Second, teach how to go about solving a decision-making case that has a strong dilemma. Third, how to apply marketing/branding concepts, used in product/services marketing, to smart city projects and urban development. Readers may find this case interesting because it demonstrates the application of branding and marketing concepts to a new area. Usually, those concepts are learned through illustrations of products or services. City branding and marketing are neither of those. The radically different aspects of applying branding concepts will help to test and improve their marketing knowledge.

Case Study: 10. **Implementing Smart City Vision: Solapur**

Publication: - The case study was selected by the international referee for the presentation and discussion, in the Strategy Track. It was at the North American Case Research Organisation (NACRA) International Conference held in **Las Vegas, USA**, in Oct 2016.

Company: - It relates to the Solapur Municipal Corporation is a part of a smart city project of the Govt. of India. The government has formed a special body to implement the smart city project, in every city.

Subject Area: - Strategy, Strategic Management, Project Management

Dilemma: - In 2015 India started working on the 'Smart City' project. It was a smart way of handling large-scale urbanization and improving the quality of life by meeting the increased needs and expectations of residents with the use of technology. Local bodies can use Smart City development to increase the efficiency of services offered and reduce their expenses. Solapur was shortlisted by the Govt of India, among the 20 cities to be considered for the Smart City Development Project, in the first round. Supriya's (the protagonist in the case) worry was about how effectively would the great vision be implemented. Was the strategy to implement the smart city project through a quasi-corporate institution, Special Purpose Vehicle (SPV) right? Or should it be implemented through Solapur Municipal Corporation (SMC)? SVP was answerable to investors, but SMC was represented by democratically elected representatives and which was accountable to the citizens who voted for the local governance. It was important to redefine the role of Solapur Municipal Corporation (SMC). How to take care of the overlaps in the authorities and responsibilities of the SPV and the SMC was the primary issue.

Related Issues: - Financing was also the major issue, Supriya was also looking for attracting private equity and Foreign Direct Equity (FDI) options. The issue was to choose between Private Public partnerships (PPP) or to go for soft loans. Where the university graduates would be employed? What will be done to employ engineers who were getting produced in big numbers? What were the steps to curb brain drain? How do develop local trade and businesses? These were the unanswered questions.

Learning Lessons: - Vision, Mission, Vision implementation, Strategy and Tactics, Environmental Scanning, and Project financing.

CHAPTER TWO

Case Learning - Not Case Teaching

The Case study method as pedagogy is like medication. One has to understand the rationale and strictly follow the spirit behind every step, in totality, in order to be effective. The critical success factors for the case study pedagogy are -

- Relevance of the case study to the curriculum in general and the subject in particular.
- Quality of the case in terms of dilemma, context, plot, articulation, facts, adequacy, the authenticity of data, external validity, diction, and flow.
- Availability and quality of the teaching notes.
- The expertise of the faculty conducting the class discussion.
- Attitudes, talent, coachability, zeal, diligence, and purpose of the students.
- Diversity, Interpersonal chemistry, class dynamics, and classroom management.
- Class layout, availability of discussion rooms, and other infrastructure.

All these factors are explained in the further my book, "**Decisions: Leader's Footprints - Excellence in Decision-Making Through Case Studies**", at length. (It is available on Amazon, Flipkart, and Notion Press site for sale.) This book is a part of the series of books that I have written for 'Leadership Development'. I have adopted a Harvard method. At Harvard Business School for every subject, they provide three books: Text Book, a Book of reading, and a Case Study Book.

- The textbook covers theories, concepts, models, numerical methods, etc. It covers most of the syllabus for that subject. Harvard publishing comes out with such course modules (or notes in Indian terms) by encouraging the faculty members to write them concisely.
- Book of reading is a nice collection of articles and papers related to that subject and syllabus. It provides the application angle along with a critique.
- The third book is the book of Case studies. Those are written by the faculty members based on their research and consultancy work. These cases are published in the Harvard Business Review. These cases are carefully mapped to suit the syllabus.

The answer key to these cases is called Teaching Notes (TN) or Instructor's Manual IM). TN or IM are only given to the subject faculty who are teaching that course. Professors are expected to sub-consciously lead the classroom discussions in the direction suggested by the case study author in the TN.

"There is no single standard answer for the issues highlighted in most of the cases. In that case, the answer will be obvious. In case of a dilemma, any solution will always have a flip side or side effects. It is the call of the decision-maker to make a choice based on his situation, decision-making parameters, and above all, the available options. The optimum answer is required to be synthesized in the classroom. But a lot of homework is required to be done before the class begins."

Students need to read the case 3 to 4 times and prepared their personal solutions to the issues. Then they need to form small groups (about 7 students in each group). The small group has to brainstorm and prepare their common group solution. With this much preparation, students are well equipped to participate in the class discussion on the case study.

"The faculty is at an advantage because he knows the thought, purpose, additional resources, expected questions, and answer keys to them. The authors equip the faculty (through IM/TN) to conduct the class discussion on the case study. But faculty are not expected to super-impose authors' views on students. He/she has to explore the fresh and creative minds of students. Faculty can't be the 'Lecturer' she has to be

the facilitator and coordinator and at times, controller, if the discussion gets derailed. "

The faculty has to take the class in two phases. He has to initially cover the divergent views. It calls for inviting different views from different sub-groups or students making them substantiate their claims with the data given in the case. Students aren't allowed to consider any other facts from books, journals, papers, or other resources. They have to base their argument only on the facts and data given in the case study text and annexures.

The fundamental difference between case study discussion in the Indian classes and Harvard classes is that, In India, we focus on 'teaching' the case study. At Harvard, they facilitate 'learning' it. We have an obsession with the solution. They want to master the process. We manufacture managers they produce leaders because managers emphasize domain knowledge and quick-fix solutions. Leaders explore possibilities, probabilities, and the joyful journey toward finding the sustainable, feasible, optimum, and acceptable solution rather than just trying to out-fox others with some answer key more than the solution.

Since the class was already divided into a few sub-groups and that sub-group had developed consensus before the class began, there isn't chaos in the class. There would be 12 to 15 clusters of opinions in the class depending on the class strength and the number of formal sub-groups formed earlier. Finally, the class listens, considers, and ponders all the views. It discusses, debates, and deliberates on the primary and secondary issues in the light of the given facts and apt decision-making parameters while the faculty maintains the discussion on track, triggers questions to instigate thoughts, and adds key inputs to lead the discussion in the direction desired by the authors. At the end of the 90-minute class discussion, they arrive at the class solution which is the collective wisdom of the entire class. The sharper the differences longer it takes to resolve them and the better will be the learning from it.

"At Harvard, the case study discussion is not just an event but is an experience or journey that leads everyone toward excellence in decision-making. It is partly skill but mostly wisdom of leadership and management."

CHAPTER THREE

How is the Case Study Written?

The excellence in the case writing is the function of: -

- The authenticity, complexity, and generalization possibility of the business dilemma.
- Inclusion of facts that are relevant and required for the decision.
- Quality of dilemma, issues, and plot.
- Quality of fiction, diction, articulation, flow, or in other words quality of the write-up. While reading the case study the readers should feel as if he is reading fiction.
- Possibility of developing a number and quality of alternative solutions to the dilemma.
- Relevance of the decision-making parameters.
- Clarity on mission, vision, core values, structure, policy, systems, and non-negotiable principles of the organization.
- Apt depiction of the cultural context, business environments, leadership style, regulation, and management functioning.
- Diversity of the industry, issues, and dilemma.

I have focused on these parameters while writing the case studies.

As explained here the quality of the case study is of paramount importance. Care has been taken to write case studies in different industries like the two-wheeler industry, apparel industry, pharmaceutical industry, software industry, automobile industry, branding of the city, and the smart city project.

CHAPTER FOUR

Decision-Making and Problem Solving

Leadership is not only about making choices though decision-making is the most important leadership function. These are other important facets of leadership. Read my books, "**Leadership Kaleidoscope**" and "**Leadership: From Telescope to Microscope**" (books of reading for the course on decision-making). They are a collection of 75 articles that highlight different facets of leadership.

Likewise, decision-making is also not just one skill. It requires a set of skills. Many of them are supplementary and many are opposite in nature. Meaning it would be difficult to find people with both such skills together. Harvard Business School pedagogy understands this fact and addresses this aspect through well-laid down guidelines for writing and discussing the case studies. Skipping any step will miss the development of a certain skill. Hence it is very important to follow their methodology in the spirit. The different skills that are developed or honed by the case study method and those are part of the decision-making skill are as follows: -

- Skill to understand materiality - It is the ability to segregate things based on their importance and highlight those which are more important. Such skill is very important because it helps a person or organization to focus attention, resources, and energy on those important things or issues. This skill helps in prioritizing things so that important and urgent things can be attended to first saving costs, time, and energy and reducing losses. The case study method embeds key issues by mixing and matching them with other less important or less urgent things. This skill helps to identify those material issues as key elements, called primary or key issues requiring immediate decisions. It also helps to identify other related issues and also non-issues that have no bearing on the final decision, costs, and losses but they are minor irritants and required to be resolved even if they have lower priority.

- Analyzing skills - examining something to find out what it is and how it works
- Logical skills - Logical thinking is the skill to use reasoning to allow to come to a viable solution. This skill allows one to accurately analyze a situation, make connections between data, and use the information gathered to solve the issue or dilemma.
- Comprehending skills - It is skilled relating to reading, listening, or absorbing things from sensory organs, and constructing bridges to understand the meaning. It is about understanding the articulation, diction, and tone, summarizing the understanding, and paraphrasing it.
- Paraphrasing skills - are an ability to define things so that they become easy to understand. It is an ability to express the meaning in different words so that those who are stuck with a phrase or words will understand it better.
- Problem-solving skills - It involves identifying issues that are creating problems. Understanding their ramifications and gravity of importance, arranging them in the order of importance and urgency, developing solutions to resolve them, and ensuring that they won't reoccur or can be handled easily if reoccur.
- Skills to infer - This is an ability to draw conclusions using the logical skills that establish relationships. Inference involves a focus on key parameters because of the major trouble or variation.
- Skills to synthesize: - It includes collecting and arranging different things to form a meaningful body of knowledge. It involves careful selection of those parts and creatively arranging them in a structure to create a synergetic impact, as that things mutually supplement each other to form a larger and more meaningful structure.

CHAPTER FIVE

Fixing Fevicol: An Endavor of Polygel

It was 3rd March 2010. Supriya[1], Marketing Head of Polygel Industries was sitting with Nishant, the Strategic Advisor, at the Mumbai office, in India. They were discussing plans to acquire the number two position in the Indian furniture adhesive market. The dilemma was whether to extrapolate success in the niche market, to the $ 400 million mass-market or make a paradigm shift in strategy.

Company Profile

Polygel Industries was a young and dynamic organization, manufacturing specialty chemicals. The company was the market leader in 'Telecom Cable Gel' in India and had established a strong brand name within a short span. Products were also being exported to Europe, Middle East Asia, and the Far East. The core business philosophy of the company was, "Recognizing the specific needs and delivering tangible value to customers". Polygel started as a single product company, manufacturing cable gel for optical fiber cable manufacturers, in the mid-nineties. It developed a fairly good basket of products by 2006. Most of these products were adhesives for industrial markets. The company successfully developed a customer base in the automobile, engineering, and footwear industry, in India, for Synthetic Rubber (SR) and Polyurethane (PU) adhesives.

Senior Team Members

Mr. Shah, the young Managing Director was leading the Polygel team. He was a first-generation industrialist. He started Polygel with his twin brother.

They were in their early twenties when Polygel was incorporated in 1995. Capt. Raichand, a veteran of the Indian Navy and known golfer, was the chairman of the board. His contacts helped the company during the initial critical phase. Polygel commissioned a state-of-the-art factory at Silvassa near Mumbai. The head office was situated in the Fort area of South Mumbai which was the business district of the commercial capital of India. In 2003, Supriya joined Polygel as the Head of Marketing. She was Engineer-MBA, IIT-Delhi product, and was having 15 years of experience, in Industrial Marketing, with multi-national engineering and petro-chemical companies like L& T, Cummins, and Royal Dutch Shell. By 2006-2007 Supriya could attract qualified and experienced professionals to form the team Polygel with appropriate structure and systems.

Product Portfolio: Cable Gel to SR

Polygel product portfolio included Gel for telecommunication cables, Titanates (for paints, printing inks, and coatings), Adhesives and Sealants, Specialty Products like Mould Release Agents, Wood Finishes, etc. Till 2003 Cable Gel remained in the number one position in the sales mix of the company, thereafter, Polygel realized the demand-supply gap which prevailed in the SR adhesives industrial market. It was due to the short supply of synthetic rubber (SR), the key raw material. There were only four manufacturers of SR, globally. It was a minor product from refineries and not on the priority list of the major petrochemical refineries, due to its tiny market size compared to other refinery products. As a result, SR became a supplier-driven market with unfair commercial terms for buyers. In India, the price realization was better in the retail market for SR adhesives than in industrial markets. The market leader, Pidilite Industries, diverted its industrial business to retail. Industrial customers were facing problems like poor availability, inconsistency in quality, and frequently rising price. Polygel started focusing on SR adhesives. By 2006, SR Adhesives replaced Cable gel as the flagship product of Polygel.

Contract Manufacturing

In 2004 Polygel embarked on a contract manufacturing business by manufacturing SR Adhesives for Kores India Ltd. This initiative was taken to ensure capacity utilization of the Silvassa factory with assured cash flow.

In 2006, the need was felt to enhance the production capacity for the adhesives. This was mainly due to the success of the company in the SR adhesives industrial markets. Secondly, multinational company, Huntsman offered the opportunity to manufacture Polyvinyl Acetate (PVA) Adhesives (also called furniture adhesives or white adhesives, or wood adhesives).

Huntsman wanted to encash on the brand franchise created by its brand, 'Araldite' but did not want to get into production. 'Araldite' was an epoxy-based adhesive and was suitable for quick fixing. It was the number one brand, in its category, nationally. Almost every hardware store in India was selling the brand. Since these shops were also selling furniture adhesive, The Company saw an opportunity for brand extension. Huntsman was prepared to share the technical knowledge with Polygel Industries for sourcing of their proposed new brand, 'Araldite- Karpenter'. Polygel started manufacturing the PVA adhesives for furniture. For one year they manufactured it exclusively for Araldite only.

PVA: The Furniture adhesive

Launched in 1959, 'Fevicol' was the first white glue introduced in India. Initially, the Fevicol brand was launched as easy-to-use glue for carpenters. Before Fevicol, adhesives made from animal fat, colloquially known as Saresh, were used. These had to be boiled before application. Apart from being a cumbersome exercise, the fumes that emanated had a bad odor.

Fevicol came as a welcome change. Furniture adhesive was a synthetic resin adhesive, easy to apply, even non-experienced carpenters could work with it comfortably. It could be used in bonding various materials. Furniture adhesive strongly bonded wood, plywood, laminate, veneers, MDF, and all types of boards, cork, etc. It was also used in sports goods manufacturing and bookbinding. The bond provided handling strength in ten hours and cured fully in 24 hours to become strong. If hit hard on the bond the wood gave away without affecting the bond. Owing to the success of Fevicol, the company launched extensions to the brand, like Fevikwik, Fevwastik, Fevicryl, Fevibond, and others.

The Furniture Adhesive Market in India

In India, customized furniture was preferred over readymade. Furniture was made of plywood, laminated on top with designs. Laminate manufacturing companies supply laminate sheets of 8 feet by 4 feet size with colorful designs and various thicknesses. Plywood manufacturing companies supply plywood sheets of different sizes and thicknesses. The end customer assigns the furniture work to a carpenter who was referred to as a 'contractor'. Work was either allotted only by paying labor charges to carpenters or they took it on a turnkey basis. In either case, carpenters bought plywood sheets from the plywood store of their choice. Laminate colors and designs are selected by the end customer. The furniture manufacturing activity was carried out by the carpenters, on-site, with the help of carpenters. After the plywood was cut into pieces the laminates were glued on the exterior surface so that the furniture looked attractive and lasted longer. Sometimes veneer was glued to plywood instead of laminate to give natural look. Furniture adhesive was used to glue laminates and veneer to plywood. That was the largest market segment for PVA adhesives hence it was commonly referred to as 'furniture adhesive'. The furniture adhesive market in India was $ 400 million. There was a proper industry structure in place. Pidilite Industries was the market leader with 'Fevicol' as its flagship brand. 'Jeevanjor' and 'Araldite-Karpenter' were the only national players other than Fevicol. Others were regional players focusing on certain geographies. The furniture adhesive retail marketwas segmented based on buying behaviour. Carpenters were habituated to buying furniture adhesive in large pack sizes, along with the plywood, from the same plywood stores. However, for top-ups, they preferred hardware stores. Top-up quantities were hardly 10 to 15% of the total adhesive requirement and were bought in small pack sizes. Therefore, hardware stores preferred to store 2 kilograms (Kg), 1kg, and half a kg furniture adhesive jar. Plywood stores preferred stocking bigger jars of sizes 50 kg, 30 kg, 20 kg, 10 kg and 5 kg. Stationery shops also sold white (PVA) adhesives but in very small pack sizes. The most sold stock-keeping units were tube packs with less than 125 grams quantity. The product for that segment was of lower grade and in liquid form rather than in cream form. The higher viscosity indicated a lower quality. Paint shops sold small quantities of furniture adhesives (PVA). It was mixed with some paints to improve the bonding. Only a few paint shops stocked furniture adhesives.

Fevicol: Bond with elephant muscle

Besides the first mover and product innovation advantage, consistent quality, widespread distribution networks, excellent customer relations and award-winning advertising had given Fevicol legendary status. It became the generic name for the product category. The illiterate carpenters referred furniture adhesive product category as 'Fevicol'. Any brand of furniture adhesive was referred to with 'Col' as a suffix. Fevicol enjoyed more than two-thirds of the market share despite aggression from many national and multinational companies. Two elephants pulling a joint in opposite directions was the brand mascot hence Fevicol brand got strongly associated with elephants, in the minds of carpenters and retailers. Fevicol was ranked number one in the Household Care segment of the Most Trusted Brands in India for 2007-08 by the Economic Times and overall ranked the 20th Most Trusted Brand. Pidilite, the makers of Fevicol, ranks 131st among India's Top 500 listed companies (ET 500, published by the Economic Times in March 2007).

Taking the elephant by the trunk

There was hardly any brand occupying the number two position, nationally. Vam Organics Ltd attempted to get into the 'number two' slot with its brand 'Vamicol', in the early eighties. They were the first adhesive brand in India to advertise on national television channels. Fevicol responded by higher advertisement spending and with better creativity. Fevicol foiled Vamicol efforts to acquire the number two spot. Vam Organics was part of Delhi based Bhartiya group, it changed its name to Jubilant Chemicals as they diversified into Biotechnology, Pharmaceutical and many other chemical businesses. With failure, they changed Vamicol with another umbrella brand, 'Jeevanjor'. It again tried to take Fevicol head-on but was soon exhausted and decided to focus on the pharmaceutical business. Stationery giant, Kores India Ltd (Brand name - 'Kores Vishwas') and the multinational paint company, ICI Paints Ltd (Brand name: 'Woodlock') tried to challenge Fevicol but could not succeed. They remained restricted only to the Western Indian and Southern Indian markets respectively. Both the brands were sold by their creators within five years from inception.

'Woodlock' was bought by another multinational company, Henkel-Loctite, a global leader in adhesives. They soon realized the acute need to create an entirely new distribution channel through plywood stores as their adhesive was sold through the hardware stores. Henkel finally sold 'Woodlock' to Pidilite Industries. Thus, Fevicol swallowed one more possible threat. Huntsman USA also jumped into the market with their brand 'Araldite-Karpenter'. They thought they could get distribution synergies. The company adopted a 'Push type' selling strategy with attractive schemes to retailers. Hardware stores supported the brand with the hope that the Araldite brand magic will work in furniture adhesive as well. But the brand could not create a pull in the market from carpenters as they were not the target customers for Araldite products and hence lacked brand loyalty. Huntsman couldn't extend the brand image to the new product category. They couldn't create space in the minds of carpenters, the decision-makers and shelves of plywood stores, the main distribution channel. Their focus on hardware stores and overemphasis on the push-type strategy led to stagnation of sales. The brand could barely survive, that too only in a few geographic pockets. Looking at the quantities sold through their distribution channels, the plywood manufacturers also attempted to launch furniture adhesive. Century Ply Ltd and Kit Ply Ltd were respected names in the plywood business, in India. These companies launched 'Century Adhesives' and 'Kit-Col' respectively. They took the outsourcing route. The small-scale manufacturers could not match Fevicol quality. There were quality issues in the earlier phases. The companies were over-dependent on the push given by their retail counters. The demand generation support from the brand owners was lacking. They failed to provide concrete reasons for shifting Fevicol loyalty. They were just 'me-too' products without unique selling propositions (USP). They did not draw lessons from the failures of others against the mighty power of Fevicol. Their efforts were perceived as half-hearted. Fevicol proved to be too tough to be taken head-on by other national players. However local brands fought successfully in certain pockets. 'Bluecoat' from Ahmadabad, 'Falcofix' from Rajasthan, and 'Unicol' from Nasik could snatch the leadership position from Fevicol in respective geographies. However, they could not replicate their success even in adjoining markets. The factors that emerged as dominant in the study of the furniture adhesive market were: Brand strength, Channel relationships, Promotion Schemes, and Distribution reach.

The successful regional players leveraged local relationships with retailers. Regional brands offered lucrative trade promotional schemes to generate the retail push. They reduced the retailers' stocks by offering faster deliveries of smaller order quantities and extended credit terms reducing the capital blocked by retailers in stock. Their sales team regularly visited the sites and ensured redemption of the money-back token scheme for carpenters. Fevicol was weak in these areas. The local players exploited the complacency of the Fevicol sales force and the lack of a localized approach. However, most of the carpenters were immigrant laborers from Rajasthan, UP, and a few other states. They spoke Hindi and not the local language, Marathi. They took off on the 'no-moon day' and visited the temple of Lord Vishwakarma (considered the God of artisans, particularly carpenters, who worked for Indra, the King of Gods, and created heaven.)

Polygel - Why Retail?

Polygel entered the wood-adhesive industry but not the market, as a contract manufacturer for the India division of Huntsman, USA. Huntsman had a funfair start. They spent a couple of years filling warehouses, godowns, and retail shelves. However, poor offtake at the retail stores stagnated their sales thereafter. They lacked relationships in the plywood distribution channel as hardware was their main distribution channel traditionally. Orders from Huntsman shrunk creating a capacity utilization crisis for Polygel. The capacity created for furniture adhesive could not be used for any other product due to differences in the processing technology. Polygel was not having any other order for contract manufacturing of furniture adhesive. Due to the industrial recession, SR adhesive sales also stagnated and there was mounting pressure on price realization. It became mandatory for Polygel to look for a new product. The primary study indicated that the furniture adhesive retail market was 250% bigger than the industrial market. Margins in retailing were higher both at gross and net levels. Polygel decided to get into the furniture adhesive retail market. But the entry barriers were high. The company was exclusively in Business to Business (B2B) selling and was lacking retailing competencies, exposure, and infrastructure. Supriya remembered her good old friend, Nishant, who spent enough years in retailing. Nishant was pursuing Doctoral research in retailing. Nishant joined the Polygel team as Head of Retail operations.

Nishant's research competency was useful to the company in the market study and in devising a strategy for the retail venture. Supriya and Nishant jointly devised the strategy for entry into the furniture adhesive market based on the research conducted by Nishant, in 25 cities of India, immediately after his joining. Some of the findings of his study were as follows:

1. Plywood retailers were not earning their margins in the case of "Fevicol ". Their tactic was to use Fevicol as a "Loss Leader" product to create a 'value for money' image of their store in the minds of carpenters. This was done because Fevicol was the only common brand, available across the plywood stores, and it was difficult to compare quality-price equations of different brands and grades of plywood. In most of the markets retailers were selling Fevicol even below their landed price as a result there was a lot of discontentment in the minds of retailers.
2. Retailers were not pushing other brands of furniture adhesives even though they were getting better margins. Retailers knew carpenters well. They were so loyal to Fevicol that, should the retailer push some other brand. and feared that the carpenters may not even buy plywood and other items from their store. Retailers would only stock brands when contractors and carpenters demanded it.
3. The influence of the retailer was restricted to only a few carpenters.
4. In every market, there was a certain number of contractors who were getting the major contracts for furniture and other woodworks. This number was usually in two digits. Every such contractor consumed at least 300 Kilograms of furniture adhesive every month. In some cases, this figure was as high as 2 to 3 Tons. In Nasik, 60 contractors were buying around 12,000 kilograms of furniture adhesive every month, which was one-fourth of the total furniture adhesive retail sales in Nasik.
5. There were 3 communities of carpenters: **Vishwakarma:** They are originally from the Hindi Speaking Regions of India. **Jangid:** Originally from Rajasthan, and preferred for their quality workmanship. **Aachari:** Originally from Tamil Nadu, speak Tamil, and work in southern India. These carpenter communities were minorities and had good community bonding. They were religious by nature and went to the community temple positively on 'No moon day'. Carpenters could be classified as contractors, 'A', 'B' and 'C' Categories.

6. Furniture adhesive was usually distributed through the following channels:

- Plywood Retailers
- Hardware Stores
- Stationery Marts
- Paint Shops
- Supermarkets and other grocery stores

The major distribution was through the plywood retailer network followed by the hardware stores. In the stationery segment, the brand preference of the user was very critical and a relatively lower grade of furniture adhesive was sold. The distribution through paint shops was a characteristic only in certain cities. The quantities per store were poor in the case of supermarkets and other grocery stores.

7. The end customers hardly played an influential role in the buying process. Carpenters were the decision-makers. 'C' category carpenters, who could be referred to as 'Applicators', were also influencers and could make the contractors or "A" category carpenter change their brand preferences. Fevicol had not changed or advanced the basic furniture adhesive category. Even though their 'Marine' and 'Speedex' versions were targeted toward quick-drying, the sales volume was low and the product was not widely available. No competitor had ever come out with the theme of a superior product than Fevicol. The focus of the competition was either on the price or the sales promotion schemes targeted towards 'B' and 'C' category carpenters and retailers.

Any brand whose maximum retail price (MRP) was low could be perceived as an inferior furniture adhesive. Successful local players had MRP higher than or equal to that of Fevicol. They focused heavily on the "Tokens in the packs" sales promotion strategy. It was seen that plywood stores were the primary channel for the distribution of furniture adhesive to the carpenters. Carpenter bought furniture adhesive along with plywood and other wood, in bulk quantity. Only the top-ups are bought, in small pack sizes, through the hardware store.

Investment by Venture Capital Fund

Supriya and Nishant were eager to launch a furniture adhesive brand. They studied the market carefully and also understood competitors' strategies leading to success and failure. They developed an understanding of consumer buying behavior, the power of influencers, and channel preferences prevailing in the furniture adhesive market, in India. Supriya knew that such a venture, rather a misadventure against one of the strongest brands in India, would need a strong investment with deep pockets. She actively started looking for a strategic investor. Polygel came across a venture capital division of a reputed bank from India. The senior team could convince a Venture Capital Division of Canara Bank, to invest in the retail initiative of Polygel. The bank not only provided requisite equity but also supported additional debt on liberal terms.

Marketing Strategy

Realizing that consistent quality was the main reason behind Fevicol's brand loyalty, Polygel decided to go for tight production standards. The factory head was confident on these grounds and the team could trust him because of the track record of contract manufacturing for Huntsman which went through without any quality issues. Polygel's strategy was based on the strong foundation of its contract manufacturing experience, analysis of the failures of national and multinational companies against Fevicol, analysis of factors behind the success of some local brands, and the insights provided by Nishant's research.

Nishant opened up his strategy presentation to the board with the statement, "Marketing strategy is making decisions on STP and 4 Ps, by understanding 5Cs." Supriya provided him with important exposure to preparing strategy documents. The strategy document was made with STP (Segmentation, Targeting, and Positioning) and 4 Ps (Product, Price, Place, Promotion) and after a critical analysis of 5Cs (Customers, Company, Competitors, Collaborators, and the Context)[2]. Polygel decided to use the 'Flanking Strategy' for Kushal. The idea was to avoid ire from the market leader while the brand was in its infancy. It also decided to use a combination of the 'Focus' and 'Differentiation' strategies suggested by Michael Porter.

The focus would be on a niche market that included only certain geographies and quality-conscious carpenters in it. The differentiation would be in terms of product. The strategy document was as follows:

Segmentation

The furniture adhesive market was segmented on distribution channels, product grades, and geographies.

- Based on grade: Super Premium, Premium and Economy. The economy grade was the cheaper adhesives used by readymade furniture manufacturers who were least bothered about durability. The paint industry and stationery industry were also using this grade. 'Fevicol-SH' and most other national/regional brands were in the Premium segment. That segment was overcrowded.
- The Super Premium segment was having scope for growth. Even Fevicol failed to get into this segment through the launching of 'Marine' and 'Speedx'
- Based on the channel: Plywood stores, Hardware stores, Projects, Paints stores, and stationery stores. Plywood stores were selling the most quantities in larger pack sizes. Hardware stores sold smaller pack sizes.
- Based on geography: Metros, Major cities, small cities, and towns. In Metros brand image played a major role whereas in small cities and towns relationships were critical.

Targeting

For its 'Kushal' brand, Polygel decided to target the Super Premium segment and Plywood stores channel. It wanted to place 'Kushal' in the higher slot than 'Fevicol-SH' in the value chain so that it can demand the price premium. Polygel realized that for its scale of operations, commercial viability could only be achieved by selling 'Kushal' at prices higher than 'Fevicol-SH'. Other brands which were launched nationally could not support and sustain the promotional budgets required to snatch market share from 'Fevicol-SH'. The sales volumes were possible only by targeting plywood stores. Even though per kg price realization was better in the case of smaller packs they could not provide the scale.

Positioning

Polygel decided to hit on the weakness in the strength of the leader. While giving consistent quality Fevicol failed to offer the benefits of modern technology to customers in the form of product development. Their flagship product, Fevicol-SH, was a 50-year-old design. The technology brought many changes in the furniture industry but 'Fevicol-SH' was unchanged. The attempts were made to launch 'Fevicol- Marine' and 'Fevicol-Speedx' but customers were not amused. They refused to accept the development. The strong brand position created by 'Fevicol-SH' did not allow the brand owners to move up the value chain. This was the weakness in the strength of 'Fevicol-SH'.

Polygel decided to focus on opinion leaders. The research inferred that only a few carpenters, in every city, contributed to major sales of furniture adhesive. They were referred to as 'Contractors'. They were opinion leaders and their carpentry skills were appreciated by others in the city. Polygel referred to such contractors as 'Kushal'. The word in the Hindi language means 'skillful'. Polygel named its brand after this opinion leader, 'Kushal'. The brand positioning statement was designed, in Hindi as "*Kushal Karigar ka sathi*" meaning "friend of a skillful carpenter". Skillful carpenters were always in the search of better tools, methods, and materials which will in turn improve their workmanship. Others carpenters emulated these opinion leaders hence convincing them was a critical task.

Other brands only tried to motivate to buy in terms of freebies but carpenters wanted the reason to change the 'Fevicol-SH' loyalty. In absence of strong reason, the danglers offered by other brands were futile. 'Kushal' was designed to offer such reasons before motivation.

The company designed a mascot that resembled a cartoon of a carpenter. The weaving bird which stands for skillful workmanship was taken as the brand symbol. Polygel decided to focus on features incorporated as the fruits of modern technology. The objective was to create a 'superior to Fevicol-SH' brand image. The product strategy was designed to create that differentiation.

Product

Research indicated that time was the important parameter for on-site activity. End customers wanted carpenters to finish off the carpentry work at the earliest. Readymade, imported furniture aroused this need by focusing on the nuisance created by on-site furniture manufacturing activity. Carpenters were under time pressure. The only work which could not be accelerated by deploying additional manpower was gluing laminates to plywood. 'Fevicol-SH' took up to 10 hours to form a bond. 'Kushal' focused on this latent customer need and promised a strong bond in three and half hours. That time was almost one-third the time taken by 'Fevicol-SH'. Besides satisfying the end customers by completing work faster, It also saved a lot of labor costs for the contractors. This 'quick drying' feature was liked by contractors and carpenters.

Termite protection to furniture was a critical issue. Anti-termite herbal extracts were added to 'Kushal'. As a result, the furniture was secure from termite attacks for 15 years. The herbal extracts ensure a lack of any bad odor or harm to carpenters' eyes, unlike other anti-termite chemicals. Usually, 1 kilogram of 'Fevicol-SH' or equivalent furniture adhesive was required for fixing up 8 feet by 4 feet laminate sheet to plywood. 'Kushal' was formulated to improve coverage. It penetrated better into the porous plywood increasing the area of the bond and hence the bond strength. By doing this, only 650 grams of 'Kushal' was required to glue the same size laminate thereby giving at least 30% saving on furniture adhesive consumption. The study showed that up to 15% of furniture adhesive was wasted or pilfered during the site work when large pack sizes were bought. 'Kushal' was therefore supplied in pouches of 1 kilogram. A jar of 50 kg contained 50 such pouches. This packaging innovation saved pilferages and on-site losses, created convenience in material handling, fetched better recycle prices for the plastic jars, and created ease in stock-taking and accounting. Carpenters were applying adhesive to laminate and plywood by non-standard methods. 'Kushal' started giving an applicator with every jar to facilitate better workmanship. The factory head was given due credit for designing customer-centric products and packaging. The factory delivered its promise of giving consistent quality of 'Kushal' which was critical in the fight against Fevicol.

Price

The pricing of Furniture adhesive was determined by Fevicol pricing in the market. All the players used to keep the Maximum Retail Price (MRP) of their products in line with Fevicol. However, Fevicol being the strong brand enjoyed demand and availability in all the outlets and was a must for the outlet's survival. Fevicol offered thin margins along with the attractive cash discounts that were almost compulsorily to be availed by the distributors. Fevicol was rarely sold at the MRP from the outlets. The actual retail selling price (Market Operating Price) was a function of the customer's overall value to the retail outlet in terms of order quantity, assortment bought, payment terms, and the relationships of carpenters. Kushal was positioned above Fevicol with a price 8% higher than Fevicol. The channel margins were also kept higher, to motivate the channel partners. The strategy was to upgrade a certain percentage of Fevicol customers to Kushal; develop the muscle of double-digit market share and slowly reduce the channel margins, as the volume grows, to increase realization for Polygel and net earnings for the channel partners.

Place

Initially, Polygel thought of offering a retail market entry opportunity to its existing Industrial business agents and distributors. The objective was the share the fruits of growth with loyal channel partners by offering them distributorship even for the retail business. Some channel partners accepted the offer. Some were confused. A few channel partners started working and then realized that it was not their cup of tea. Polygel focused on generating demand by focusing on Contractors/ Carpenters, who were the major consumers of wood adhesive. Converting a small base of contractors who were the opinion leaders for the other carpenters would make them demand Kushal from retail outlets. Thus, 'Kushal' would automatically find placement for itself on retail shelves. During the early stages, retailers were not showing interest in 'Kushal'. But over a period of time, as the key contractors demanded Kushal, the retailer support began. 'Selective Distribution Strategy' was used to avoid price undercutting at the retail level. Only select retailers were given Kushal in every market.

Promotion

The promotion focus was on the top contractors of the town. A detailed database of such contractors was prepared for all cities where Kushal was being sold. Advertising on national television was ruled out due to limitations on promotional budgets. The method of promotion used was creating awareness through 'contractor meets' and personal visits to sites, for creating awareness. 'Contractor meets' were arranged in small groups for better communication and one-on-one interaction. The best hotel in every town was selected for such meetings to ensure the attendance of contractors.

Product demonstration, in the form of free trials on-site, followed contractor meets. The product superiority could be demonstrated with such trials. It was critical for the conversion of contractors and carpenters. The field force was trained in soft selling on site. They were provided with a 'Flip chart', a visual aid developed for the sales call for effective communication.

What Happened in Niche Market?

Nasik, a town north of Mumbai was selected for launch. The response to promotional activities was very positive from the contractors. However, over a period of a few months 'Polygel' realized 'Kushal' was not finding enough placement on the shelves. Hence, the initial good work of convincing carpenters was not yielding the expected results. A local manufacturer was very strong and blocked placement successfully. There was a similar experience in the Pune market, dominated by another local player. Working with retailers called for a large sales team and their relationships with retailers. Kushal was then launched in a different part of the country in a phased manner. Locations like Indore, Rajkot, Jalandhar, Amritsar, Ludhiana, Mysore, Satara, and Baroda started well. In the year 2008, Polygel came across an opportunity to take over an existing business in Retail competing with 'Fevicol' in the market. The brand was 'Vishwas', which was launched in the market with big fanfare in the year 2003-04. A lot of brand-building expenditure was made. However, as the focus of the brand owner altered, 'Vishwas' was put on sale.

Polygel considered it a good opportunity for the following reasons:

1. 'Vishwas' enjoyed good brand recall in the market and had no clash with the positioning of 'Kushal' as 'Vishwas' was positioned against 'Fevicol' to take it head-on. Hence, 'Vishwas' had complementary positioning.
2. 'Vishwas' had a good distribution network in most of the important pockets of the country. However, the channel was starved of products since management had lost interest in business and further many related operating issues had cropped up.
3. A large sales team with excellent market relationships was in place which was much needed for retail business.
4. A new manufacturing facility augmented the capacity with substantial benefits coming from tax holidays.

After the 'Vishwas team was merged with 'Kushal' the sales picked up in Gujarat, Mumbai, Navi Mumbai and other outskirts of Mumbai. The retail presence of 'Kushal' got strengthened and sales galloped to 125 Tons per month, which other competitors took over 5 years to achieve. 'Kushal' clearly became a success in the niche market. It could be corroborated by the following facts:

1. It was the first brand to be sold at a higher price than the market leader in the history of Furniture adhesives, in India.
2. 'Kushal' commanded a 5 to 20% market share of total market size and 30 to 80% of the Super Premium segment in targeted geographies.
3. There were negligible performance complaints in comparison to any other brand entering the market.
4. Any carpenter who once used 'Kushal' asked for it again.
5. Market leader's sales team acknowledged it by using pressure tactics with retailers or offering tempting promotional schemes.

From Niche to Mass Marketing

Enthused by the success, Polygel raised its ambitions to enter the mass market and take the number two position all over India. This required taking 'Fevicol' head-on at least in some markets which required a lot of financial strength. Raising debt was hardly an option because that investment would go into brand building, an intangible asset.

Various options were debated. Finally, Private Equity (PE) emerged as the optimal solution. Careful short-listing of interested Private Equity funds was done. Enthused by the growth track record and plans of Polygel, 'Arcapita Bank', a Bahrain-based Multinational investment bank, invested USD 15 Million in Polygel equity.

The Dilemma

No sooner did they receive a positive signal from the investor, than Supriya and Nishant's thought process began on building a comprehensive strategy. Supriya was confident about the 'Kushal' strategy used in the test marketing phase since it was tried and tested. Supriya argued, "Now that we have seen the success of Kushal's strategy, we should expand its scope to untouched territories. I am sure we will continue to reap the benefits." But Nishant had a different view. He argued, "Mass marketing was a completely different ball game. What worked in niche markets, may not be extrapolated to mass markets. It needs a radical rethinking of strategy. Gross generalization is of no use and can harm us too." Supriya lamented, "Come on Nishant, our product has been tested all over India. It was performing well in the heavy rainfall areas of Mumbai, at the 48-degree centigrade ambient temperature of Rajasthan and also in the chilling cold of Punjab. Our selling propositions are accepted by carpenters all over the country. Most importantly, we are selling at a price higher than Fevicol. Now, why are you apprehensive of extrapolation of the strategy?" "Precisely, the threshold for the transition from a mid-size company to a mega-corporation depends upon how the strategy was transformed. Most businesses fumble while shifting from niche markets to mass markets. The successful niche players may not always be the successful mass marketers. The failure can happen because of the inability to identify, forecast, and manage the variables which are critical in mass marketing. Success in the niche market may become a blinder that hampers the vision. What worked in the niche market may not work in the mass market. Our success in the niche markets can be largely attributed to the product. But in mass marketing, it can be treated as a 'product orientation' disease. Here we have to strike a balance in the marketing mix." Replied Nishant.

Nishant continued his argument "Things that worked in niche markets may not work in the mass markets. I doubt whether we can promote our product by personal selling method. Contacting and convincing carpenters all over India would need a huge size of salesforce. It worked for us in the niche markets but for the mass markets we might have to go for mass media as a main promotional tool."

Supriya interrupted Nishant, "Just forget it. Let us not repeat the mistakes done by other brands while competing with Fevicol. Advertising in mass media is the best way to untimely instigate Fevicol and invite trouble. Vamicol did this before and got killed prematurely. I would rather go step by step and go on swallowing as we digest it but wouldn't change over to mass advertising. What may go against us in mass marketing? Can we not forecast and manage those variables successfully?"

Supriya asked. "As a national player, we have to deal with the market leader, followers, the regional players, and the unorganized sector. All of them have different propositions. Can we fight the war only with a single brand and limited range? We might have to consider multiple brands or at least develop an umbrella brand," said Nishant.

"Do not forget, we have achieved Kushal sales volume in just two years for which others took more than five years." Supriya smiled and spoke. "That's fine. But as a national player, we have to play a multi-brand strategy. We can't be selling only super-premium grade. We will have to cater to premium and economy segments as well. In mass marketing, having a range is a must. We will have to segment the market, target different brands for different segments, and differentiate every brand with a unique positioning." Nishant elaborated his point further, "Targeting different brands to different segments will be critical for the success. We will have to ensure that our brands don't cannibalize each other. We need to sort out the issue of whether to go for a multi-brand strategy or an umbrella brand strategy. Of late, Pidilite Industries adopted a multi-brand strategy and launched brands like Parcel, and Woodgrip to fight the competition from the lower end of the value chain. Their efforts of extending the brand to the super-premium category have failed. They could not make customers move up the value chain and buy Fevicol-Marine and Fevicol-Speedex."

"Precisely, only 'Fevicol-SH' grade is sold. They couldn't succeed in transforming Fevicol into an umbrella brand. Their multiple brand strategy also met limited success. If they can reach to number one position with a single brand, why can't we be number two only with Kushal? Not only Fevicol but Jeevanjor also did not succeed in its umbrella brand strategy. Kores Ltd. failed in multi-brand strategy" Supriya argued with conviction. "I am not convinced that these players gave serious try to their strategy. It only remained on paper. I feel there was a 'Knowing-Doing gap'. Look outside our industries for better examples."

"Look Nishant, commercial viability was the issue in case of lower grades. The gross margins do not make business sense. The production capacity gets blocked in commercially non-viable, economy brands. Secondly, supporting promotional expenses becomes a tough task at the market price levels. I would rather make efforts and spend money on upgrading the market by educating carpenters. Nishant, do you think people will try to save money in adhesives, which was not even 5% of their furniture cost, and face the risk of de-lamination?" Supriya said.

"Few more issues. What should be our central strategy initially? Should we take 'Fevicol' head-on or look for the soft targets and attack 'Jeevanjor' and 'Karpenter' brands nationally?" asked Nishant. "I think we have to do both. Let that be the decision of middle-level managers who will act based on factors specific to markets locally," replied Supriya.

"Secondly, should we target the super-premium segment of Fevicol where they market brand extensions like Fevicol-marine and Fevicol-Speedx which generate hardly any volume for them, or 'Fevicol-SH', their breadwinner in the premium category?" While responding to this issue Supriya clarified, "We will attack their breadwinner with a brand which has better specifications and features than their super-premium upgrades. We will educate the market that we are adding value with just a marginal price increase. The value differential would out-weigh price differential."

"Lastly, how do we promote Kushal nationally, for mass marketing? Should we take the 'Fevicol' route and advertise heavily, on national television channels, at premium timings? Or continue following our method of awareness creation through carpenter meets and personal visits of field force?" Nishant asked.

Supriya replied, "Initially we may not advertise. In absence of a strong distribution network nationally, there will be a lot of advertisement wastage. Secondly, product trials on-site were vital in the success of niche markets; therefore, I suggest, we should continue doing what we did earlier. We shall focus on 'In-shop meetings' of carpenters and 'Canopy campaigns' at retail stores for creating product awareness. 'Product trials' to create interest and 'incentive schemes' to effect the action of the retailers and end-users."

While Supriya had a strong conviction about extending the earlier strategy to new markets, with certain refinements, Nishant demanded a different and comprehensive strategy that should be meticulously executed. They agreed to seek advice from a veteran marketer, Mr. Prem Mehta, who joined the Polygel board recently.

Mr. Mehta was ex-chairman of Lintas, one of the largest advertising agencies in India. He was known for his marketing wisdom in Indian corporate circles. Supriya had to forge a consensus and present a strategy during the scheduled board meeting on 24th March 2010.

Foot Notes: -

[1] Names of the Marketing Head and Strategic Advisor have changed.

[2]IACOBUCCI, MM What's Inside: Marketing Management - A South Asian Perspective

Appendix 1: Product Portfolio

Adhesives: Synthetic Rubber (Brushable-SR & Sprayable-SP), Polyurethane (PU), White (SH), Epoxy etc.

Engineering Adhesives: Anaerobic, Cyno (Fevikwik type), UV Curing, Electronic Grades

Silicone & PU Sealants

Speciality Products: Mould Release Agents, Wood Finwashes etc.

Turbofix was the brand introduced by Polygel in 2003 with many extensions.

TURBOFIX SR –ADHESIVES (Brushable grades)

Synthetic Rubber base brushable adhesive was used for various kinds of applications, like leather and footwear, flooring, auto upholstery, Luggage, foam furnishing etc. SR-based adhesives are also used for Ply laminating and other carpentry Work. TURBOFIX SR-900, SR-400F, SR-500F.SR-700P are recommended for such applications.

SR-900 and SR-700P can withstand higher temperatures hence recommended for those applications where the substrate was exposed to atmospheric temperatures.

TURBOFIX SR –ADHESIVES (Sprayable grades)

TURBOFIX –SP was BENZINE FREE Neoprene rubber base Sprayable adhesive. Major applications are automobiles, carpeting, seating system, foam, fabric etc. For such applications, SP-ASP, SP-RT, and SP-SX are recommended.

The TURBOFIX-PU:-Polyurethane-based adhesive was used for Footwears.

TURBIFIX SEALANTS:-Used for various industrial applications

TURBOFIN WAX: - Used as a release agent and polwash for some specific applications.

Appendix 2: Carpenter Profiles

Category	Consumption of Furniture adhesive (per month)	Profile	Number of employees handled
Contractor	300 kilogram plus	He was the fellow who used to be a carpenter earlier. However, his profile has changed from technical to commercial. He bids for the tenders floated by public and private institutions along with major carpentry work in the domestic sector. It was seen that most of them stayed in a bungalow, had a four-wheeler and their kids went to English medium schools.	15 skilled carpenters Semi-skilled team of helpers. (3 sites per month)
'A' Category	100 to 250 kilograms	He was a fellow who undertaken jobs of woodwork and furniture in shops and houses. The carpenters working under him belong to his community.	10 Carpenters (2 Sites per month)
'B' Category	50 To 100 Kilograms	This fellow preferred to work at one site at a time and his teammates are his relatives.	5 to 7 Carpenters (1 Site)
'C' Category	Less than 50 Kilograms	This fellow works for others rather than doing his own business.	-----

Appendix 3:

- **Kushal Mascot and Punch line.**

- **Kushal Brand Symbol**

Appendix 4: Pricing Structure: Furniture adhesives

Price	Fevicol Unit Price %*	Other National Brands Unit Price %*
Maximum Retail Price	100	100
Market Operating Price	97	94
Retailer Margin	-3 to +5 **	7 to 15
Distributor Margin	5 (Cash Down Payment)	7 (Min 60 days Credit)
Taxes and Duties	15	15
Promotion Schemes	4 to 6	10 to 20
Promotion Spend	2	3 to 10
Mass Media Advertisement	2	Nil

*Since pricing structure was a sensitive subject all pricing numbers are converted in % points.

**Some retailers treat 'Fevicol' as a 'loss leader' and sell it at loss to attract footfalls.

Appendix 5: Fevicol advertisement- Sample of creativity

In the background, you can see Fevicol hoarding on the train as if people are glued to the Mumbai local train because of Fevicol.

CHAPTER SIX

Carving a Niche in a Crowded Market: e-Emphasys ERP

It was Friday, 15th January 2010. Milind Bagade, the CEO of e-Emphasys was sitting with his younger brother and COO, Sayam Bagade, in their head office situated in Weston Parkway, Cary, North Carolina, USA. They had just concluded a very bumpy financial year which was making them think harder about their business model. e-Emphasys was into IT consulting services for the BAAN platform, since its inception. The IT industry was going through a tough time because the US economy was facing a banking crisis and recession as a fall out of the subprime mortgage crisis. Additionally, they couldn't launch 'e-Emphasys ERP', as per the strategic plan. In the year 2005, they had decided to carve a niche for 'e-Emphasys' in the crowded IT sector by developing a product. It was a proposed ERP software for the 'construction heavy equipment and vehicles' dealers and rental companies, to integrate their business processes with a standardized ERP product of their principals, the manufacturing companies. It was based on BAAN ERP (Presently known as Infor ERP $_{LN}$) platform. There was an unfulfilled need in the market because these dealers and rental companies were not using ERP, whereas their principals (the manufacturers of this equipment and vehicles) were operating businesses on sophisticated ERP. For many years, the manufacturers had wanted to take the ERP implementation to the next level of the supply chain. They were after the dealers and rental companies to install ERP but no such standard product was available in the market to suit their need. 'e-Emphasys ERP' was targeted towards plugging in this hole in the market. The product was to transform e-Emphasys from IT consulting services to an IT product company, which was Milind's dream. However, they were struggling to develop it since the year 2006.

They had already invested $15 million in the development but things were not going their way. Many factors in the ecosystem and under the client's control posed challenges over and above the background and limitations of e-Emphasys. Milind had a gut feeling that they were very near to the final step, whereas Sayam felt they were leaping in the dark. Sayam was losing out his patience and wanted to challenge the strategy. Bagade brothers had agreed to re-think their 'Mission- 2020' and the strategy to accomplish it. They were back from a two-week Christmas and New Year vacation with fresh minds. It was time to debate. Milind wanted to transform e-Emphasys into an IT product company, whereas Sayam wanted to continue the existing consulting services business and become a leading player. Their challenge was to develop collective wisdom, translate it to mission 2020, and design a well-crafted strategy.

Family Managed Businesses and Entrepreneurship

Milind and Sayam Bagade were brothers. Milind had a background of working in the product development function of BAAN ERP whereas Sayam was a computer engineer who worked for a decade in IT consulting services on the BAAN platform. Their background provided them with insights and conviction. Their father Raghunath Bagade was a hardworking engineering draftsman who migrated from a rural area of Western Maharashtra to Mumbai at a very young age. He worked at Bhabha Atomic Research Centre (BARC) and resided in Kalyan with his kids. Mr. Raghunath Bagade was a very enterprising man and got very good support from his wife, Prabha. She was a brilliant lady and was known for her prudence, cleanliness, and cooking skills. She was raised in a poor family amongst 4 siblings and couldn't complete her education but nevertheless, she was committed to the education of her children. Raghunath and Prabha manufactured Agarbattis (Indian scented candles). Raghunath would sell them in his office and to friends, relatives, and neighbors. (See **Exhibit 1**). Milind was the elder among the two sons. He completed his under-graduation in the Science discipline. Sayam became a Computer Engineer. Both brothers were enterprising like their parents. Milind's wife Manisha and Sayam's wife Sanjana strongly supported their husbands and took complete responsibility for family matters. Their sacrifices and strong support were the foundation of the success of e-Emphasys.

In 1991, Sayam who was 23, and Milind 27, started a business of providing satellite TV connections to people, while also working as salaried professionals. They successfully convinced a couple of developers and builders in Thane (a suburb of Mumbai) to provide a satellite TV connection to all the apartment residents. These realtors included that offer as a feature to attract new customers who wanted to buy an apartment in their project. Milind got married to his childhood love, Manisha and the family shifted to Thane from Kalyan. Their satellite TV connection business was doing very well. In 1993, Sayam secured a good job in software development in the Netherlands with BAAN Corporation, which was the leading Enterprise Resources Planning (ERP) company in Western Europe. Milind and Manisha continued to work and also run the cable business with the help of their parents. Soon the local gangs and goons started entering the business of providing satellite TV connections and the business lost its social status. In 1997, Milind decided to sell the business. Meanwhile, Sayam had migrated to America but was still working on the BAAN platform. Sayam was working for a BAAN partner in the USA. Milind took a major decision to shift his career and started working on the BAAN platform too. Manisha joined Patni computers and both Milind and Manisha got into the international traveling jobs.

Evolution of Enterprise Resources Planning (ERP)

In the 1960s, when computers and operating systems were in infancy, companies started using them for the purpose of inventory control. In the 1970s, Material Requirement Planning (MRP) emerged as a powerful tool to take an integrated approach to manage material as an important resource. Xerox and IBM laid the foundation of ERP. In 1973, a German company, SAP developed a product to help businesses manage their processes in the areas of mass production and marketing. This software was called Enterprise Resources Planning (ERP). In the 1980s, with the advancement of computer technology, companies started using ERP software to manage business processes and increase productivity by optimizing resources. The real growth of ERP was triggered in 1990. During the 1990s ERP vendors added more modules and functions as "add-ons" to the core modules, giving birth to the "extended ERPs."

These ERP extensions include advanced planning and scheduling (APS), and e-business solutions such as customer relationship management (CRM) and supply chain management (SCM). The worldwide license and maintenance revenue for ERP systems was US$21.5 billion in 2000, which represented a growth of 13.1%[i] for the top 10 ERP companies (See **Exhibit 2**).

BAAN ERP Systems

In 1978, Mr. Jan Baan developed software in the Netherlands to integrate various business processes into a single integrated system. The objective was to provide financial and administrative consulting services. His efforts were supported and financed by a Dutch church. BAAN ERP system was more customer friendly, flexible & easy to customize. BAAN System became popular in the early 1990s. In 1994 BAAN bagged a mega order from Boeing and became a threat to the market leader, SAP. In 1995, it became a public company, registered on Amsterdam & NASDAQ share markets. BAAN started taking over other software companies. It took over about 5 companies. The sales were on rising every year. In 1997, BAAN enjoyed a 5% market share in the global ERP industry. In 1998, their business was almost $750 million. During this year, BAAN employed 3000 software professionals. However, by the year 2000, the company was in deep trouble with many lawsuits against them and financial losses for 7 consecutive quarters. Finally, the company was sold to Invensys for $ 700 million. In June 2003, SSA Technologies bought BAAN from Invensys for just $ 130 million and changed the name of the company to SSA ERP Ln. They reworked BAAN software and launched a new product SSA ERP Ln 6.1. In the year 2006, an Atlanta-based ERP giant, Infor Global Solutions bought SSA.[ii] Infor started its operations in the year 2002 and became a leading ERP company within a decade.

Friendly assignment with BAAN Japan

After 1997, Milind was traveling frequently to Japan and Netherlands from India for BAAN clients. In a short period after joining BAAN, he rose to a leadership position in R & D. In the year 2000, the ERP business was at its best.

The 'Y2K bug'[1] created a massive opportunity for the software industry. Y2K compliance concerns at the turn of the millennium also served to hasten the growth of the enterprise software industry (Jacobs and Weston Jr. 2007). But BAAN was in trouble and couldn't encash the opportunity.

Milind was in Japan and his friends told him about a performance issue with one of the BAAN's customers in Japan, Tokyo Electron, who had a performance issue. To generate a production order, it was taking 36 hours. BAAN tried very hard to identify the problem and resolve it but they couldn't. They gave up, leading the customer to halt the global project. Milind's friend in BAAN Japan wanted to buy some time and hence they requested Milind for help, knowing his technical competency.

Smelling the Business Opportunity

Milind discussed the problem with Sayam. Both of them smelled an opportunity to demonstrate their competency. Sayam took a leave from his office and flew to Japan immediately. On his arrival, the customer, Tokyo Electron, gave details of the exact issue. The brothers decided to take up the challenge right on the spot. BAAN Japan arranged for a computer server on the same day. They also made arrangements to stay in a nearby hotel. Without any break, both the brothers worked hard for 3 days and nights non-stop. Sayam didn't sleep for 41 hours at a stretch. In 3 days, Sayam changed the software. The production orders were created in 4 hours instead of 36. Japanese were happy to see the change but they requested further improvement. They wanted to complete this process even quicker, in a couple of hours (from 36 hours). The Bagade brothers had other commitments and hence had to go back but they promised the Japanese to bring the processing time closer to two hours. The customer bought a new flight ticket from Tokyo to Raleigh, NC. This was the first business class trip for the brothers but both slept throughout the journey.

Birth of e-Emphasys

It was December 2000. After Sayam returned to the USA, BAAN Japan gave him a great surprise. The entire R&D ERP server of BAAN Japan had arrived at his home by FedEx. Sayam managed to reduce the processing time to 54 minutes without altering any functionality.

This was never heard of in ERP. Both were extremely excited even though it was just a friendly assignment. Everyone at Tokyo Electron and BAAN was in utter disbelief and was thrilled. Within 3 days, the customer sent a cheque for $100,000 for all the efforts. This was another pleasant shock because the brothers had neither seen nor expected such a high-value cheque. Finally, Tokyo electron did continue with the BAAN solution, which they are using happily, even in 2018. Sayam and Milind deposited that cheque in the bank and ventured into the business of developing software, on the BAAN platform.

They registered a company 'e-Emphasys Technologies, Inc.' at Sayam's residential address in North Carolina, USA. e-Emphasys was formed with a three-stage strategy; no outside funding, building a global presence and finally building its own products to ensure long-term sustainability. In 2001, Sayam decided to focus on e Emphasys. He gave up his job.

Company History

Fifteen days after the formation of e-Emphasys in America, Milind decided to give up his job in BAAN and return to Mumbai to focus on developing software for internet banking. His friends from BAAN Corporate in the Netherlands requested Milind to visit the Netherlands office on his way back to India. They asked him to present the entire BAAN technology platform to the Invensys team, a $14bn company in 2001, which was planning to acquire BAAN. Milind presented the technology. Invensys team was happy with what they saw and they requested BAAN to provide Milind's consulting services in the US after the takeover. Two of Milind's friends from BAAN joined e-Emphasys. They were also deputed on the Invensys consulting services project by Milind. Invensys had also asked IBM to do the same pilot project in parallel to e-Emphasys. IBM lost the race. Later on, Invensys also asked e-Emphasys to provide a bigger team for a longer term. Simultaneously, Tokyo Electron hired e-Emphasys for the implementation of ERP and also for integrating BAAN ERP with other third-party software such as I2 Factory planning, Windchill PLM, etc. By 2001, e-Emphasys was firmly established in consulting business of 'ERP implementation and integration services' on the BAAN platform. They were paying BAAN the license fees.

Why BAAN?

There were many other ERP systems developed by giant companies like SAP, Oracle, Microsoft, etc. but Milind and Sayam did not give up their faith in BAAN. Their conviction in the quality and flexibility of BAAN helped them to develop the technical competencies which became the foundation of the success of e-Emphasys. Both Milind and Sayam had mastered the BAAN system technically. Their technical competencies were respected by BAAN itself and also by the important customers of BAAN. The top management of BAAN in the Netherlands was supportive of Milind and Sayam. The brothers knew the expertise of different people working in BAAN and also working on the BAAN platform. They could scale up manpower on the BAAN platform for any mega project in the future and could also train professionals. Their networking with customers and suppliers using the BAAN system could help them in the consulting business. Most importantly, BAAN ERP had a huge global customer base which was in thousands. These customers required services and consulting advice on maintenance, upgradation, and other support. But BAAN was busy with its own problems. Sayam thought consultancy business based on BAAN ERP was a once-in-a-lifetime opportunity for e-Emphasys. They were at the right place at the right time and wanted to leverage their expertise in BAAN systems. Most of these BAAN customers could be sold 'add-ons', 'extended ERP', and upgrades in addition to the maintenance services. There was a lot of potential to develop an IT consulting services business and Sayam was keen to do so.

Business Entry Strategy and Early Success

When the Bagade brothers started e-Emphasys in 2000, they wanted to get into the development of the internet banking software business. Due to the success and opportunities, they got from BAAN customers in Japan and USA, e-Emphasys always remained on the BAAN platform in an IT consulting business. They started their company by focusing on the consulting business. It was a very difficult year for the IT industry. The industry saw many closures. But e-Emphasys remained on the development path from the year 2000 until the year 2004.

It gained exceptional goodwill, cash, and reputation in the ERP world with large corporations trusting e-Emphasys such as Boeing, Tokyo Electron, Invensys, Komatsu, etc. By the year 2005, 'e-Emphasys' was in a good shape on the basis of the IT consulting services business. It had 3 major development centers, a strong global BAAN customer base in multiple countries, and 50 employees. At the beginning of the year 2005, Milind and Sayam reviewed the performance of their business and realized that they had successfully climbed the first step. Most of the teething problems were over. They decided to take up a higher risk and jump to the next level. Milind decided to move to America with his family in 2005.

BAAN: An Opportunity for e-Emphasys

Implementing the ERP systems was a big market in the year 2000. However, in the new millennium ERP systems were posed with challenges. The growth and success of ERP adoption and development were dependent on the capability of the ERP systems and also on emerging extended modules like Customer Relationship Management (CRM), Supply Chain Management (SCM), and integration with the Internet-enabled applications.[iii]

After 2003, BAAN was not doing great in the ERP business. The company was sold frequently, changing management. Due to this, BAAN talent started seeking opportunities in other technologies. The customers who earlier bought BAAN ERP were actively looking for support to refurbish their ERP system in the light of their changing needs and expanding businesses. Due to the scarcity of skilled BAAN developers, other companies couldn't cater to all such inquiries.

Sayam wanted to grab this opportunity and develop e-Emphasys strongly around these customer needs and increase the business by many folds. His dream was to develop e-Emphasys as a leading IT consulting services company and to join the elite club of successful Indian software companies such as Infosys, TCS, and Wipro. He gave up his job in 2001 and started focusing on such opportunities under the e-Emphasys umbrella. His consulting area was BAAN installation, servicing, maintenance, support, and upgradation to the next level of ERP to modernize it. He felt by tapping the potential of BAAN globally company could develop a global scale.

Plugging the Hole in the Market: Developing the Product

Milind had worked with BAAN in the product development function. He developed a passion for product development, particularly on the BAAN ERP platform. He was thinking hard about developing a few products and customers to create a niche for e-Emphasys in the ERP business rather than trying to compete with big companies in the consulting services space. During his job, Milind was interacting with the construction heavy equipment and vehicle manufacturers globally (See Exhibit 3). Most of the heavy construction equipment and vehicle manufacturers like Komatsu, Hitachi, Volvo, Caterpillar, etc were using ERP systems for many years. But their dealers and rental companies, who were directly in touch with the customers, in the marketplace, were not a part of their ERP systems. They were using basic software and couldn't provide the required data to the principals. This gap in database management was making it difficult to forecast and manage business processes in the dynamic and fluid business environment. Milind felt the need to develop an ERP system for dealers to connect the missing link and make it compatible with the ERP system of the Original Equipment Manufacturers (OEM). He had already developed an integrator that was required to use e-Emphasys extended ERP software along with other ERP systems of SAP, Microsoft, Oracle, etc.

Komatsu's Support

Japanese companies turned out to be very lucky first customers for e-Emphasys. They ventured into the IT consulting services business by getting the first order from Tokyo Electron. Another Japanese company helped e-Emphasys to get into the IT product business. Komatsu, the second largest construction heavy equipment and vehicles manufacturer in the world after Caterpillar (from Japan), took initiative and provided an impetus to e-Emphasys to develop an ERP for their dealers and integrate it with Komatsu's ERP system. This push provided a great business opportunity for e-Emphasys. Komatsu was using BAAN ERP and hence the development and integration of ERP for their dealers seemingly didn't pose a challenge.

Developing an 'e-Emphasys ERP': A Rough ride

Shriram Rajagopal, who was VP – Of Product Management for e-Emphasys, was working with Milind in the product development department of BAAN Netherlands. He was one of the first associates who developed faith in the entrepreneurial abilities of Milind and Sayam. A few other employees also joined the company in the early phase when there was no surety of success. Going forward they rose to key positions in the company structure. (See **Exhibits 4 and 5**) Milind and Shriram started developing a product for Komatsu dealers and rental services companies. Surprisingly it was taking much longer than Milind and Sayam expected. They conceived the idea in 2005 and started seriously working and investing in it in the year 2006. They invested over $ 15 million in 3 years but the bug-free product was not getting ready even in 2009. Post-Subprime Mortgage Crisis a major economic recession hit the US economy. The software industry was affected badly. Sayam was losing out patience. In his view, the company couldn't sustain the product development expenses. He wanted to discuss the fate of the product with Milind once and for all. He suggested sticking to the IT consulting services business rather than moving focus to product marketing. He felt the demerits of product business outnumbered the merits. There were huge untapped opportunities in the field of IT consulting services that required to be encashed on priority.

The Crossfire: IT Products or IT consulting services

On 15th Jan 2010, during the strategic planning meeting, Milind and Sayam decided to involve Shriram who was heading the product development function. After a cup of tea, Sayam started the conversation, "Milind, we had decided to develop a product and shift to 'product marketing' business rather than 'IT consulting and services' in a phased manner. We have already invested about 5 years of our net earnings, during the last 3 years, in product development. But it is not working out for us. It was a collective decision to develop this product and hence nobody is to be blamed for the collective failure. But I feel we should not stay hooked to the product. We must move on and develop the IT consulting services business and try to accelerate it." Milind replied, "Yes, we have not yet developed the product but that doesn't mean that we failed in developing the product. I feel that we are very close and our dream can be a reality any day."

Milind was referring to the launching of 'e-Emphasis ERP'. Sayam said, "I feel that we are barking the wrong tree. Our core competency is IT consulting services. We should develop our business around that strength. Our sales in 2009 have, in fact, come down to the 2007 level due to the loss of sales." Milind said, "I think we need to refine that view. Our core competency is the technical capability of the BAAN platform. We can enter any software development business which uses the BAAN platform. The ERP that we are developing is also the same effort. Secondly, please don't mix up two issues. Our sales in 2009 were down because of the weak performance in the consulting services business which is sensitive to economic fluctuations. We took a hit because of the economic recession which was followed after the subprime mortgage crisis. Everybody in the IT industry got beaten up. We can't be at peace when the world is at war. Delay in product development has no bearing on this economic crisis. We know those reasons, we have worked on them and soon we will over-power them." Sayam said, "That is true. I am not saying losses are due to product development but the fact is that the delay is pinching us more because of the bad business environment and we are unable to invest in opportunities in the current business. How can we not be worried when we have invested years of our hard earnings in product development and achieved nothing visible until today?" Shriram added his argument, "We are investing heavy resources in product development because we want to reduce our over-dependence on consulting services business. The current situation attests to our concerns and supports our vision. It only proves that our worries are realistic and we must develop products to shift our focus and dependence."

Sayam asked a question to Milind "Don't you think we are restricting ourselves by focusing on a very narrow segment and will lose out on the other business opportunities? I am unable to attempt many opportunities in consulting services because of the resource constraints posed by the product development budgets." Milind replied, "That is the trade-off we have to do when we are planning to use a 'Niche Marketing strategy'. Remember, you can't be everything to everybody. We are just making a choice. There will be a cost associated with this choice." Shriram added, "I think we are through with almost 80% of the development. It is too late to go back out now. If we stop development then we will lose $15 million. We deserve a chance to recover it by going ahead."

Sayam said, "I don't deny that but we need to take a call. If we don't succeed in developing a bug-free product then we will face real embarrassment over and above the financial loss. My concern is that such failure will harm our confidence in our technical capabilities."

Shriram said, "But our team will be equally demoralized if we abruptly stop the product development by doubting the technical competencies." Sayam said, "That may be very true. We need to handle it well and back out with grace." Milind said, "Every innovation goes through similar phases. Those who continue even after everyone else has given up winning the race. We know that the one who is beaten up badly ultimately wins in boxing. I think we need to develop that stamina." Sayam pointed out, "there are many external factors like volatile business environment, lack of clear business processes at the dealer end, variability in their work methods, etc. These factors are making things difficult for us." Milind said, "We are required to re-engineer the business processes of the customers before developing the ERP system and hence the process of developing the product turned out to be much more difficult, time-consuming and costlier than expected." Shriram added to Milind's argument, "We also had our share of learning. BAAN is basically designed for a company with a manufacturing setup. Our product caters to the dealership. The change of such orientation also makes a difference." Milind nodded and said, "The developers are from India and they took some time to understand the American situation. Their lack of industry knowledge has also added some time and cost."

Sayam said, "You guys need not defend the delay and cost over-runs. It is a part of life in our industry. My view is that we could have afforded experiments during a boom time. In a recession, we need to go easy on expenses and investments. Can we put the project in the refrigerator for a couple of years and take it up for development once the market improves?" Shriram looked at Milind and said, "Milind has to take that call but from the development team I feel that such a hold can be damaging."

Milind said, "I strongly believe that no opportunity is lost, the competitors will grab it. The construction heavy equipment and vehicle manufacturers are so desperate that they will route this new product development through our competitors and we might lose the war forever. Komatsu and others have given us this opportunity just because of our relationships. They are suffering due to lack of ERP system at the dealership and they don't want to continue suffering." Sayam asked a question, "We were lucky that we got to identify an exact hole in the market. How will you identify another product when we will be saturated with this product? Remember, products have life cycles. Technological products have shorter life cycles. An IT product company has to always be innovative and commit heavy investments to R&D and product development. My point is that this situation in product development is not unique. It will be a way of life if we decide to be in IT product. Do we have enough market potential and reach to encash our innovation? Are we prepared to stay with the uncertainty associated with innovation?" Milind laughed and said, "It will be a problem in the next decade. We will have enough business with these dealers if we sell globally. As a matter of fact, we need to increase our selling team to grab this opportunity. I was about to talk to you about this. Just a couple of days back our research agency gave me the report on number of dealerships and rental companies with an exact number of their employee strength. (See **Exhibits 6 and 7**). They have classified them into 4 groups: Top (with 3000 employees each), Mid (with 500 employees), Semi-Mid (with 125 employees), and small (with 50 employees). If we assume that the dealers will pay for the license of just 50% of their employees, the market potential is more than 1.6 million licenses. Globally there are 38500 companies to be convinced. Just calculate how many sales persons we would need and what kind of structure will be there in our global sales organization?" Sayam said, "This sounds interesting. But I feel the IT consulting services business is more stable in the long term. Our own performance attests to this fact. (See **Exhibit 8**). There may not be a cap on the growth potential. We can be Infosys tomorrow."

Milind laughed and said, "What if, we don't succeed? Behind every Infosys, there are 100 companies that couldn't be Infosys. In the IT product business, we will have better control of overall operations, sales, and profitability. Once our product development costs are written off, we will have fantastic profits." Shriram added, "Plus the marketing costs will be minimum. We can also have variable selling cost by paying higher commissions than salaries." Milind continued, "My plan is to carve out a Niche in the IT industry for our business. We can't be a challenger to SAP, our market leader. They are too big a bull to take by the horn. There are enough followers in the industry who are focusing on the products and markets which are left by SAP or where SAP is not strong. I don't want to be just another company in the crowd. If we do that and accept the follower's status then our strategies and survival are driven by the market leader. I strongly wish e-Emphasys to be associated with a unique brand position, such as an ERP solution partner for heavy construction equipment and vehicle dealers and rental companies. If we can't be the leaders in the entire ERP market, we can certainly lead this niche market for years. We can be a niche player in the current industry structure." Shriram supported Milind, "Fortunately, we have identified the market which can be a very good niche for us. As Milind explained, the market size is good enough for us to do business but other big players may not get into it soon. Plus, there are technological entry barriers for the newcomers which will make their entry difficult. We can rule the segment at least for a few years."

Sayam pointed out, "the sales of the construction heavy equipment and vehicle industry have come down drastically in 2009. In the year 2008, the global sales stood at 900,000 units which came down to below 700,000 units in 2009, a $22 billion loss of sales in dollar terms. If the trend continues then our estimates will go for a toss. Such drop can be very harmful to a niche player because the customers will cut down on investments in new software." Milind replied, "This drop is also a result of the subprime mortgage crisis. During my last visit to the exhibition of construction heavy equipment, most of the manufacturers gave me hope. They were all bullish about the sales growth. The market will be on the upswing soon. There are positive trends from Asia, particularly from China and India." Sayam was still not satisfied. He asked, "How are you confident that SAP or other major ERP companies will not launch ERP in this segment? If so, then the niche markets will become a mass market." Milind replied, "My logic is simple. If we have taken more than 3 years to complete 85% of the product, I don't expect them to take anything less than that. They haven't started development yet. We will have at least 3 to 5 years of lead time before any major competitor becomes a threat to our niche."

Suddenly the discussion was interrupted because Milind got an important international call. Sayam told Shriram, "We have to take a final decision today. Let us seal the strategy for the next 5 years."

Foot Note:

[1] All the computers were programmed for years starting from digit 1 but the change of millennium required to considering digit 2 initially. The change of the date format was mandated in all programs. There were fears that the computers will stop working creating chaos. All software companies took massive projects to update the date format. It was referred to as the Y2K project.

Exhibit 1: - Timeline

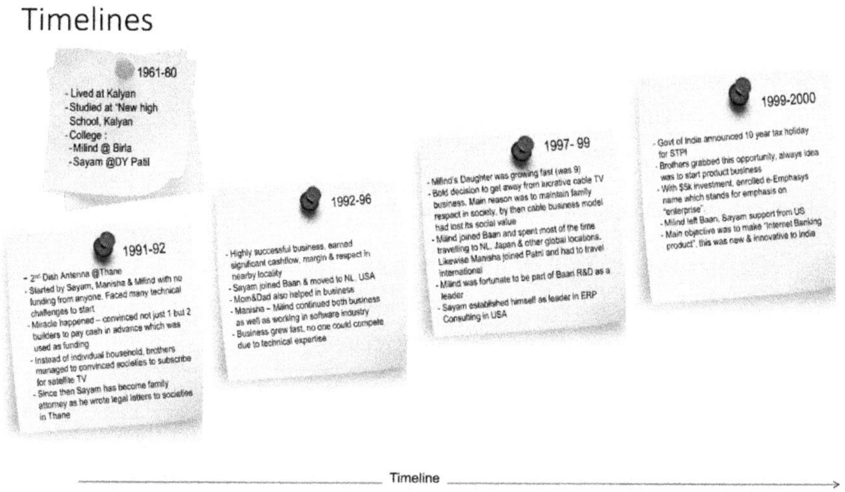

Exhibit 2: Top 10 ERP Companies

Top 10 Global ERP Companies in the World in 2009			
Sr. No.	Name of the Company	Revenue in Million USD	Market Share in %
1	SAP	5094	25.30
2	Oracle	2414	12.00
3	Sage	1342	6.70
4	Infor	1011	5.00
5	Microsoft	856	4.30
6	Kronos	458	2.30
7	Yonyou	356	1.80
8	Totvs	303	1.50
9	Unit 4	279	1.40
10	Concur	248	1.20
	Others	7767	38.60

Source: Analyst Report 2009-2013 (Chris Pang, Yanna Dharmasthira et al., 2009-13)

Exhibit 3: Construction Equipment and Vehicles

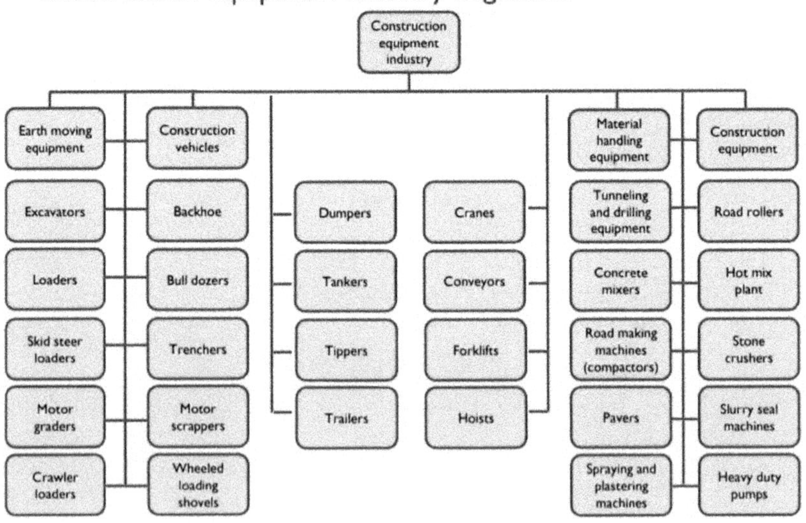

Source: Company reports

Exhibit 4:

e-Emphasys' Global Corporate Structure

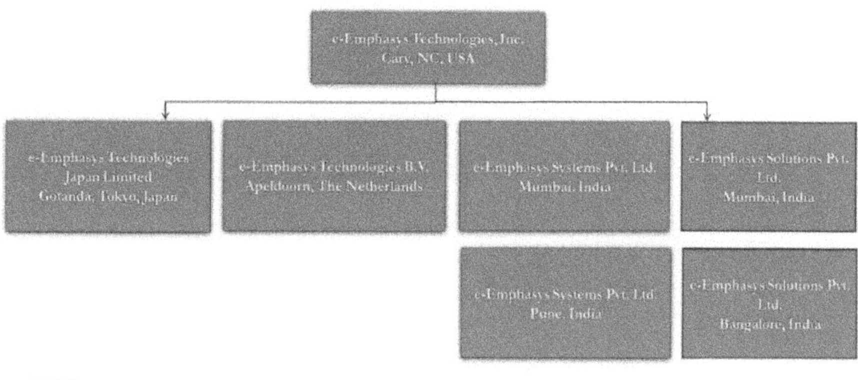

Exhibit 5:

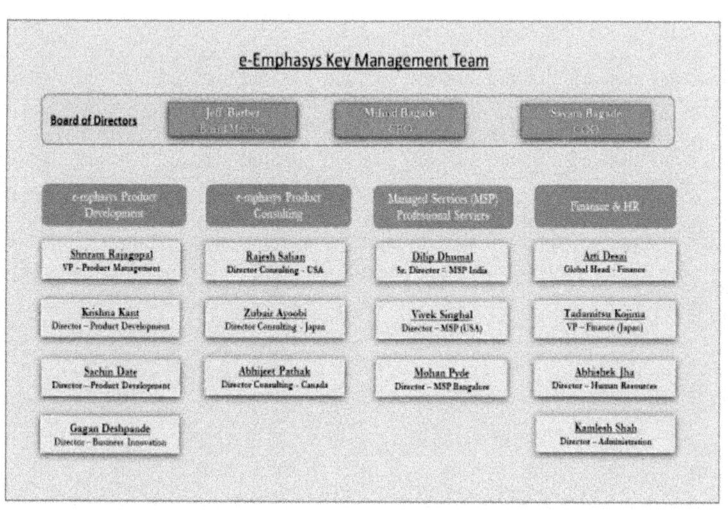

Exhibit 6: Demand for ERP software for Dealers and Rental companies of the Construction Heavy Equipment and Vehicles

Global Market Size

Market Stratification	# of Companies	% of Companies Opening RFP (Avg. Year)	# of Potential Deals/Year	Avg. # of Employees	Avg. # Concurrent Users	# Potential Mrket Size (Users/Year)
Top	300	25%	75	3,000	2100	157,500
Mid	3,200	25%	800	500	350	280,000
Semi-Mid	13,000	25%	3,250	125	80	260,000
Small	22,000	25%	5,500	50	20	110,000
						807,500

Source: Company Internal Reports

Exhibit 7: Average Spending on IT by Dealers of Heavy Civil Equipment and Vehicle Dealers

IT Spend – Why are we here?

- Average IT spending with in dealerships:

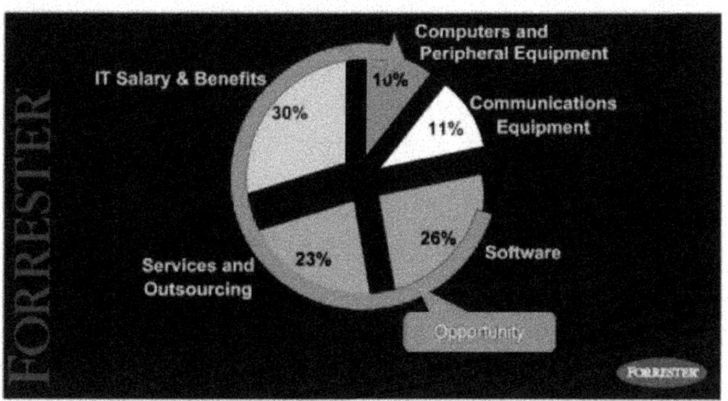

8 eXtend

Source: Company Internal Reports

Exhibit 8: e-Emphasys Revenue

Exhibit 8: e-Emphasys Revenue

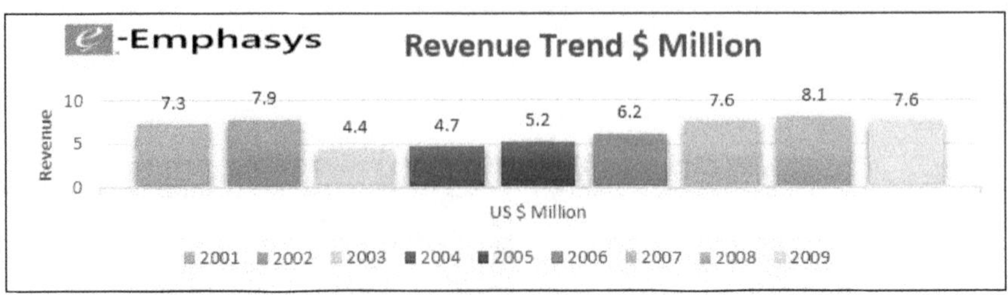

References

---

[1] Mohammad A Rashid et al, "The Evolution of ERP Systems....", Massey University Albany, New Zealand report.

[2] https://en.wikipedia.org/wiki/Baan_Corporation

[3] Mohammad A Rashid et al, "The Evolution of ERP Systems....", Massey University Albany, New Zealand report.

CHAPTER SEVEN

Follower's Dilemma: Indian Pharmacy Warfare

It was February 2005. Ajay Piramal was sitting in his Mumbai office, finalizing the business strategy for Nicholas Piramal India Ltd, NPL. The Piramal group diversified into the pharmacy business in 1988, by taking over a small company. Within 15 years they featured in the top five pharmaceutical companies in India. The Government of India committed to the WTO that it would shift from process patents to a product patents regime, beginning in January 2005. This change in the macro-environment would pose a challenge to Indian pharmaceutical companies. A radical rethinking of the business model and strategy became necessary. Mr. Ajay could either choose the 'status-quo' or play the 'second-fiddle' to multinational pharmacy companies by focusing on 'In-Licensing/Contract manufacturing' and distribution. The third possibility of forwarding integration, organized pharmacy retailing, was attractive. All three strategic options had flip sides.

Group History

The Piramal family was traditionally in the business of textiles and owned textile mills in Mumbai, India. During the notorious '*Textile Labour strike,*' in the early 1980s, the textile business in Mumbai went through a painful experience. Many textile companies went out of business; others shifted their base outside the city. Only a few could survive the strike. The Piramal family was one of them. The labor strike taught many lessons to mill owners. They realized the importance of modernization of the textile units to improve quality, quantity, and productivity at the global level. Ashok Piramal, the elder brother of Ajay, was heading the business.

He had a vision of taking the textile business to a truly global level but at the same time reducing the over-dependence on textiles. In the late 1980s, they diversified into Pharmaceutical, Electronics, Glass, and Engineering.

Pharmaceutical: - Journey from Marginal Player to the Industry Leader

Piramal Group bought Nicholas Laboratories, an Australian company, operating in Mumbai. The company was a niche player and had a good brand portfolio. In 1988, it had a turnover of $50 million, PBIDT of $ 0.7 million, and PAT of $0.25 million. The Company was ranked 48th in the Indian formulations market.[1] The factory was located in Mumbai and this mid-size company was known for its quality products and healthy industrial relations. Mr. C.M. Hattangdi was brought in as the Managing Director and CEO. He had had a rewarding career of almost 30 years with multinational pharmaceutical companies like Park Davis, in India. He had a critical role to play. He was the only person on the new board with techno-commercial knowledge.

Backward Integration

Getting quality glass bottles for the packaging of tablets and syrups was critical. The company was facing problems in the market due to the poor quality of bottles. Various suppliers were tried but the efforts were in vain. In 1990, Ashok Piramal decided to takeover Gujarat Glass Ltd, an ailing glass company. He also decided to get technological know-how from a company in Europe, which was the leader in pharmaceutical bottles. The commercial production of bottles started in 1990. By 1992, the company acquired a sizable share in the Gulf and Africa. Ajay Piramal completed his MBA from the reputed Jamnalal Bajaj College of Mumbai and joined the business in 1988. He started working with his brother.

New Team, New ambitions

Suddenly, in Jan. 1991, Ashok passed away due to cancer. It was a great shock to the family and their developing business. Ajay Piramal joined the board and became the Chairman and Managing Director; Mrs. Urvi Piramal was appointed as his deputy.

Success in the first venture in the pharmaceutical industry gave a lot of confidence to the top management. Ajay Piramal, Urvi Piramal, and Mr. Hattangdi complemented each other very well and formed an excellent team. In 1993, they opened a new plant in Madhya Pradesh. The production capacity was almost doubled. The sales in the financial year 1994-95 stood at $180 million. Neither the product mix nor the sales volume was large enough to keep distributors and retailers loyal to the company. They were required to increase product lines, even for survival. Encouraging developments took place in the Indian pharmaceutical industry around that time.

- In 1970 India came out with a patent law. But it was a process potent law rather than a product patent law. It allowed Indian manufacturers to produce less expensive copies of the world's best-selling patent-protected drugs. Indian drug producers became experts in 'reverse engineering' and increased their supply. India's pharmaceutical industry grew even in a highly regulated environment with government prices.
- In the mid and end 1980s, global pharma companies gave up hope and started abandoning the Indian market by selling their Indian arms. The exit of MNCs became an opportunity for Indian companies to take over.
- The Indian government decided to do away with the price regulation.
- The Indian market for pharmaceuticals was projected to grow at an average annual rate of between 15 and 20% from 2005 to 2010. The surge in production was driven by legislative reforms, the growth in contract manufacturing and outsourcing, value-added foreign acquisitions and joint ventures, India's mastery of reverse engineering of patented drug molecules, and India's efforts to comply with its World Trade Organization (WTO) Trade-Related Intellectual Property Agreement (TRIPs) obligations. When India joined the WTO in 1995, its pharmaceutical exports were valued at less than $600 million. It started growing by leaps and bounds. (By 2004, its exports had grown to $3.7 billion and accounted for more than 61% of industry turnover.) Indian pharmaceutical companies started producing 22% of the world's generic drugs and offered 60,000 finished medicines and nearly 400 bulk drugs used in formulations. India garnered a worldwide reputation for producing high-quality, low-cost generic drugs.

Ajay Piramal saw business opportunities emerging due to this critical policy change followed by positive market developments. He started scouting for more pharmaceutical companies. In Jan. 1994, he got another breakthrough. The group took over a French pharmaceutical company, Rhone Poulenc, India.

Getting Into the Top 20

The newly acquired company had a strong presence in the cough and cold, anti-dysentery, and anti-nausea markets. In just one stroke, the Piramal group was able to increase its therapeutic presence.

Though their brands were not market leaders, most of them were among the top three in their respective segments. The top brands of the company contributed around 90% of sales. There was a good scope to launch brand extensions.

With the takeover of the second company, the group appeared in the top 20 pharmaceutical companies of India, with respect to sales but Mr. Ajay Piramal wanted the company to be amongst the top five. A search for companies for the takeover was initiated.

The rising input costs, sluggish demand, poor economic conditions, increasingly demanding unions, the regulatory authorities, etc helped the group to identify many such potential takeover targets. Mr. Hattangdi was busy with the techno-commercial teams of the top management, in evaluating the proposals. Two Joint ventures were finalized; one in the Mid 90s and the other at the end 90s. The organic growth was complemented by acquisitions. In the year 2000, the group acquired 40% shares in another European Pharmaceutical Company. The stake was purchased from a Life Sciences company, which was also a global pharmaceutical giant. Up to 2002, the company acquired nine businesses. It demonstrated its ability to:

- Choose the right deal,
- Integrate the acquired businesses and
- Grow better through the acquired businesses.

The company occupied top standing in Therapeutic categories that comprised more than 85% of the Indian Pharmaceutical market. The company had products in almost all the higher growing chronicle ailment segments. These deals put the company in the top league of the Pharma industry. The combined sales touched $0.36 billion (FY2002), pushing it into the top five in the Indian Pharmaceutical Industry. Its number of brands in the list of ORG top 300[2] to sixteen and it became the company with the second-most number of brands on the list.

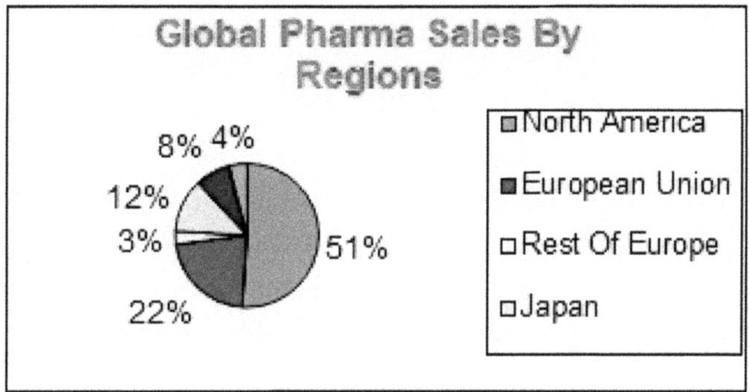

Sales by Region

In 2003,the size of the global pharmaceutical industry was $430 billion, to which North America and Europe contributed three-fourths, Japan contributed 12%, Latin America 4%, and the rest of the world 12%, India was the fourth-largest pharmaceutical market in the world. But 13th in value terms, which showed that it was one of the cheapest markets for pharmaceutical products. NIPL had strong growth in sales and profits. In 2000-01, the company outperformed the industry and grew at 14% a year. For 16 years the company was on a relentless growth drive. The Compounded Annual Growth Rate (CAGR) during this period in Sales and PBIDT was over 31% and 35% respectively, whereas in PAT it was 41%. The top 30 brands in their portfolio contributed to 50% of the domestic branded formulation sales and the top 10 brands formed 30% during 2003 –2004. The company was committed but selective in new product launches and was among the first four to market. NPL launched 22 new products and combinations. New products contributed 7% of branded formulation sales.

'In-Licensing' and 'Alliances' were the important strategies. The company entered an alliance with the third largest global company in biotechnology. The company had one of the largest field forces in India. About 3,000 sales representatives covered 65,000 chemists and 162,000 doctors. The scope for cross-selling of products was good.

New Horizons: - 2003

Behind the scene, the core management team was debating the business strategy of the company in the light of the dynamic macro-environmental factors, Vision, and Mission Statement.It was necessary to respond to the emerging trends in the global and Indian pharmaceutical industry.

Patents Regime in India

- With effect from 1st Jan 2005, India committed under the World Trade Organization (WTO) agreement to switch to the 'Product Patent Regime' as opposed to the 'Process Patent Regime' that existed.
- The government allowed the Indian Pharmaceuticals sector enough lead-time to prepare itself for the day - it was now almost a decade since India signed the WTO agreement in 1995.
- Though the Patent Act has existed since 1970, the government had deliberately kept pharmaceuticals out of the ambit of product patents. The new law would change that situation.
- Earlier companies could 'Reverse Engineer' a patented product, get permission under the Indian process patent regime, and launch it in India or anywhere else in unregulated markets. But under the new law, product patents demand registered in any WTO signatory country would have to be respected, for the first three years of the life of the product.
- Companies of all sizes - small and large - would have to stop 'Reverse Engineering', provided the original patent holder registers its product in India, after the first three years.

Three-fourths of the total sales of the company came from domestic formulations; hence it was important to critically evaluate the business strategy in the light of the new Product Patent Law[3], and choose an appropriate business model to succeed in the dynamic macro-environment.

India Pharmaceutical Industry

At the time of independence in 1947, India's pharmaceutical market was dominated by Western MNCs that controlled 90% of the market primarily through importation. Approximately 99% of all pharmaceutical products under patent in India at the time were held by foreign companies. Drug prices in India were among the highest in the world. The market remained import-dependent through the 1960s until the government-initiated policies stressing self-reliance through local production. At that time, 8 of India's top 10 pharmaceuticals were subsidiaries of MNCs. To facilitate the supply of pharmaceutical products the government of India founded 5 state-owned pharmaceutical companies. After the mid-1990s India's pharmaceutical industry was doing very well. The share of MNCs, which dominated the market with 90% share in 1970 came down to 28% in 2002.

Industry Structure

The Indian pharmacy industry was highly fragmented. The industry was broadly classified into organized and unorganized sectors. It had grown rapidly due to a lenient patent regime and low-cost manufacturing structure. This gave rise to an environment of intense competition, high output volume, and low prices. In 2002, around 24,000 small, medium, and large-scale companies were producing drugs in India. The leading 250 pharmacy companies controlled 70% of the market, with the market leader having only 7% market share. The top 10 companies covered around 31% of the pharmaceutical market.The Indian pharmaceutical industry was expected to grow from $6 billion in 2002 to $9 billion in 2005. This growth reflected the growing importance of India on the global pharmaceutical map. India was the 5th largest manufacturer of bulk drugs, according to Ernst and Young's Global pharmaceutical report, 2002. Up to December 1994, the pharmaceutical sector was governed by the Indian Patent Act (IPA), 1970 which did not allow product patents on medicines, agricultural products, and atomic energy. India became a signatory of the GATT (now WTO) in 1994 and therefore a signatory to the TRIPS agreement. The government of India was under compulsion, by the TRIPS agreement, to abolish the process patents and introduce a product patent regime in 2005 after a transition period of ten years. India shifted from process patent to product patent on January 1, 2005.

Ranbaxy: The Leader

Ranbaxy was the largest pharmaceutical company in India. Annual sales touched US$ one billion in the year 2003. It produced and marketed branded generic pharmaceutical products and Active Pharmaceutical Ingredients (APIs). It was a research-driven company, with 6% of revenues going towards it. The focus on research and development resulted in several approvals in developed markets.

Ranbaxy's continued focus on European and US markets helped it build deep product pipelines in both markets. The company sold products in over 70 countries and had an international portfolio of affiliates, joint ventures and alliances, ground operations in 34 countries, and manufacturing operations in 7 countries. The revenues achieved a 24% CAGR in the past five years, while the net profit had recorded a 42% CAGR. Looking into different geographies, the US was the largest contributor to top-line growth (about 35%). The total ANDA filings of the company in the US stood at 127 ANDAs, out of which 92 have been approved. The pipeline of the company was one of the largest in the US market, which indicated the potential growth prospect from this region in the form of new drug launches.

In Europe, the company's performance was again exciting, with contributions from the French market coming in for the first time after the company acquired RPG Aventis, France. The European market grew by 107% with revenues of US $139 m. The French market was the third largest for the company after US and India. The company has increased its regulatory filings to more than 14 products to date through various regulatory channels in Europe. With the inclusion of 10 more countries in the European Union, Ranbaxy would be able to expand its market with the same regulatory approvals. Coming to India specifically, sales growth in the first nine months of 2002 was impressive at 15%. The company had expanded its presence in top generics markets globally. The growth drivers continued to be the US and the European markets. Going forward, Ranbaxy may see strong competition putting pressure on margins. Though it would be compensated by strong volume growth. The R and D efforts of the company would also show benefits in the long run.

Dr. Reddy's Laboratories: Growth through innovation

Dr. Reddy's Laboratories, a leading pharmaceutical company, was present in the entire pharmacy value chain - basic research, finished dosages, generics, bulk actives, biotechnology, and diagnostics. They filed 64 patents and were the first Indian company to out-license a molecule for a clinical trial. The company was the first from India to get an Exclusive Marketing Right (EMR) in the US market. The company exported bulk drugs and branded and generic formulations to 60 countries. Export contributions to total revenues were 65%. Active Pharmaceutical Ingredients (API) constituted 40% of the business. The formulation business was another big contributor to revenues (39%). Its generics business in regulated markets contributed 22% and the rest came from diagnostic, critical care, and biotechnology business. The company was passing through a rough phase in 2003-04, profitability and sales growth had come under pressure. The revenues remained stagnant, which was due to a huge fall in generics sales in the US market (down 16%). This drop in sales was largely attributed to intense competition. Also, sales of Fluxotine, and Tizinadine, which were the mainstay of the company in the US market, saw a decline of 41%, as new players launched generic versions. Revenues from bulk drugs declined by 10%, both in local as well as global markets. The decline in revenues from API caused the decline in revenues from the European market (down 58%), due to lower sales of 'Ramipril', which saw tough generic competition, and price decline. Ramipril was used to treat high blood pressure (hypertension). However, the domestic market performance saw a decline, led by a fall in sales of high revenue generating products from key therapeutic areas of Gastrointestinal, cardiovascular and anti-infective. The lackluster top-line performance led to an even worse bottom-line performance. The operating margin of the company came down from 23.8%. The major reason for this was an increase in R&D expenses and higher other expenses. The R&D expenses of the company grew almost by 25% and were at 11% of revenues. The increased R and D expenses were due to the clinical trials of one of its molecules, which the company initiated recently. The sales and distribution expenses grew by 29%. However, the increased expense heads were seen as an investment for the future. Adding to the woes in top-line, as well as in operating margins, the net profit of the company was down by 48%, year to year. The loss on the foreign exchange side lowered other income. Tax exemption on the R and D expenses and new bulk drug facilities in tax-exempted areas stopped the further slide in the profits. Dr. Reddy's Lab (DRL) was going through a trial by fire on the stock market. The share prices of DRL had plunged by 30%. Mr. Anji Reddy, one of the most respected personalities in the Indian pharmaceutical industry, was under attack. Some investors rejected his vision of 'Discovery Led Success'. The criticism was on the premature R and D investments, results of which wouldn't be immediately forthcoming. Striking a balance between profit and vision was critical to the successful business model. DRL needed to grow a bit more to be able to pay for the 'High Risk-High reward' innovator game. Indian Pharmaceutical industry had been built on reverse engineering of the successful molecule. No company had taken a big bet on innovator products like DRL. It had consistently increased R and D expenditures to 12% of the revenue. It was close to what multinationals spent on research. The research DRL was doing for tomorrow was paid for by the business it is doing today, 'Marketing the copy-cat products worldwide. It was unfortunate that DRL was taking longer to establish its business model. With a couple of breakthroughs and the world would have been different for DRL. They already had eight new molecules either at the pre-clinical or clinical level of development. Some global companies would shift their business models away from developing blockbusters,[4] toward more specialized products that require less promotion. Roche had thrived by selling drugs for hepatitis, HIV, and cancer. They required smaller marketing budgets since the patient populations were smaller, and the specialist physicians were fewer. Roche's drugs were selling well because they addressed serious medical needs. Roche's sales would grow by 6.2% annually over the next several years as against Pfizer's 1.4%.

Growth Model for Nicholas Piramal Industries Ltd

Ajay Piramal's mission was to create value for his shareholders and become a value generator, rather than focusing on just one industry. He was always counter-intuitive. In the 1990s and early 2000s, when everyone was into reverse engineering, he partnered with the global pharma giants rather than going against them. Buying and selling companies had been his nature. Ajay Piramal took over Indian arms of Aventis, Rhone Poulenc, Roche, etc, and subsequently Rhodia, Pfizer Morpeth, and Avecia.

This strategy helped to build a reputation and international presence in custom manufacturing and earned the trust of the reputed MNCs in the pharma space, globally[5]. The company developed competencies in the area of contract manufacturing. It also invested in research and development but realized that a different mindset is required for the same. The company hired McKinsey in 2003. They came out with the international contract manufacturing blueprint which was based on the premise of patent non-infringement and collaboration in drug development and manufacturing. McKinsey proposed using India for cost arbitrage but leveraging a global footprint to stay closer to the customer. Sensing that the innovators were lacking the infrastructure to outsource too far, Piramal started investing in the manufacturing bases in America in early 2000. They acquired manufacturing facilities in the US and were to invest USD 1 Billion in the next decade. Mr. Piramal was thinking hard about how to grow his company and offer value to his shareholders who trusted him with the leadership. He had three major options.

Option One: Playing Second Fiddle [6]

Some business executives were suggesting a conservative business model, for NPL. They felt it would be better to partner with innovator companies in the global markets rather than compete with them in the product patent era. The success of NPL, in the last decade, should be leveraged to attract better clients who are looking for outsourcing. The conservative outlook on the business model could be summed up as below:

- India could certainly play a role in research by offering country advantage like low cost of research particularly in the areas like Clinical trials, which was a costly proposition in the western world.
- The mass database of patients in India could be of great value in the research.
- They strongly advocated the plan of offering India advantages to the global innovator companies, by providing end-to-end outsourcing solutions to them from custom chemical synthesis, APIs[7], and intermediates up to formulations.
- They proposed to go for USFDA approval for production facilities and establish a 100% subsidiary in the USA for closer customer coordination.

Investing into the R and D in the coming years for new product development would be a costly affair, particularly because of WTO regulations. The perception was, "The international laws regarding pharmaceutical research were pro-multinational companies and Indian companies would have a tough time falling in line. Basic research was luxury for Indian companies and it might not receive required returns because of the incomparable scale of operations." Global companies could easily recover the R and D overheads, which were getting divided amongst a large number of markets. Secondly, Indian pharmaceutical companies made their maximum impact while supplying bulk drugs or Active Pharmaceutical Ingredients (APIs) to the world market. It was a business model that existed for three decades and was likely to remain the most preferred model. After all, it fetched healthy net margins of 15-20% for Indian pharmaceutical companies of all types, big and small. API was done by the rebel manufacturers who made copies of patented molecules without the knowledge or formal approval. The friendly manufacturers manufactured and supplied bulk drugs for and with the approval of the holder of the patent. While the former dominated the nineties, the trend in India was beginning to gradually shift towards the latter. Post-2004, this trend to be a friendly manufacturer would intensify because at least 70-75% of the world pharmaceutical market would go under patents by then. The strengths acquired by Nicholas Piramal (NPL), over the last 15 years were:

- Operating Efficiently,
- Employing efficient chemists, in the factories, at the globally lowest cost
- Producing consistent quality pharmaceutical products as per pre-determined specifications.

More cautious analysts suggested that Nicholas Piramal should focus on core competencies and get out of the areas where they were average performers. The focus should be on the 'Live and let Live' strategy. Mutual co-existence with multinational pharmacy companies was imperative. "NPL could continue doing 'In-licensing' and distribute products of multinationals in India through their strong network and continue to profit from the distribution infrastructure which was created over a period of time, with great difficulty."

Option Two: Maintain Status Quo

The bullish view argued that if NPL could survive in the tough Indian market then it could thrive globally. There was no reason for the company to succumb to the Multi-National Companies, MNCs, in panic. It had a consistently rewarding performance for 15 years in the markets where it successfully fought against a good number of MNC subsidiaries.

In their view, the immediate threat of the new patent law to the Indian pharmaceutical industry was minimal. That was because Generics[8], (25% of the global market) was still open to manufacturers. Indian companies could go ahead with the R and D of specialty pharmaceuticals and apply innovation to develop products that would fulfill the unmet or poorly met medical needs. Even one breakthrough invention would provide billion-dollar sales in a couple of years. No other business model could offer such growth. Just two products, Lipitor (cholesterol reducer), worth $7.79 Billion, and Norvasc (antihypertensive), 3.84 billion, took Pfizer to the Fortune 500 list.[9] This school of thought believed that an incomparable size of field force that could communicate the required message and could persuade a hundred and sixty thousand doctors, a strongly knitted web of loyal and exclusive distributors, and more than sixty thousand chemists would cater to the demand generated for the hundreds of Stock Keeping Units. They suggested that In-licensing must be used very selectively and should be discouraged to the maximum possible extent. In their view, the MNCs may have the competitive advantage of having new molecules with global patents and a well-established R and D back up but they would take a minimum of 5 to 7 years to match distribution capabilities in India. The challenge for Indian companies was to utilize this lead-time and set off the edge enjoyed by MNCs. Why should global companies get everything on the platter?

There was nothing wrong with 'Contract Manufacturing' however. The philosophy should be to look for opportunities to add value rather than working on vendor-type manufacturers. "We should look for partners who will give us chance to contribute and learn when we do contract manufacturing for them. They should also offer us other opportunities like country-specific marketing rights, contract research, and process development contracts."

The largest change in the post-2005 scenario would be the unprecedented number of drugs going off-patent. Between 2005 and 2010, the patent of many widely used drugs would expire. This implied a huge potential in national and international generic markets. NPL had strong infrastructure facilities to manufacture these generic drugs. NPL's advantages in this field were:

1. Bulk drug manufacture base,
2. Low manufacturing and capital costs,
3. Skilled manpower,
4. Optimal use of process research skills,
5. Focus on exports and niche therapeutic areas.

NPL had manufacturing practices approved by the US-FDA to ensure success even after the introduction of the product patent. This group of strategists believed that the pharmaceutical sector wouldn't be decimated by the new law and there was enough in the market.

Less than 5% of the drugs available in the Indian market where copies of patented products hence Indian pharmaceutical companies need not agonize over it. NPL could focus on the least developed countries for exports, where the product patent regime would not be operational until the year 2016.[10] Even though their average per capita income was $268, which indicated lower purchasing power, it's an opportunity nevertheless. The Indian pharmaceutical industry would go through a restructuring in the product patent era. Many small and medium players would be forced to sell off their factories. The supply side would be better organized with a smaller number of players remaining in the fray. They would not be in a position to create an unfair advantage by exploiting the loopholes in the legal and tax structures. Additionally, the Govt. would be forced to relook at the industrial policy, which was pro-small-scale and created hurdles in the progress of mega-size companies. This would ease competitive pressures to some extent. This view believed that it was unnecessary to raise doubts about the present business model, which had been tried and tested even in the toughest of times. They suggested the status quo, definitely with a few required adjustments to take care of the emerging post-product patent scenario.

Option Three: Thinking Out of the box – Forward Integration

The third view believed that the status quo with minor adjustments in the strategy was not enough. Radical rethinking was required at this crucial juncture in the current business model. However, focusing only on possible threats to the environment was not a great idea. Other opportunities in the environment must be seriously looked at. Only out-of-box thinking would help the company in selecting an appropriate business model. The prospects for organized pharmacy retailing in India were promising. Piramals could go for forwarding integration and create pharmaceutical retail chains like CVS Pharmacy and Walgreen[11].Taking the first-mover advantage in the organized pharmaceutical retail in India was important. Highlighting the megatrend in the Indian Pharmaceutical industry the group of experts argued, "The future trade channel will evolve in such a way that there will be value migration from suppliers to retailers, the reason being the proximity retailers will have with the end customer. As the role of the intermediary diminishes, retailers will become stronger in their negotiating power than manufacturers and the only way for companies to keep this bargaining power is to enter into retailing themselves. The growth of the pharmacy retail store is bound to increase as it leads to more accountability and professionalism in the industry." Morepen Laboratories' acquisition of the retail chain Lifespring, as well as the new launches, 98.4 from Global Healthline and Consumer Retail Services (CRS) Health Division from SAK Industries, exemplify this new trend. SAK CRS is aiming to operate 150 outlets in the country in the next five years, while Global Healthline is planning to open 40-50 stores. Indian Pharmacy Retail Scenario was as follows:

- India had 5.1 million retailers, of whom only 15 percent had pharmacies.
- Indian patients are not always sure of the originality of the medicines due to adulteration.
- Due to the growing mall culture, customers in metropolitan cities were getting used to heavy discounts and prices below MRP on grocery, FMCG products, apparel, etc. But they were not getting any discounts on pharmacy products even after buying them in bulk. Customers having loyalty Walgreen cards, by contrast, saved an average of 27% on prescriptions.

- There was not a single pharmacy chain store operating in India. All the pharmacy shops were stand-alone and did not get the advantage of scale.
- The manufacturers had an upper hand in distribution that they exploited to fulfill their interests.
- The initial response to the medical sections in the Hypermarkets in the metro cities was encouraging. The small medical stores in close proximity to the hypermarkets suffered major sales loss, despite the many shortcomings in the medical counter of the hypermarkets like missing inventory, lack of discounting, no self-service, and no store brands.

The prevailing macro-environment in India was very much conducive to opening pharmacy chain stores. The benefits that a company could get from such diversification were:

1. The group could have control of entire value and supply chains.
2. The company could launch many new generic products, which would be sold through the chain stores, and hence success could be achieved faster. This could have been an important strategy in the product patent era where the focus of the company would be on generics.
3. The company could also launch many Over-The-Counter (OTC) products. In OTC products the distribution and getting shelf space on retail counters are the keys to success.
4. The chain store network could be leveraged to attract positive responses from multi-national pharmaceutical companies for In-Licensing.
5. The prime land, available to NPL in the metropolitan cities due to the shifting of the production bases in the interior areas and which couldn't be sold freely due to legal and political pressures, would be best utilized to improve Returns on Investment (ROI) of the pharmaceutical company.
6. Availability of exclusive distribution channels for their related products could also benefit other group companies like textiles because a typical pharmaceutical chain store sells non-pharmaceutical items up to 40%.
7. After streamlining pharmaceutical retailing and achieving a critical mass, the company could get into manufacturing private brands at a later date.

The Crossfire

Choosing the right business model in the volatile and dynamic environment became further complicated with many strategic options available to management. When the company was losing its grip on the current business in the post-product patent scenario, pharmaceutical retailing could be a good alternative to regain the grip. But the retailing option was investment intensive. The capital market was unstable and was not in the mood to help a pharmaceutical company in the post-patent era. Selling a part of the real estate at premium locations in Mumbai and divesting non-core business units were the only options left for raising funds. Additionally, retailing is a volume game, margins were wafer-thin. A sustaining power, in terms of deep pockets, was required at least for an initial 7 to 8 years. The real worry was whether the strained business could support retailing efforts on its own for such a long period. Joining hands with an overseas pharmacy retailer could be a better option. Though getting into pharmacy retailing was a good ambition, it was too early to begin. Following hurdles were identified in pharmacy retailing expansion:

1. In most of the areas, hospitals, dispensaries, and chemists had an understanding between them. The Medical practitioners direct the customers only to specific medical stores. Organized retailers could not compete on such a basis.
2. Getting into pharmacy retailing might send wrong signals to the pharmaceutical distribution network and the channel members might get demoralized, hurting the sales growth.
3. Most of the medical stores were successfully avoiding payment of taxes. An organized pharmaceutical retailer wouldn't be able to do so.
4. Some medical stores were offering monthly credits to select customers. Due to limited penetration of credit cards, Pharmacy retail chain stores would not be in a position to extend credit facilities to the masses.
5. There were many laws, which were practically not possible to follow. Small medical shops were manipulating them but chain stores could not.
6. Usually, the pharmacy stores have up to 40% of their stock as non-pharmacy Stock Keeping Units (SKUs). Identifying such SKUs and managing them is a separate business in itself and needs different skill sets which were not readily available in the organization.

7. Selecting the right foreign partner would be most critical. Walgreen and CVS were not operating outside the USA. Selecting a marginal player wouldn't help in getting an early breakthrough but selecting a too strong foreign player might invite trouble when the business starts performing well after initial teething problems.

Some thought the risks associated with the first mover in organized pharmacy retailing outweighed its benefits.

Follower's Dilemma

As the chairman of the board of directors, Mr. Ajay Piramal, spoke at the Annual General Meeting in 2004, "A continuing dominant presence in the Indian market is not only healthy business proposition – it is essential to hone chemistry, innovation and marketing ability of any Indian pharmacy company that has global aspirations. NPL has decided to partner with innovator companies in global markets, rather than compete or patent-litigate against them. Over the past 16 years, we have demonstrated an unrelenting commitment to our partnerships with global innovator companies across products, IPR, and technology in the domestic market. This has won us their faith and confidence. Our export model delivers India's advantage to global innovator companies. We will provide end-to-end outsourcing solutions across the pharmacy life cycle. We recently completed a review of our strategic direction ahead and have named the initiative- Project '*Agya Chkra*'."

Ajay Piramal was in deep thinking. He had to come out with an appropriate business model to steer his successful organization through the volatile macro-environment. He had to convert the dynamic macro-environment to strategic advantage rather than becoming a victim to it. He had to ensure that the next 5 years would not dilute the momentum of the past 16 years.

Exhibit 1: - Ratio Analysis

Management Efficiency Ratios					
Year	2000	2001	2002	2003	2004
Adjusted Net Profit Margin (%)	10.74	11.73	8.03	14.62	14.55
Cash Profit Margin (%)	12.92	14.18	9.82	16.68	17.31
Gross Profit Margin (%)	14.52	15.39	13.86	17.61	17.05
Operating Profit Margin (%)	21.35	20.55	19.57	21.14	19.72
Profit Before Interest and Tax Margin (%)	19.17	18.09	17.79	19.07	16.96
Return On Capital Employed (%)	20.61	20.57	30.48	34.66	34.60
Return On Net Worth (%)	15.38	17.03	21.89	51.16	54.88

Liquidity And Solvency Ratios					
Year	2000	2001	2002	2003	2004
Current ratio	2.68	2.42	1.55	1.48	1.51
Debt Equity Ratio	0.33	0.28	0.64	0.94	0.79
Long Term Debt Equity Ratio	0.32	0.28	0.48	0.67	0.65

Management Efficiency Ratios					
Year	2000	2001	2002	2003	2004
Debtors Turnover Ratio	6.19	6.49	9.00	7.80	8.34
Fixed Assets Turnover Ratio	2.03	2.05	2.81	2.83	2.78
Inventory Turnover Ratio	6.33	6.07	7.65	7.15	7.84
Total Assets Turnover Ratio	1.07	1.14	1.71	1.82	2.04

Debt Coverage Ratio					
Year	2000	2001	2002	2003	2004
Interest Cover	2.81	3.51	3.11	5.39	6.35

Exhibit 2: - Mission and Vision Statement

Mission

Making a difference to the Quality of Life by reducing the burden of disease.

Vision

To become the most admired Pharmaceuticals Company in India with leadership in market share, research and profits by:

Building distinctive sales and marketing capabilities

Evolving from licensing to global launch of own patented products

Being the partner of choice

We shall pursue world-class standards in our People, Products, Processes, Partnerships and Performance

Encouraging Innovation and Nurturing Intellectual Capital

We seek quantum growth to lead in the domestic market and enhance our international presence.

Source: Company Report

Exhibit 3: - Sales Analysis

	Net Sales Break up	% Total	% Growth in 2004
I	Domestic		
1	Formulation	75.8	31.0
2	Generics	3.2	(7.4)
3	APIs	0.9	177.5
4	Vitamins and Fine Chemicals	5.1	(8.9)
5	Diagnostics	6.1	17.0
6	Others	0.5	-
	Sub –Total	91.5	26.4
II	Exports		
1	Formulations	1.8	6.1
2	Generics	0.5	84.7
3	APIs	4.9	337.7
4	Vitamin and Fine Chemicals	1.0	84.1
5	Others	0.3	-
	Sub –Total	8.5	136.4
	Total	100.0	31.6

Source: Company Report

Exhibit 4: Important players in Indian pharmacy manufacturing:

Drugs	Domestic Market	Exports	International Alliances	Strategic Thrust
Cipla:				
Wide product range in domestic market, antibiotics, anti-bacterial, anti-asthmatics, anti-inflammatory, antiretroviral, anthelminites, anti-cancer and cardiovascular.	In domestic formulation market, antibiotics were the mainstays.	Concentrated on developing speciality bulk drugs for export markets	Strategic alliance with major generic manufacturers such as Watson, Mylan, Barr and Ivax for the supply of bulk drugs.	The largest pharmacy company in the Indian retail market as per ORG survey. Strong presence in formulations and bulk drugs.
Glaxo:				
Revenues from two segments viz. pharmacy and animal healthcare. Leading brands like Zinetac, Betnesol, Cobadex and Zevit in the domestic pharmacy market.	The pharmacy segment grew by 21% owing to the effect of the merger of Burroughs-Wellcome The parent signalled its willingness to launch new products in the Indian market	In line with the guidelines by the parent company.	The parent company, is the second-largest pharmacy company in the world, with an R and D chest of US$ 4 billion.	The largest MNC pharmaceutical company in the Indian market.
Aventis:				
Chronic (diabetes, CVS) and critical-care therapeutic segments.	It was the 6th largest domestic player with a market share of 2.9%. Aventis had relatively few but very strong brands in the country. Over the years. 6% growth in the domestic market continued, in 2004. Opportunity for the compa terms of launching new pr from its parent's portfolio new patent regime.	supplied bulk drugs to its parent, which constituted about 26% of the company's sales. Exports lead the charge; sales growth was largely driven by strong performance on the exports front. It grew by 63% on the back of demand arising from higher supply to its parent company. Their products were sold in Russia and CIS countries	50% subsidiary of Aventis SA, France	2nd largest pharmaceutical MNC in India with a turnover of over Rs 7 billion.

Exhibit 5: Ranbaxy – A Global Pharmaceutical Company with Indian Roots

In January 2004, India's top drug maker Ranbaxy Laboratories made a big-bang entry into France's $800-million generics market. It went from being a nobody to France's fifth largest marketer of off-patent drugs by acquiring RPG Aventis from the Franco-German Aventis Pharmaceuticals. The coveted top league in France - the world's fifth largest generics market, after the US, Japan, Germany, and the UK- has a hefty price tag. Ranbaxy reportedly paid Aventis $84 million (nearly 1.4 times the target company's 2003 sales) for a 100% stake. That made it the largest overseas acquisition by an Indian drug maker. In the following months,

Hyderabad's Dr. Reddy's and Mumbai's Wockhardt made acquisitions in Germany and the US. In 2003, Zydus Cedilla had bought a company in France, Wockhardt in the UK, and Glenmark in Brazil. Was that the right time for Indian Pharmacy companies to go global with a vengeance?

In 1993, when the then Ranbaxy Laboratories chairman Parvinder Singh and his trusted lieutenant D.S. Brar scripted an ambitious roadmap to take the company global, very few of their peers were thinking the same way. With marketing and sales infrastructures in as many as 45 countries (being increased to 100) and manufacturing plants in seven countries,

Ranbaxy was more global than any other Indian company. Going forward, it would perhaps be more global than what Parvinder Singh had planned. Only 22 per cent of Ranbaxy's nearly $1.2-billion revenue came from domestic operations. It had a non-Indian CEO, Brian Tempest, with global experience. The company's global headquarters for intellectual property and legal affairs had been set up in Princeton, New Jersey. And its market research headquarters is in London. It was listed in India and the Luxembourg Stock Exchange, and 18 per cent of its 9,500 employees were non-Indians.

Exhibit 6: Walgreen - CVS

- One third of the pharmaceuticals retail sales in USA was controlled by only two retailing giants Walgreen and CVS Pharmacy. They have been developing at a rapid pace for last decade. More than 30% of their sales was non-pharmaceuticals products and services.
- Walgreen, whose fiscal 2004 sales totalled $37.5 billion, operated 4,682 stores in 44 states Of USA and Puerto Rico. It planed to open about 450 new U.S. stores in fiscal 2005.Every 19 hours; a new Walgreens was opening – all on carefully selected sites. In last 10 years only 2 stores were closed due to poor sales. Around 55 million people lived within a mile of Walgreen store and billion Americans drive past Walgreen high traffic corners every week. Study showed maximum distance Americans wanted to travel for buying pharmacy was 2 miles or less. Walgreen had therefore kept a target to open 7000 stores by 2010. Walgreens filled 443 million prescriptions in fiscal 2004, an increase of 10.8 percent from the previous year. Walgreen received 8.2-million prescription requests online, 21% growth over last year. Convenience is central to the success, and to the customers that means freestanding stores at major intersections, drive-thru pharmacies and ample parking that's safe, secure and a short walk to the store's entrance.
- People of all ages can access Mayo Clinic Health Information on Walgreens.com, which included articles on disease states, healthy living and self-care. They also air "Walgreens Health Corner" on WGN-TV in Chicago and nationally on the WGN Superstation. This program, available to 56 million families each week, probes topics such as heart disease, healthy eating and flu prevention. Generics account for approximately half the prescriptions Walgreen fill. Generics lower costs for patients and third party payers, and provide the retailer with better gross profit per prescription. Financially, they're good for the bottom line. But because generics are less expensive, they also lower sales line. This, in turn, distorted expense ratios when measured as a percent to sales.
- CVS Pharmacy operated 5,383 retail and specialty pharmacy stores in 36 states of USA with Annual sales of $ 27 billion. It opened 275 new stores in a year 2003.CVS had highest sales per square foot. Ratio of $800 in the entire pharmaceuticals retail industry, $100 more than next

best. In 2003, CVS balance sheet remained among the best in the pharmaceuticals retail industry, with low leverage and excellent working capital ratios.

References: -

[1]Ajay Piramal, A letter from Chairman,NPL Annual Report 2004

[2]ORG is a Market research company. It publishes a list of the Top 300 pharmacy brands in India, every year.

[3]As a result of the commitment given by the Govt. of India to the WTO, a new patent policy came into effect on 1st Jan. 2005.

[4]Drugs with revenue of $1 billion annually or more.

[5] The Economic Times

[6] Options are based on the views of senior executives who requested not to mention their names.

[7]**Active Pharmaceutical Ingredient**

Any substance or mixture of substances intended to be used in the manufacture of a drug (medicinal) product and that when used in the production of a drug becomes an active ingredient of the drug product.

[8]**Generic Drug**A drug is produced and marketed under its chemical or "generic" name (as opposed to a brand name. A generic drug can be sold only after a proprietary drug goes off patent (i.e. when the patent runs out after 17 years).

There are numerous generic drug manufacturers. While generic drugs are cheaper for consumers, they still must meet the standards of GMPs as set out by the FDA.

[9]To be a Fortune 500 company the minimum required turnover as per the latest list is $ 10 Billion.

[10]Forty-nine countries are currently designated by the United Nations as
least developed countries (LDCs) on the basis of low national income, weak human assets, and high economic vulnerability.

[11] Walgreens and CVS Pharmacy both are Fortune 500 Pharmacy chain stores,
based in the USA.

CHAPTER EIGHT

Ridding the Skidding Motorcycle - Bajaj Auto Ltd.

It was May 2017. Rajiv Bajaj, the Managing Director of Bajaj Auto Ltd, was sitting with his senior team in his head office in Akurdi, Pune, in India. They were going through the sales report of the company for FY 2016-17 which ended in March 2017 and for April 2017. A major setback in the domestic (Indian) motorcycle market was a real cause of concern. In April 2017, the sales of motorcycles in the local market came down by 19%. Ever since Bajaj stopped producing scooters, in 2010, they focused on bikes and have done a splendid job in international marketing. Exports contributed to 44% of their sales. In April 2017, exports jumped up by 46% compared to the previous month. However, the sales of their motorcycles in the Indian market came down from FY 2011-12 until FY 2016-17, as a result, their motorcycle market share in the Indian market dipped from 24.3% to 18.3%. The market share of flagship motorcycle brand, Pulsar, came down to less than a half, from 27%, ten years ago, to 12%. Honda snatched the number two position, in the Indian two-wheeler industry, from Bajaj Auto, thanks to Honda's mega success in the scooter market supported by increasing market share in the motorcycle market. Bajaj was pushed to the fourth position in the Indian two-wheeler industry. After discontinuing scooters, they had an identity issue. Bajaj couldn't create a distinct image in the minds of customers for their motorcycles. Hero, the market leader, dominated the domestic motorcycle segment which was three-fourths of the two-wheeler market. The sales growth in the Indian motorcycle industry was standstill from 2012-13 to 2015-16.

However, the domestic scooter market had been growing more than 20%, annually, for the past five consecutive years. The scooter market was poised to re-capture 40% of the two-wheeler market share from motorcycles. Bajaj maintained a strong financial position of the company, though did not leverage it fully for the growth of the market share. Rajiv and his team had to respond to the decline in domestic sales. His options were limited. Rajiv had to recreate the magic around the umbrella brand, Bajaj, in the domestic market, by brand re-positioning. He had to leverage the strong financial position and also the goodwill created in the domestic scooter market from 1960 to 2000. Rajiv couldn't ignore the strong market trend in favor of scooters. Most two-wheeler manufacturers responded to the trend by launching new models of scooters. But for Rajiv, it was not an easy choice. He had been practicing and advocating the strategy of 'Focus' on motorcycles and preferred to stay away from scooters. He made Bajaj get out of the scooter market which they were ruling for many decades. Rajiv was in a fix, whether to re-launch scooters? His focus on motorcycles was working well in the export markets but was not delivering results in the domestic market. The board meeting was scheduled for two weeks. Rajiv had to prepare well for the meeting.

Bajaj Auto Ltd: A Company Profile

Bajaj was a motorcycle and three-wheeler manufacturer from India. As of April 2015, the company was the fourth largest two-wheeler manufacturer in India ("see Appendix 1") having an 18.81% market share in the domestic markets of motorcycles. The company sold 1.9 million motorcycles in the Indian market whereas 1,49 million motorcycles were exported. With sales of about 250000 units, the company was the market leader in the domestic three-wheeler market with a market share of 57.5%. The company exported 280000 units of three-wheelers. Exports contribute 44% of the business and are valued at more than $ 1.3 billion. ("see Appendix 2"). Africa was the largest international market for Bajaj Auto which contributed 43% of the total exports followed by South Asia & Middle east (31%), Latin America (20%), and ASEAN markets (6%). The company was having three manufacturing facilities with the installed capacity of all three plants of the company was about 6 million vehicles.

Bajaj Auto invested a total of € 198.1 million (Rs 12.19 billion) and acquired a 48% stake in KTM AG of Austria (KTM), the fastest-growing motorcycle brand in the world[i]. Bajaj was the most profitable two-wheeler company in the world. In 2016 the net sales of Bajaj Auto reached $ 3 billion (Rs 222 billion). Operating earnings before interest, tax, depreciation, and amortization (EBITDA) increased by 17.5% to $ 0.7 billion, making it the highest in the Company's history. The operating EBITDA margin was 22.4% of net sales and other operating income, which was the highest in the industry. At 21.1%, the operating profit margin to net sales plus other operating income was also thehighest in the industry[ii]. Bajaj had an after-tax profit of about $ 0.52 billion. Bajaj had cash reserves of $1.5 billion. For the Bajaj group, the cash reserves were more than $ 5 billion. Most of it is with Bajaj Holdings & Investment Limited [BHIL]. Even with a 1:1 debt-equity ratio, they could easily raise debt of $ 5 billion for new projects.

History

Bajaj Auto started trading Piaggio scooters in India in 1958. In 1960 the company entered into an agreement with the same Italian company to manufacture and sell Piaggio scooters in India. It started its manufacturing plant in Pune, in Western India. The joint venture with Piaggio ended in 1971. Rahul Bajaj, took charge of the business in 1965 when he returned to India by getting an MBA degree from Harvard Business School. Under his leadership, the turnover of Bajaj Auto the flagship company has gone up from Rs.72 million to Rs.46.16 billion (USD 936 million)[iii] and the company started manufacturing plants at Waluj and Pant Nagar. Rajiv Bajaj, the elder son of Rahul Bajaj joined the company, as an 'Officer on Special Duty', in 1990, after completing his post-graduation in Mechanical engineering. In the year 2000, Rajiv was inducted into the Bajaj Auto board. He started a state-of-the-art plant at Chakan. Bajaj Auto was known in India for their scooters which they designed in collaboration with Piaggio. 'Chetak' was the first brand of their scooters and they also launched other brands like 'Super', 'Cub' etc. In 1975, under an agreement with Western Maharashtra Development Corporation Ltd., a joint sector company was incorporated under the name Maharashtra Scooters Limited. A plant started, at Satara manufactured scooters in the brand name 'Priya'.

In the government-regulated production era, in the 1970s, Bajaj scooters were having a long list of customers who paid full price and waited for more than ten years for the delivery. In 1981, the 'Bajaj M80', 80 cc mini-motorcycle, called 'Step-thru', was entirely developed by the company and introduced in the market. The licensed capacity was 3,00,000 scooters during the year 1083. In 1983, Bajaj Auto entered into an agreement with Kawasaki Heavy Industries of Japan for the manufacture of motorcycle engines. It was dependent on foreign partners for the technical know-how, design, and development till that time Rajiv took over the function of product development in the mid-1990s. Rajiv and his team designed and developed the motorcycles brand, 'Pulsar' which later became their flagship model, and various versions of Pulsar was launched. A three-wheeler with a rear engine was designed and marketed in this period.

Creative Destruction: Killing the Brand Rather the than Product

Some brands become part of national consciousness. Bajaj scooter was such a brand in India until the beginning of the twenty-first century. The brand became an integral part of Indian heritage and tradition. The image of an Indian family, husband driving a Bajaj Chetak scooter, wife sitting at the pillion seat with two kids got embedded forever into Indian minds. The slogan of Bajaj Auto became popular in India. It was in the national language of India, Hindi. In TV advertisements, it ran as: '*Buland Bharat ki Buland Tasveer. Hamara Bajaj, Hamara Bajaj*' (meaning strong India's strong image: our Bajaj). Until 1983 API and Bajaj Auto were the only two scooter manufacturers in India. After that, the government opened up the sector for foreign manufacturers and other domestic business houses. Honda entered the Indian market with a scooter, Kinetic Honda. Southern business house, TVS, also came into the market with a lower capacity model. Bajaj was the clear market leader of the Indian scooter market until the year 2002. Bajaj scooter had an almost maintenance-free engine. It was designed by Piaggio of Italy as a part of technical collaboration. Though not very fuel efficient, it was highly reliable. The engine of the scooter was mounted on the left side rather than in the center. This engine mounting created problems in starting a bike and parking it on the side stand. The quantum of effort needed to park it on the stand was high. The problem persisted in all models. Bajaj never attempted to resolve this issue.

Women could not park them on the account of required physical efforts. There were quality issues with the clutch and gear cables, quality of the steel sheets used, etc. Customers had to stay with these product issues because the company did not do enough to modernize Bajaj Scooters. Ever since 1995, there had been a significant shift away from scooters to motorcycles, the market for basic scooters declined marginally, while that of motorcycles increased at a compound annual rate of 25%. In 1995-96, almost 1.2 million scooters were sold in India, versus 661,000 motorcycles. In 1999-2000, scooter sales clocked at 1.1 million, while motorcycles sales climbed to 1.6 million. ("see Appendix 3"). Even within the scooter segment, there was a shift away from traditional metal-bodied models to the sleeker scooterette . In 1994-95, a little over 96,000 scooterette were sold. Five years later in 1999-2000, sales had more than doubled to over 258,000. Bajaj Auto's mainstay was the traditional, metal-bodied, side-engine mounted, kick-start scooters. From 1995 to 2000 the company had to face a stagnant even declining market for these models. Bajaj realized that the days of resting comfortably on the high margins from Chetaks and Supers (metal-bodied scooter brands) were coming to an end. Bajaj conceived a strategy for 'creative destruction. It wanted to keep the Bajaj brand alive in the scooter market. That could be done only by killing the old product form of scooters and replacing it with modern technology scooters. Bajaj tried to develop and launch a few models of scooters and mopeds in the late 1990s like Sunny, Spirit, Saffire, etc. but could not succeed in the marketplace. Those new models failed even to attract Bajaj loyal customers who were seeking replacements. For the man on the street, it was the demise of his trusted scooter, Bajaj-Chetak. The product was designed for young males. Women loved it for the space it offered on the pillion seat and the variety of things one could carry on a scooter[iv]. Over a period the young male got attracted to a bike and Bajaj failed to attract women from the pillion seats to the front seat. They rather preferred to ride 'Honda-Activa'. By late 2009, scooter volumes for Bajaj, once a clear market leader, had dropped drastically making little sense to keep running production lines for scooters. They were selling just a few hundred units a month rather than a few hundred thousand in the 1970s and 1980s. They lost the market leader status to Honda. Rajiv took the decision to stop scooter and moped production in 2010.

The country saw a kind of emotional outpouring as if a family member[v] was no more when Bajaj scooters went out of production in 2010. Bajaj created blunders by cannibalizing its products, Chetak and Super. Failure of the company to replace those products invited trouble. It cost them their leadership in the Indian scooter market. Over a period the company became susceptible to competitive attacks. Honda was the first competitor to encash this opportunity. In 2001, it launched its scooter in the Indian market, in 2002 Honda challenged Bajaj scooters. In 2003, it sold more scooters than Bajaj Auto, acquiring the market leadership. In three years Honda demonstrated its muscle power by knocking off the market leader. After losing the market leadership the sales of Bajaj scooters started declining every year. In 2005, Bajaj discontinued the traditionally geared scooters from production. The flagship product was destroyed within four years. In 2010 Bajaj got out of the scooter market completely by phasing out even the non-geared scooter. The market leader completely vanished within eight years. Bajaj cannibalized the brand rather than the product. It created a re-entry barrier by itself by creative destruction.

Managing the Product Life Cycle – Honda Way

Scooters were introduced in the Indian market in 1955. It remained in the introductory stage till the 1960s with just two players. From the 1970s until the 1990s scooter markets saw growth. In 1994-95 scooter market in India crossed the mark of one million unit sales. saturated. Till the 1980s there were only three motorcycle manufacturers in India selling just three models. Royal Enfield sold 350 cc bike 'Bullet', Escorts sold 175 cc bike 'Rajdoot' and Yezdi sold 250 cc bike 'Java'. They sold only black-colored bikes with poor customer service and no product innovations. The government of India opened up the two-wheeler sector for foreign direct investment by the mid-1980s. Japanese motorcycle companies invaded the Indian market with lighter, trendy/colorful bikes through joint ventures. In the following decade, the customers started shifting from scooters to motorcycles. The customer profile also changed during that period. Younger customers with higher buying power started buying two-wheelers. They loved the more powerful, stylish, safer two-wheelers with better fuel efficiency. There was a significant shift away from scooters to motorcycles.

Between 1995 to 2000, the market for scooters was in the declined stage, though marginally, while that of motorcycles increased at a compound annual rate of 25 percent. In 2002 API scooter production came to a grinding halt. In 2004 the market for geared scooters remained at just 5% of the two-wheeler market. ("see Appendix 4") Bajaj Auto identified scooters as a product on the decline stage of the product life cycle and decided to harvest them rather than hold on to it. While addressing the shareholders, in the year 2000, Rahul Bajaj wrote in the annual report, "Over the last five years, the company has had to face a stagnant, even declining market for scooter models. We realized five years ago that the days of resting easily on the high margins from Chetaks and Supers were coming to an end. Expanding the market for our basic scooters would be necessary, but not sufficient in the long term. We had to make major inroads into the motorcycle and scooterette markets and that required new products, new branding, new marketing, and new investments" In the same address he disclosed that the company was making handsome profits on scooters but not on motorcycles. Exactly after five years, Rajiv closed down non-geared scooter production on account of weak sales and poor profitability. Bajaj exploited the growth stage of the product life cycle, maintained the status quo in the maturity stage and lost stamina, and gave up in the decline stage. Honda had a positive approach to managing the product life cycle. It realized that the drop in the scooter market was getting accelerated due to the inaction of the market leader, Bajaj Auto. Honda entered the scooter market when it was in the maturity stage. It survived the decline stage and finally rode the growth stage. For the first decade, post-launch, Honda-Activa grew at the cost of Bajaj scooters. Once Bajaj was out of the scooter market, Honda-Activa started to grow at the cost of motorcycles. In 1998, Honda ended up their ties with the collaborators. The agreement between Kinetic and Honda was terminated. Honda (HMC, Japan) sold their stake and started building their 100% subsidiary in India, in 2000. They had another joint venture with Hero Group to manufacture motorcycles. The company Hero-Honda was the market leader in the Indian motorcycle market. Due to the restrictions posed by the association with the Hero group, Honda could not enter the motorcycle market in 2001. They become aggressive in the scooter market and launched 'Activa'. Honda-Activa was a technically superior scooter with many new features. It took no time to dislodge Bajaj from the leadership position, but for years after Activa's launch, scooter sales continued to slide down in the Indian markets.

Honda engineers kept working on the technology, particularly on electronics, at a time when most scooter engines were mechanical in nature, steadily improving power and mileage without compromising on the unisex appeal - compact size, sleek design, and easy weight. It introduced a centrally mounted engine that gave Activa stability on par with bikes. It brought in a puncture-resistant tuff-up tube for the tires, rendering the ugly back-strutted stepney[vi], a spare wheel for the emergency tire replacement, all scooters carried at the time, In the end, Honda got the reward, regarding the market leader in the Indian scooter market. It was their effort that took the scooter market out of the decline stage and got on to the growth path again. The Indian scooter market was in the trouble since 1995. It started showing some signs of improvement in 2009. It took 55 years for the scooter market to go through a full product life cycle, from introduction to growth to maturity, to decline and finally, it again entered the growth stage. Scooters and motorcycles remained alternative products for decades. Scooters remained the preferred two-wheeler of Indian customers from the 1960s until the mid-1990s. Motorcycles out-performed scooters from 1995 until 2011, except for the decline in 2008 and 2009. Post-2011 scooters started dominating the two-wheeler market on account of the major changes in the macro-environment. Massive urbanization, women empowerment, increased buying power of the middle class, growth of vehicle finance business and uni-gender profile of the two-wheeler customers changed the game. Bajaj Auto was already out of the market when the market tilted heavily in favor of scooters. Bajaj lost an opportunity to ride on the second growth phase of the scooter market in India. Honda was rewarded for its diligent work in the maturity and decline stages of the scooter product life cycle. Ever since 2011 they saw a steady rise in their sales volume, particularly in urban India. Honda-Activa became the most sold two-wheeler in India, in 2016 with a 58% market share of the Indian scooter market. Inability to manage scooter product life cycle also cost Bajaj their position in the domestic two-wheeler industry. The share of Bajaj Auto declined by more than 10% and their rank came down to 4th position from the second. The brand Bajaj created magic with the earlier generation. The customers in 2017 were not part of that magic hence there was little Bajaj could do to leverage that customer franchise.

Changing the Generic Strategy

Under the leadership of Rahul Bajaj, the company adopted the 'cost leadership strategy' and maintained the scooter prices relatively stable even in the long term. For implementing cost leadership, the company was required to cut corners. They employed a temporary labor force in the factory, on the large scale, to reduce the labor cost. It also maintained a tough stand during the salary negotiations with labor unions. With every pay hike, the management demanded increased productivity commitments from the labor unions. As a result, the company had unhealthy labor relationships. It had labor strikes that lasted many months at Akurdi and Waluj factories. In September 2007, Bajaj Auto closed its plant at Akurdi due to many reasons. The main reason was their inability to maintain the cost leadership for the products manufactured in the Akurdi factory. Rajiv provided reasons like the impact of government policies on capacity rationalization, chiefly the regional distortions created by inconsistent tax benefits, and octroy (local/municipal tax on goods) in the state. During the same time, the company inaugurated a manufacturing plant at Pant Nagar in North India. The decision was also a part of the 'cost leadership strategy'. The plant at Pant Nagar had been set up at an investment of Rs. 7000 million, of which Rs. 1500 million were invested by the company and the remaining by its 16 vendors. It had a capacity of one million units per annum. Immediately on the inauguration of the new plant, the company reduced the price by about 10% on its value-for-money motorcycle model, Platina. While Bajaj practiced the 'value for money' generic strategy, Honda attacked them with another generic strategy, 'product differentiation'. In 2001 Honda launched a technically superior and differentiated scooter with many new features like automatic gears, button start, side stand, and hidden cargo carriage. After Rajiv took over the leadership he maintained the marketing objective laid down by his father. He maintained profit-centric business growth rather than chasing the market share. He developed those businesses which had profit in their DNA. Rajiv developed a rapport with Jack Trout, the strategy guru who advocated the generic strategy of 'Focus'. Jack became a marketing consultant. Under Jack's guidance, Rajiv changed the generic strategy of Bajaj Auto for the domestic two-wheeler market. He emphasized the strategy of 'Focus'. The brand-led strategy of Jack Trout increased the profits of the company five times in just five years' time.

Acknowledging Jack's contribution Rajiv said, "We didn't become better in the kitchen, we serve better in the restaurant," The guru was equally pleased with his student. Jack told Indian media, "After years of working all over the globe, I can safely say that Rajiv is my best student, He has read my material so carefully. Sometimes, he quotes from my books, and I ask: Did I say that?" In the international markets, Rajiv continued with the cost leadership strategy. The Bajaj motorcycle, sold in Africa, became the cheapest motorcycle sold in the world. 'Boxer' model was being sold in Africa just for the price of $350. The focus strategy worked well in exports but did not fulfill the company's appetite in the domestic market.

Efforts in the Motorcycles Market

Honda was busy planning and executing the aggressive marketing strategy, targeting the leader, Hero. Bajaj was lured by the exiting growth rate of the motorcycle market segment which had better profit margins. In the mid-1980s Bajaj had a technological tie-up with Kawasaki of Japan. The Kawasaki-Bajaj `RTZ' model was launched in February 1988. In 1991, it was upgraded to a four-stroke model with the view to improving fuel efficiency. The bike stayed in production for ten years and spawned several variants. It was replaced with the new brand, Boxer, in 1997 which was further succeeded by another brand, CT100, in 2004. 'Caliber' was launched in 1998 as an 'executive commuter bike'. It performed well. Bajaj sold 100000 units in the first year of launch. In 2003, it was succeeded by 'Wind-125', a standard street bike. It was renamed after a year as 'Discover'. The 100cc version of this bike was launched in 2006 as 'Platina'. ("see Appendix 5")

Rajiv was known for his passion for motorcycles though he took almost care not to drive the business solely for his passion. With an initiative taken by Rajiv, the company entered the Premium bike segment in 2001. It launched Eliminator and Pulsar. The 'Pulsar' brand turned out to be a huge success for the company. 'Pulsar' continued growing with many variants. In 2005 'Eliminator' was replaced with 'Avenger'. In FY2016, Bajaj Auto sold almost 3.36 million motorcycles in India and abroad[vii]. Bajaj offered motorcycles in nearly every bike segment and each body style. Platina, Discover, Pulsar, Avenger, Ninja, RE, and KTM were some of the famous brands in the company's kitty.

Bajaj also had a partnership with Austrian manufacturer KTM in which it acquired a 48 percent stake. The KTM models available in India are Duke 200, Duke 390, RC200, and RC390. In FY 2016 Bajaj sold nearly 1.9 million Motorcycles in the Indian domestic market, which was 7.2% higher than in the previous year. In the sports and performance segment, with the Pulsar and the Avenger models. The company sold 729304 such bikes and maintained the leadership position in this segment. The market share improved from 41% in FY2015 to 49% in FY2016. Bajaj used an aggressive pricing strategy in the 'Utility segment', also called the entry segment. The Company sold 865366 CT and the Platina and acquired a market share of 35%. In fact, the entire growth in this segment was monopolized by Bajaj Auto. The KTM and the Pulsar RS 200 are in the niche super-sports segment. The KTM, India's fastest-growing sports motorcycle brand, increased its sales by 32% between FY2015 and FY2016[viii] in the super sports segment. The new Pulsar RS 200 (RS for Race Sports), introduced in March 2015, had sales of over 2,900 per month. In February 2016, Bajaj Auto launched the V15, a 150-cc model to create a new, differentiated, and more powerful engine category[ix]. The fuel tank assembly contained metal from India's flagship aircraft carrier, the INS Vikrant. The company expected more customers in this newly differentiated segment.

Launching KTM Bikes

Bajaj Auto had a technology transfer agreement with Kawasaki for manufacturing 'value for money' bikes. Using the technology Bajaj developed low-priced bikes and fuel efficiency. Rajiv realized the need for strong technical support in the performance bike segment. Bajaj Auto acquired a 48% stake in Sport-motorcycle AG, an off-road sports bike brand known for its legendary racing achievements. They sold bikes under the brand name KTM which was Europe's second-largest motorcycle manufacturer. The brand was launched in India, in February 2017. Initially, the brand launched three models, Duke 200, Duke 250, and Duke 390. Prices for the new Duke lineup now start at Rs 1,43,500 for the new 200 Duke, going up to Rs 2,25,730 for the new 390 Duke. The price for the all-new 250 Duke is Rs 1,73,000.

Probiking

Rajiv realized that the Bajaj scooter dealers would be of little use to him for selling high-performance bikes to passionate customers. The dealers were neither well equipped nor well trained to provide the kind of service expected by these choosy bike lovers. Rajiv initiated a direct bike retail initiative, 'Probiking' for its complete range of high-end bikes through a well-planned network of state-of-the-art den-type bike showrooms in all metros, major tier-2 & tier-3 towns. These showrooms showcase Bajaj Technology & Products where consumers can understand, feel and experience through self-interactive displays like the Tech center, Interactive design station (IDS), and Unique Dynamometer.[x] It offered a differentiated buying experience to consumers through various touch and feel points in a cozy environment. While the Tech center provides an at-a-glance understanding of technology and products, IDS facilitated access to detailed product information, key in personal details, generate quotations, and fire a printout. Dynamometer offered an excellent indoor bike riding experience where all bike performance characteristics like Acceleration, Speed, Torque, Power & Decelerations, etc. could be tested.

Three-Wheeler Sales

Bajaj Auto ended the FY2016 with a record domestic sale of 254,995 vehicles, up by 8.8% over the previous year as against industry growth of 1%[xi]. During FY 2016, in the domestic three-wheeler passenger vehicles segment, the company increased its market share by 3.3% to 57.5%. Total three-wheeler sales which included domestic and exports, were its highest ever, at 534995 units in FY2016 — a growth of 3.1% over the preceding year.[xii]

Re-positioning the Umbrella Brand, Bajaj

The company could not convince enough customers 'why should they buy Bajaj motorcycles?' Every Bajaj motorcycle brand like Pulsar, Discover, Avenger, etc. had its set of promises to the customers and a certain number of customers were being sold on them. But those numbers were not in tune with the management expectations and also shrinking day by day. The umbrella brand, Bajaj, was not adding enough value.

Bajaj could not re-create the aura around motorcycles as they did with scooters. The meaning of the brand Bajaj was not clear to the potential customers. It was not triggering emotions in the minds of customers like it used to do with scooter customers until the late 1990s. Customers used to sing popular Bajaj jingles from TV advt. The umbrella brand was required to be re-positioned again by developing and communicating the value added by them. Various motorcycle brands created customers for Bajaj but it was not creating a synergetic effect. The total impact of the umbrella brand was missing. Success in different market segments was not adding up to the ultimate success in the domestic motorcycle market.

Scooter Market in India 2016

The domestic two-wheeler industry, in India, reported a 4.4% year-on-year growth in Q3 FY2016. The moderate volume growth is mainly attributable to the weak performance of the motorcycle segment which saw a sales reduction of 5%. However, the Indian domestic scooter market grew by 23.60% in 2016. The total sales of scooters stood at 36,16,605. The scooter market rose to 32% of the total two-wheeler market (including mopeds) in India. The flagship scooter brand of Honda, 'Activa', took the crown from the motorcycle brand of Hero, 'Splendor', and became the bestselling two-wheeler brand in India for 2016-17. It outsold Splendor with a substantial margin of 209,005 units during the last fiscal. ("see Appendix 5").

The rapidly growing scooter market had become a top business priority for companies that were looking to tap the opportunities in this segment efficiently. ("see Appendix 6") Honda crossed the monthly sales milestone of 350,000 units in September; TVS Motor crossed 87,000 units in October and Yamaha passed 50,000 units during both months. Honda remained the top performing company in the overall scooter segment with a dominating market share of 58%. It sold 21,01,197 scooters in the domestic market between April-October 2016. Other than the Activa, the Dio and Aviator models were popular among young urban buyers. Hero Moto Corp, the number two player in the overall domestic scooter segment, registered total sales of 537,111 scooters during the same period, up by 31.53% with a market share of 15%. The scooter production capacity of Hero MotoCorp stood at 100,000 units per month.

Hero Maestro, the 110cc scooter, was the third largest selling scooter brand in India. It sold 378,347 units in FY2017 against the sales of 498,754 units in FY2016. Honda commissioned a 1.2-million-capacity scooter plant, the world's largest, in Gujarat. However, the demand for Activa was so high that confirmed bookings top 20,000. Honda added a second assembly line of 600,000 units in 2015-16 to its Bangalore plant. "With another line for scooters, our cumulative capacity (including for bikes) will reach 5.4 million this year. I'm not sure if it will be enough," Mr. Muramatsu, India head of Honda two-wheelers, told Business Today. But Muramatsu was aiming to sell 5.2 million two-wheelers in India in 2016/17, besides exporting another 200,000. Activa's cumulative sales crossed the 12-million mark.

Hero doubled its annual scooter capacity to 1.5 million units. It acquired the number two position in the scooter market in India. Rural demand primarily drove the motorcycle sales volume. The income growth in the rural sector had been weak over the two fiscals, 2014-15 and 2015-16. Two consecutive drought years impacted agricultural production along with the unseasonal rains. The growth in rural wage rates adversely impacted demand for motorcycles. However, the scooter segment posted attractive growth during the same period which was mainly driven by urban demand and new launches.

Reincarnation of Bajaj Scooters?

Indian media was constantly guessing about the possibility of reincarnation of the Bajaj scooters. When asked, Rajiv Bajaj didn't out rightly reject the case. His response was political. He said the re-entry into the scooter segment was a possible strategy only if the company reached a saturation point in the motorcycle market. He did not set any timeline for the relaunch. In August 2015, in an interview, Rajiv told Business Standard, "Today, we are humble enough to accept we have to do the motorcycle game right. But if in five years we become one of the top two, how do you grow the company? After you have a 30-40 percent market share, I cannot grow motorcycle volumes. So, when that saturation is reached, a very logical space for the company to grow would be scooters."

Meanwhile, Honda was the clear leader in the scooter market hence the entry into the scooter market required an attack on Honda. Fifteen years back Honda not only snatched their market leadership but also wiped out its presence in the Indian scooter industry. Rajiv's problem was whether to re-start the lost war against the global leader by launching scooters in the Indian market. It was more difficult this time because even the national leader, Hero, was on the battlefield, up against Bajaj.

Rajiv could also not ignore the strong market trend in favor of scooters. Although most of the two-wheeler manufacturers responded to the trend by launching new models of scooters, for Rajiv it was not an easy choice. He had been practicing and advocating a strategy of 'focus' on motorcycles and preferred to stay away from scooters. He was instrumental in Bajaj withdrawing from the scooter market which they were ruling for many decades. Rajiv changed the strategic direction of the company. How could he switch his stand and request the board for the reincarnation of scooters? In that case, he had committed the blunder of wasting ten to twelve valuable years, giving up the core competencies acquired over decades of diligent work, and letting the competitors walk away with the cake without any fight. It would undermine his leadership ability. He was always evaluated against the tall personality of his Harvard MBA father. Relaunching scooters could be seen as a leadership failure of Rajiv.

On the other hand, Bajaj would be reduced to a marginal player if they refused to get into the scooter market. Their competitors would gain a strong edge over them and would be in a better position to manage product lifecycles by maneuvering these alternate products. Refusing the scooter market meant settling down with a follower or niche player's position in the industry structure and giving up on becoming the market leader or at least the challenger in the Indian two-wheeler industry.

Rajiv's options were limited. His domestic motorcycle business was in trouble. The Bajaj motorcycle was skidding on the domestic roads (markets). Ridding such a skidding motorcycle could only mean scale-up the brand in the global motorcycle markets which meant taking Honda head-on. A global war against Honda could be played in the motorcycle market. It was Rajiv's aspiration ever since he joined Bajaj in 1990.

Though he had been working on it for the last 25 years, the attack would be premature. It required a paradigm shift in the approach, from international marketing to global marketing. Bajaj had to improve technology, product range, a number of markets served internationally, dealer network, and after-sales service. They required much stronger global brands with proper brand architecture and a boost in advertising and sales promotion. Presence in all the global market segments of motorcycles and achieving critical mass in every segment were a must. A strong alliance with the brands like KTM, Kawasaki, and globally spread manufacturing facilities were required to match Honda in technology, branding, and global reach. Rajiv had to write a story of another successful Asian brand.

Rajiv's problem was not limited to choosing between motorcycles or scooter market but he was required to specify his mission in clear words. If the mission was to fight for global leadership in motorcycles then his option had to be, 'riding in the motorcycle market'. If he wanted a respectable presence in the Indian market then he couldn't ignore scooters. In an interview with Forbes Rajiv said, "Even we were a part of the 90 percent (product) failure rate. Then we looked at the difference between the ones that succeeded and those that failed. And we realized that the difference was that the 10 percent were the ones with the first mover advantage that created categories. The rest were followers that tried to take some share of the category created by the rest."

The domestic market was waiting for the categories which Bajaj Auto would create for their survival. Meanwhile, the guns of the competition were blazing on the battlefield with great force.

Two-Wheeler sales in India in 2015			Difference	
Company	CY 2015	CY 2014	Units	Growth (%)
Hero MotoCorp	62,96,920	64,44,542	-1,47,622	-2.29%
Honda Motorcycle & Scooter India	43,14,558	41,72,717	1,41,841	3.40%
TVS Motor Company	21,48,025	20,82,676	65,349	3.14%
Bajaj Auto	18,09,612	18,85,263	-75,651	-4.01%
India Yamaha Motor	5,94,608	5,66,749	27,859	4.92%
Royal Enfield	4,44,527	2,96,380	1,48,147	49.98%
Suzuki Motorcycle India	3,28,423	3,37,620	-9,197	-2.72%
Mahindra Two Wheelers	1,50,927	1,94,516	-43,589	-22.41%
Piaggio Vehicles	27,830	26,998	832	3.08%
Harley-Davidson Motor Company India	4,445	4,080	365	8.95%
India Kawasaki Motors	1,312	851	461	54.17%
Triumph Motorcycles India	1,135	1,055	80	7.58%
TOTAL	1,61,22,322	1,60,13,447	1,08,875	0.68%

Appendix 1: Two-wheeler sales in India in 2015

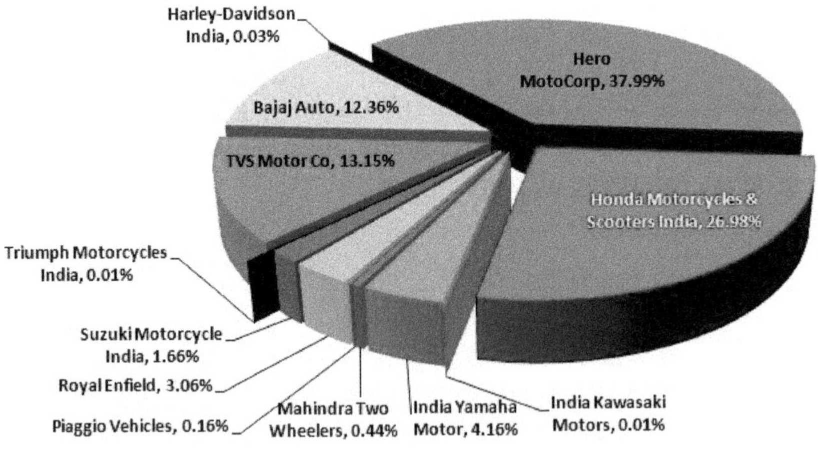

Appendix 2: - Two Wheeler Exports in India

Two-Wheeler Exports in 2015			Difference	
Company	CY 2015	CY 2014	Units	Growth (%)
Hero MotoCorp	1,89,493	2,01,122	-11,629	-5.78%
Honda Motorcycle & Scooter India	1,93,941	1,90,426	3,515	1.85%
TVS Motor Company	3,58,085	3,11,519	46,566	14.95%
Bajaj Auto	14,69,090	15,59,143	-90,053	-5.78%
India Yamaha Motor	1,61,966	1,71,842	-9,876	-5.75%
Royal Enfield	8,287	6,221	2,066	33.21%
Suzuki Motorcycle India	54,418	24,691	29,727	120.40%
Mahindra Two Wheelers	17,330	10,954	6,376	58.21%
Piaggio Vehicles	799	9	790	8778.00%
Harley-Davidson Motor Company India	3,704	0	3,704	NA
India Kawasaki Motors	0	0	0	0.00%
Triumph Motorcycles India	0	0	0	0.00%
TOTAL	24,57,113	24,75,927	-18,814	-0.76%

Appendix 3: Annual Sales of Two-wheelers in the Indian market

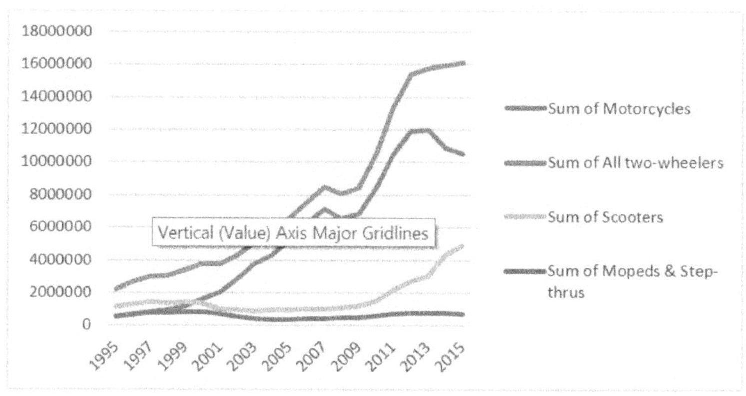

Source: Society of Indian Automobile Manufacturers (SIAM)

Appendix 4: The annual scooter market in India

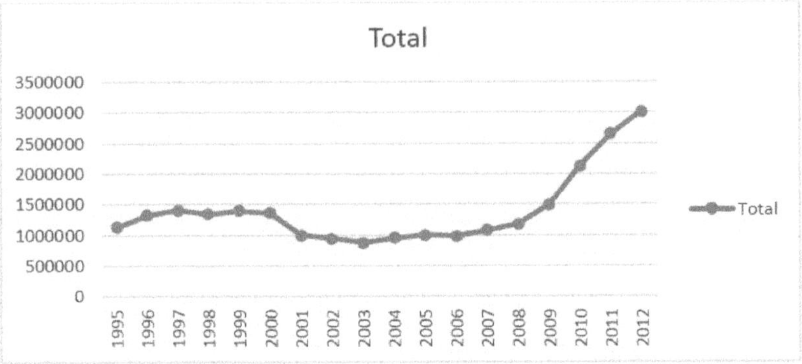

Source: Society of Indian Automobile Manufacturers (SIAM)

Appendix 5: Top 10 two-wheelers in India

Top 10 selling two wheelers in year 2015					
Model	**Year 2014**	**Rank**	**Model**	**Year 2015**	**% Change**
Splendor	2504264	1	Splendor	2489336	-1%
Activa	2085835	2	Activa	2409166	16%
Passion	1382641	3	Passion	1186621	-14%
HF Deluxe	1102690	4	HF Deluxe	1081851	-2%
CB Shine	872894	5	CB Shine	799490	-8%
TVS XL Super	774150	6	TVS XL Super	718296	-7%
Discover	693570	7	Glamour	628288	18%
Pulsar	627904	8	Pulsar	624182	-1%
Dream	614280	9	Jupiter	499905	51%
Glamour	530389	10	Maestro	497276	4%
					Source: SIAM

Appendix 6: Players in the Indian scooter market and their market shares

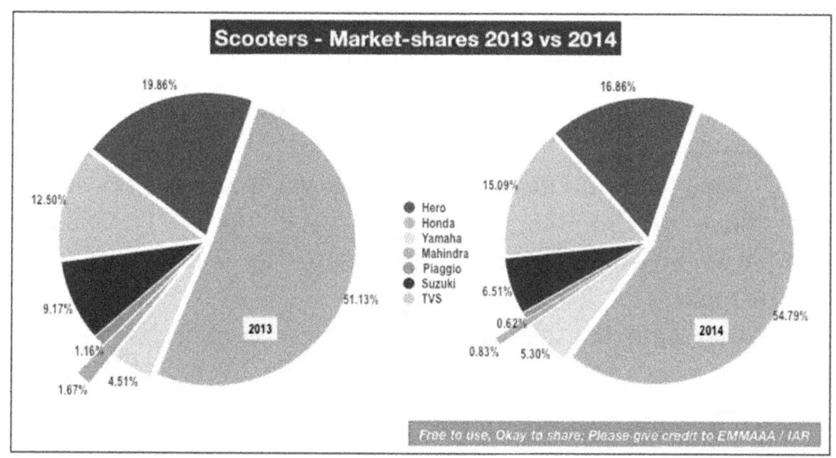

References

[i] "Check out the Bajaj auto ltd Management Discussions | Live ..." Insert Name of Site in Italics. N.p., n.d. Web. 17 Jun. 2017 <http://www.indiainfoline.com/company/bajaj-auto-ltd/management-discussions/28074>.

[ii] Check out the Bajaj auto ltd Management Discussions | Live ..." Insert Name of Site in Italics. N.p., n.d. Web. 17 Jun. 2017 <http://www.indiainfoline.com/company/bajaj-auto-ltd/management-discussions/28074>.

[iii] "36421489-Bajaj-Auto-Ltd-Business-strategy-case-study-ppt ..." Insert Name of Site in Italics. N.p., n.d. Web. 17 Jun. 2017 <https://www.coursehero.com/file/6595549/36421489-Bajaj-Auto-Ltd-Business-strateg>.

[iv] "Bye bye Bajaj - The Hindu." Insert Name of Site in Italics. N.p., n.d. Web. 17 Jun. 2017 <http://www.thehindu.com/features/metroplus/society/Bye-bye-Bajaj/article16853949>.

[v] "Bye bye Bajaj - The Hindu." Insert Name of Site in Italics. N.p., n.d. Web. 17 Jun. 2017 <http://www.thehindu.com/features/metroplus/society/Bye-bye-Bajaj/article16853949>.

[vi] "Road to Resurgence - Yahoo India Finance." Insert Name of Site in Italics. N.p., n.d. Web. 17 Jun. 2017 <https://in.finance.yahoo.com/news/road-resurgence-114155484.html>.

[vii] "Check out the Bajaj auto ltd Management Discussions | Live ..." Insert Name of Site in Italics. N.p., n.d. Web. 17 Jun. 2017 <http://www.indiainfoline.com/company/bajaj-auto-ltd/management-discussions/28074>.

[viii] "Bajaj Auto Ltd 2015-16.pdf - Business Responsibility Report..." Insert Name of Site in Italics. N.p., n.d. Web. 17 Jun. 2017 <https://www.coursehero.com/file/19696310/Bajaj-Auto-Ltd-2015-16pdf/>.

[ix] "Bajaj Auto Ltd 2015-16.pdf - Business Responsibility Report..." Insert Name of Site in Italics. N.p., n.d. Web. 17 Jun. 2017 <https://www.coursehero.com/file/19696310/Bajaj-Auto-Ltd-2015-16pdf/>.

[x] "PROBIKING STORE EXPERIENCE | Bajaj Auto." Insert Name of Site in Italics. N.p., n.d. Web. 17 Jun. 2017 <http://www.bajajauto.com/probiking_store.asp>.

[xi] "Check out the Bajaj auto ltd Management Discussions | Live ..." Insert Name of Site in Italics. N.p., n.d. Web. 17 Jun. 2017 <http://www.indiainfoline.com/company/bajaj-auto-ltd/management-discussions/28074>.

[xii] "PROBIKING STORE EXPERIENCE | Bajaj Auto." Insert Name of Site in Italics. N.p., n.d. Web. 17 Jun. 2017 <http://www.bajajauto.com/probiking_store.asp>.

http://www.autocarpro.in/analysis-sales/india-sales-analysis-cy2015-wheelers-10312

http://www.autocarpro.in/analysis-sales/india-sales-wheelers-2016-20335

CHAPTER NINE

Bajaj Auto- Handling Marketing Myopia

It was June 2017. Rajiv Bajaj, the Managing Director of Bajaj Auto, was sipping a cup of coffee with his father and the Chairman of the company, Mr. Rahul Bajaj, in their corporate office, at Akurdi, Pune, in India. They were debating certain aspects of the proposed scooter launch. Bajaj Auto was the market leader in the Indian scooter market from the 1960s until the year 2003. After that, they were dethroned by Honda. Bajaj Auto partially closed the scooter production in 2005 and completely closed down the scooter division in 2010. Ever since they closed down the scooter division, the scooter market in India started soaring. Although motorcycles were dominating the Indian two-wheeler market, the predictions were that by 2020 the scooter market would constitute 40% of the market. Bajaj could not afford to stay away from such a valuable segment for long. There were two views in the strategy team. 'Seniors' wanted to launch a petrol scooter. 'Youngsters' thought of creating a new category by launching an electric scooter. Seniors maintained that Bajaj Auto was known in India for producing quality petrol two-wheelers. Seniors thought the electric scooter was not just a new product but total diversification. They wanted the company to 'stick to the knitting' rather than diversifying into electric vehicles. Youngsters viewed that opinion as a 'marketing myopia'. In their view, it was not an apt business definition. They defined the business in terms of the customer needs Bajaj Auto was catering to. Youngsters believed that their business was to provide convenient, economic, reliable, stylish, and fast personalized public transportation. They pointed out to the news that Norway resolved to ban vehicles with hydrocarbon fuel (petrol, diesel, etc) from 2030. China has stopped the registration of new petrol scooters in main cities like Beijing, Shanghai, etc.

They were sure that electric vehicles would be the future of two-wheelers in India. Team Bajaj was doing a great job in the international motorcycle market but was losing business in the domestic market. They were also weakened by their absence from the scooters and moped segments. Bajaj was overdue for launching scooters in India. The only point of debate was which technology to bet on, petrol or electric. They were to decide and release a press note along with the half-yearly quarter review report which was due in Oct 2017.

Bajaj Auto Ltd- History

Rahul Bajaj took over the charge of Bajaj Auto in the mid-1960s after completing his MBA from Harvard Business School. He leveraged his family's network during the era when the government-controlled industrial production under the planned economy model of development. Rahul Bajaj developed the business and gave a global scale to it. Bajaj Auto was known in India for its scooters and three-wheelers. Bajaj scooter was the most popular family vehicle of the Indian middle-class family, whereas their three-wheeler was a part of public transportation. Bajaj Auto's focus was urban India. Most of their vehicles were used in Indian cities. In the 1970s, Bajaj customers used to wait for over a decade to receive the delivery of their scooter. In the early 1980s, Bajaj Auto partnered with Kawasaki of Japan and started manufacturing and selling motorcycles in India.

Bajaj was the market leader in the Indian scooter market. Honda took over that title from them in 2003. In 2005, Bajaj stopped production of their geared, metal-body scooters[1]. It tried to market the modern-day format of scooters by launching it under the brand name 'Kristal' but could not succeed. Bajaj Auto completely stopped the production and marketing of scooters in 2010. Exports remained the focus of the company. Three-fourths of the exports were done to a specific geographic belt, Africa, the Middle East, and South Asia. Bajaj also broke open South America (20% of the exports) and Far eastern markets (5% of the exports). The contribution of exports to the company's overall sales was 44%, which was valued at about $1.3 billion in Financial Year[2] (FY) 2015-16. Bajaj Auto exported 1.46 million motorcycles and 280,334 three-wheelers, in the same year.

Bajaj Auto was leading the domestic three-wheeler market with a market share of 57.5%. The national market share in the motorcycle market stood just under 19% and they were ranked third, behind Hero and Honda. Rajiv Bajaj, the elder son of Rahul Bajaj, joined the company in 1990, after completing his engineering education. Initially, he worked in the product development department. In 2000, he acceded to the board of Bajaj Auto. Rajiv was passionate about motorcycles; under his leadership, they developed the model 'Pulsar' which became the flagship product. In FY 2015-16 the company exported 313,000 units of Pulsars in the international markets. The motorcycle business was flourishing in the global markets but losing ground in the domestic market. From the year FY 2011-12 till FY 2015-16 the motorcycle business of Bajaj Auto, in the local market, showed a declining trend. Rajiv and his team were required to boost up the sales in the local market. However, domestic motorcycle sales went up in the financial year 2016-17, by 5%.

Evolution from Production to Marketing Orientation

Bajaj Auto started off in the 1960s with a *'production orientation'*. They could sell whatever they could produce. In fact, Bajaj had a long list of customers who waited for a decade to get their vehicle delivered. They were more focused on production, productivity, and cost-cutting. Bajaj Auto maintained a lean cost structure and practiced the 'Cost leadership strategy'. As a result, they were aptly rewarded. Bajaj was the most profitable two-wheeler manufacturer. In FY 2012-13 their profits were twice the profits of the market leader. In the 1980s the government opened up the automobile sector for competition. With the increasing competition, Bajaj graduated to *'product orientation'*. In an interview with Business Today Rajiv candidly admitted, "I was an engineer. I thought if I made a better product, it would sell. If Hero had a bike that gave 80 km to a liter, and I made one that gave 87, it should sell. But in reality, no one comes to buy it. This I did not know earlier."[1]

In 2001, Honda launched Activa. As the competition became fiercer, Bajaj got into the next phase. It developed *'Selling orientation'*. They tried hard-selling scooters. Rajiv tried all sales gimmicks but could not stop Activa. Finally, he gave up and decided to stop production of geared, metal scooter brands Chetak, Cub, and Super in 2005.

He also tried to hard sell other scooter models like Kristal but could not succeed to regain the lost scooter empire by selling routes. Activa couldn't be defeated because it always had a marketing orientation. Honda had graduated to marketing orientation while selling products globally.

Rajiv came a long way ever since Bajaj Auto failed in branding scooters in the domestic market. Rajiv learnt his marketing lessons and became a successful marketer after the mega success in the export markets and also from the lessons by Jack Trout. In 2011, Rajiv got in touch with the brand guru, Jack Trout, who started advising him on branding. He developed a better understanding of customers, their preferences, and how to respond to them. He understood the power of marketing and also the scope and limitations of tools of marketing. Rajiv made efforts to give Bajaj '*marketing orientation*'. In the interview given to the Business Today magazine, he elaborated his wisdom about marketing, "Pulsar is a complete market leader in sports bikes in India with 50 percent share. Honda, Yamaha Suzuki, everyone has products there. But they can't do anything. In Indonesia, the same products as Honda and Yamaha are there. Pulsar is also there but has only a two percent market share. Products that succeed are good products. But most of the products that do not succeed are also good products. That was when I realized the importance of marketing."[2]

The Two-wheeler Market

India overtook China to become the world's largest market for two-wheelers. A total of 17.7 million two-wheelers were sold in India, in FY 2016-17, an average of just under 50,000 units a day. China sold 16.8 million units in the domestic market. Chinese two-wheeler market reached a peak of 25 million units. And then it started declining. It was due to due to the fast-paced growth in car sales and the curbs on petrol two-wheelers in top cities. Indonesia was the third-largest market with annual sales estimated at 6 million units. The volumes slipped from 6.5 million units in 2015.

In India, easier finance options, newer and more fuel-efficient models, rising incomes, and new business models, such as e-commerce also helped purchases.

The growth of infrastructure in smaller towns and non-urban areas[3] helped the demand growth along with the massive government spending on rural programs and large road-construction projects leading to a pick-up in volumes in smaller towns and villages[4]. In metros and major cities, the sales were also being aided by the choked infrastructure. People in cities were buying two-wheelers for shorter commutes, even if they had a car. It was hard to move around in congested cities and even harder to get a parking space. So, two-wheelers were increasingly becoming the second vehicle in the household. It was projected that the two-wheeler market would grow at 11% for FY 2017-18. See **Appendix 1** for two-wheeler sales.

Installed Production Capacity and Capacity Utilization

The automobile industry operates on economies of scale. The manufacturing capacities play a critical role in business development. When the competition gets fierce, companies fight for volumes, and production capacities become critical. Any quantum addition to capacity would take 3 to 4 years, losing out on the business opportunity and more importantly letting the competitor grab it. Capacity utilization is the actual production. Higher utilization of capacity distributes overheads, eases out the price pressures, and increases profitability. The unused capacity shows the potential to grow but it creates pressure on the performance of the management. The market leader needs the highest installed capacity and capacity utilization. Inadequate capacities reflect poor coordination between the sales forecast/budgeting, production planning and control, and the project management team which creates capacities. Refer to **Appendix 2** for the production capacities and utilization of the market leader, Honda and Bajaj Auto.

Alternate Products: Motorcycles and Scooters

Motorcycles and scooters were alternate products. Both were different forms of two-wheelers, they were designed to satisfy the same customer need for a personalized and quick commute. Due to the swing in customer preferences, the demand for motorcycles adversely could affect the demand for scooters and another way around. In the late 1990s, the demand for motorcycles grew at the cost of scooters. Post-2010, the scooter market in India started outpacing the motorcycle market.

Refer to **Appendix 3** for the details of the scooter market in India. In 2017, the Scooter market was about one-third and the motorcycle was the rest in India. By 2020, it would be 40%, pushing down the motorcycle share further.

Hero MotoCorp India was the market leader in the Indian two-wheeler market but its leadership was firmly challenged by the number two player, HONDA Motors and Scooters India (HMSI). Refer to **Appendix 4** for the profile note on the market leader and the challenger. From the year 2001 to 2015, the motorcycle brand, 'Splendor', manufactured by 'Hero Motors' (Until 2010 it was 'Hero-Honda') ruled the Indian two-wheeler market as the most sold vehicle. In 2017, 'Honda-Activa' became the most sold two-wheeler in India. Refer to **Appendix 5** for the list & sales of the top 10 two-wheeler brands in India.

Bajaj Auto: Experimenting with New Scooter Launches

Before and after closing down the production of Chetak and Super, Bajaj Auto tried to develop and market a few scooter brands. But Bajaj could not develop a great reputation in making variator gearbox[3] scooters. They experimented with Saffire, Spirit, and Wave. All did little or no business. Bajaj kept constantly trying to earn a name in the scooter market. They finally unveiled the Bajaj Kristal DTS-I but could not make a dent.

When Bajaj was experimenting with these new scooter brands, the Indian market for scooters was not doing well. Too many scooter brands were trying to chase too few inquiries. Honda outfoxed the competition with the state-of-the-art product, Activa. It acquired a unique position in the minds of customers. Honda developed the brand equity for Activa by R and D, market analysis, customer research, and feedback. It leveraged the global exposure, experience, and expertise to over-power the local competitors who never sold scooters outside their own country. The post-mortem showed many inferences about Activa's success over Bajaj scooter brands. Indian customers loved power. In automobile language, they wanted a scooter with 110 - 125 CC.

Activa was of those capacities whereas Bajaj Kristal was just 95 CC. Customers were also not prepared to trade off fuel efficiency for power. Activa had a fuel efficiency of 60 km per liter against 49 km per liter of Kristal. Indian customers used scooters to transport more than two persons on many occasions. They need higher torque and broad and long seats to accommodate a child and parents or a teenage friend. Kristal was perceived as a smaller scooter even though Bajaj tried to project it as a sleeker model. Honda focused on delivering quality electrical and electronics.

Kristal had starting problems and issues related to battery and electrical, like other models of Indian scooters. Bajaj struggled with the targeting and positioning of Kristal scooter. Customers compared it with the brand 'Scooty' of TVS Suzuki. It was considered a moped (the smaller version of the scooter). Though Bajaj was targeting Kristal as a scooter, the customers were looking at it as a moped.

Bajaj experimented a lot with different brands of scooters and motorcycles in the Indian market. They tried Hudibaba (Calibre 118), Wind 125, Saffire, Spirit, Wave, Sunny, and Kristal brands. Awareness was created through advertising and promotions for most of those brands but didn't back up any of these brands for more than two years. Bajaj never demonstrated a conviction in these brands as they did with 'Pulsar'. The multiple branding strategies with often switching of brands created confusion in the minds of customers. Against that, Honda maintained the brand Activa consistently ever since it was launched in 2001. Honda went on upgrading the product, using extensions like Activa 110, Activa 125, Activa 150, Activa 3G, Activa 4G, etc. This consistency and continuity paid off for them. A senior executive noted on the condition of anonymity, "Why Bajaj did not modernize and extend the successful market leader brands like Chetak, Super, Cub remained a mystery. In the car segment companies like Toyota maintained brand names Corolla, and Camry for decades and leveraged the brand equity. Honda did the same in scooters. Successful brands cannibalize their products but keep the brands intact. Baja did it the wrong way. They killed the brands, which they developed for decades, for nothing. Bajaj paid a hefty price for their amateur approach in brand management."

Electric Scooters

HistoryElectric cars first appeared in Europe in the late 19th century. They virtually disappeared due to the nexus between car manufacturers and the petroleum lobby. Since the increase in the price of the latter, the situation has changed. Contrary to popular belief, the electric car is not a modern invention. The first models of electric passed the symbolic speed of 100 km/hour in 1899.[5] Lower maintenance requirements, as well as superior quality and reliability initiatives, increased product popularity among consumers. These vehicles are vibration-free due to fewer moving parts as compared to traditional products, thus eliminating periodic servicing requirements.[6]

The causeElectric scooters were the eco-friendliest vehicles because of the absence of hydrocarbons (fossil fuel), there were no engine lubricants and oil. They helped the cause by reducing the carbon footprint and providing a clean and green environment by reducing greenhouse gases. According to the calculation of Bywin (a well-known Chinese manufacturer from Shandong Province).[7] The carbon emission reduced by riding on an electric two-wheeler equaled the cleansing effect of 12 trees. Given the current Bywin five million users worldwide, the carbon dioxide emission cut in ten years surpasses the cleansing effect of 60 million trees.

Electric scooters were noise free hence reducing sound pollution. The weight of the electric scooter was less in the absence of heavy engines and related parts. Due to less weight and no engine, the vibrations were also less. It was considered a uni-gender vehicle. It could be parked quickly and required less parking space hence suitable for metro life and for the major cities. The focus areas of these scooters were environment friendliness, economy, and convenience.

ProductThe body of the electric scooter resembled traditional scooters. The main parts of the electric scooter were an electric motor and a battery. Motor ran on a battery and it was required to be charged by an external charging source. Sealed lead acid batteries were used initially due to their benefits such as robustness, tolerance to abuse, and low costs.

Properties such as bulkiness and the likelihood of overheating due to charging were some of the disadvantages of lead acid batteries,[8] which made them discharge quickly even without handling heavy loads. In China, as in many other Asia Pacific countries, lead-acid batteries, much cheaper than Li-ion batteries, occupy the vast majority battery market for electric two-wheelers. However, Li-ion is cleaner, much lighter, and of longer life circle.[9] Electric motorcycle and scooter prices varied due to a high battery and motor costs. The batteries could be recharged from any external source of electricity and frequent charging was required as vehicles had a shorter driving range. The technology focused on reducing battery costs by using solar energy. Electric motorcycles and scooters market included both commercial and personal use cases.[10]

Globally, regulatory bodies encouraged the adoption of eco-friendly, electric scooters by providing tax concessions. In the annual budget, the government of India made a provision for subsidizing electric scooters. The European government was planning to increase sales of electric vehicles to improve the air quality of the region. Twenty-seven EU countries started imposing taxes on carbon dioxide emissions related to vehicles whereas 15 nations were providing tax incentives for electric vehicles. Governments were also aiding the rise of hybrid and electric scooters by offering attractive incentives and subsidies to the owners of such scooters. For instance, in China, the government offered a subsidy of US$ 600 to US$ 1,000 to customers on every purchase of an electric scooter or a hybrid scooter, depending on the size of the battery pack. Major cities in China such as Beijing and Shanghai offered free registration plates to the customers of electric scooters.[11]

In the United States, the government allocated grants of about US$ 2.4 Billion for the development of hybrid and electric vehicles and high-density batteries. The U.S. administration has also given incentives to customers of electric vehicles and scooters in the form of tax credits amounting to a maximum of US$ 7,500 based on the type of battery of the hybrid or electric vehicle.[12]

Global Electric Scooters Market

China, as the world's largest electric two-wheeler manufacturer and exporter, accounted for 92% of the global market in 2012 (Pike Research, 2012e). Although as a No.1 exporter, China itself consumed the vast majority of its output. In 2012, the output was 35 million, with an annual growth of 26.3%, generating revenue of $6.9 billion. As predicted by Pike Research, global sales in 2018 would reach 47 million units and $11.9 billion in revenue (Pike Research, 2012d).[13] Consumers' demographic features varied a lot among different regions. Drivers from Europe and North America tend to see electric two-wheelers more as a lifestyle or style choice (being green and fitness workout), while those from the Asia Pacific, Middle East, Africa, and Latin America used electric two-wheelers more as a practical transportation means.[14] Regarding age group, North American consumers were around 45 - 65 and affluent, while consumers from other regions were younger and working (Pike Research, 2010). The Chinese export in 2012 was 1.29 million. The major export destinations were the Netherlands (USD 60.5 million), Germany (USD 46.2 million), the US (USD 41.7 million), Italy, Bangladesh, Japan, Belgium, Brazil, the UK, and Spain. The Netherlands was the largest export destination, taking up 14.2% of the total export of China.[15]

According to MA Zhongchao, chairman of the China Bicycle Association, the number of e-bicycles in use in China now reached 142 million. These figures had not counted those converted ones, which were normal bicycles by adding a battery pack and a motor, either by the consumers themselves or by some specialists. The lack of a charging infrastructure hindered electric scooters' market growth. This increase in electric bicycles in China was less technology-driven and more policy-driven. It was facilitated by favorable local regulatory practices in the form of gasoline-powered motorcycle bans and loose enforcement of electric bicycle standards. The alleged justifications for these bans included relieving traffic congestion, improving safety, and reducing air pollution. Many Chinese cities started to ban or restrict motorcycles and scooters using a variety of measures: some cities suspended the issuance of new motorcycle licenses, others banned the entrance of motorcycles and scooters into certain downtown regions or major roads, and some capped the number of licenses and then auctioned the license plates that were available.

These bans were imposed on all motorcycles, regardless of their power sources, and since electric bikes were categorized as non-motor vehicles they were exempted from the prohibitions. According to the motorcycle committee of the Society of Automotive Engineers of China, the use of motorcycles was banned or restricted in over ninety major Chinese cities.[16]

A well-established traditional two-wheeler market in Asia Pacific countries, such as China, Japan, South Korea, Indonesia, Taiwan, Vietnam, Thailand, Malaysia, etc., were passing on the market share to electric two-wheelers. In China, there were approximately 2,600 licensed whole-vehicle manufacturers and assemblers, by 2011 among which, 800 were of high productivity. Up to 50% of the total output comes from 50 manufacturers.[17] Global Market Insights, Inc. forecasted Electric Motorcycles & Scooters market size was poised to exceed USD 55 billion by 2024.[18]

Electric Scooters in India

In 2006, Electrotherm, a company based in Gujarat, launched the first electric scooter in India, under the brand name 'Yobykes'. It was powered with a 100% Electric Power Train and did not require any fossil fuel. YObykes offered an Economical, Eco-friendly, Convenient, and Safe personal mobility solution. As of FY 2016-17, it sold over 100,000 vehicles in India.[19] The hero became the first national scooter manufacturer to launch 'Flash', the electric scooter in Feb 2017. A lead acid battery powered the Flash e-scooter. The Flash, could travel for 65 kilometers on a single charge and had a top speed of 25kph. It was launched at an introductory price under $ 300.[20]

The price was inclusive of the government subsidy of $ 200 for electric vehicles. It was done in collaboration with the Department of Science of the Govt. of India, and the Society of Manufacturers of Electric Vehicles (SMEV). Flash was a limited-edition model with just 2,000 units for sale. Depending on consumer preference, there was also a provision to offer a lithium-ion battery-powered Flash e-scooter within a few months.

The price differential between the two battery-powered scooters was around $ 250. After the government subsidy, the price of the Lithium battery electric scooter almost matched the price of the traditional petrol scooters otherwise it would cost more. Hero Electric was gearing up to launch two new products. The first is a high-end smart scooter powered by a lithium-ion battery and Bosch power train. The second is a low-speed, high-end e-scooter with a lithium-ion battery. Both with a range of about 60-70km, the smart scooter would have a top speed of 55kmph. The battery was to be sourced from Korea, China, or Taiwan.[21]

The Issues with the Electric Scooters in India

YObike and Hero were the only electric scooters available in India. The customers were not happy with those models. The range of these e-scooters was less. They could hardly run for 50 km after the charging which took 6 to 7 hours. They were not using Li-ion batteries, as a result, their batteries were bulky, polluting, and would leak sometimes. Most of the scooters were parked in the open spaces and had no covered parking where the charging point could be available. The public charging stations were practically non-existent, even in the major metros. Those scooters were having feminine looks and men were not very comfortable riding them. The maximum speed was low and the scooters starve for power. They were too light and used to vibrate on the road when a heavy vehicle passed by. The road grip and braking power were also not up to customer satisfaction.

The Final Attack

Rajiv had been struggling to compete with Activa for over a decade. He tried sales tactics and launched many new brands but nothing worked. His dream was to be the number one motorcycle company in the world. He couldn't realize it unless he overpowered Honda globally. If he could defeat Honda, in scooters, in India, it could be a replicable simulation. His morale then would go up and he could convince the board members and his team to try to repeat the performance on the global Warfield. Rajiv and Rahul were discussing the action plan. This time, Rajiv wanted to provide strong reasons to customers for shifting their brand loyalty from Activa to Bajaj scooters. 'Why customers should buy Bajaj scooters?' He was not getting a convincing reply.

Rajiv said[4], "I've often pondered over a critical question: Why do 90-95 percent of all new products fail? This is a very fundamental issue because if the failure rate is so high, it means there is something wrong with the tools with which we operate. For instance, would you go to a cardiac surgeon who has a reputation of 90 percent failure? For me, there's only one conclusion: Our management tool kit is outdated."[22]

Rahul Bajaj did not agree. He had a different opinion. He thought nothing was wrong on their part but the environment was not right. The scooter market was declining in India. However, Rajiv knew he was overdue to change the toolbox which Bajaj was using in the domestic market. He was required to make a paradigm shift in his perspective, approach, and philosophy. This was the final attack he was planning for survival in the domestic market. He didn't want to leave anything to chance.

Rajiv said, "For us, this wasn't just an academic discussion though. In 2008, we were in all kinds of trouble. We had a string of failures, with the XCD, Calibre, and Wind. On the face of it, we had done almost everything right. We did all the R&D right. We had done all the manufacturing right. Our costs were under control. We had at least one version of marketing right? We backed the products with big ad spends, a large dealer network, and a good service and parts policy. So, what was the issue?"[23]

Rahul Bajaj was listening carefully to the pearls of wisdom his son was sharing. "The best way to create brands is to create a category. So, if you create a category of sports bikes, the name you give it — Pulsar — also eventually becomes a brand. It is always about the path less taken, always about being different rather than the same. We are always taught in school that familiarity builds contempt, whereas in business we behave as if familiarity builds desire. And we learnt this when most of the products we made failed."[24]

Rajiv candidly admitted that he was also a part of the 90% failure rate. Rajiv was very clear, he did not want to launch another *'me-too'* scooter which would be an addition to the list of failed brands. He wanted to create a new category in the scooter market. During the final attack, Rajiv's concern was the *'point of difference'* and the response time.

He wanted to design a scooter that was distinctly different and first of its kind and which would create a category. He wanted to position it differently in the minds of customers by providing logical and emotional reasons to buy. Most importantly, he wanted to be the first brand in the new category to do so. He admitted, "We looked at the difference between the ones (brands) that succeeded and those that failed. And we realized that the difference was that the 10% were the ones with the first mover advantage that created categories. The rest were followers that tried to take some share of the category generated by the rest."[25]

He knew the risk associated with the commercialization of electric scooters in India but he was ready to dare. Rajiv had dared a similar thing earlier. The Pulsar was a power bike at a time everyone was making mileage bikes. It had a 150cc engine, an 18-liter fuel tank, and delivered 12 BHP of peak power at a time when the norm was 100cc, 10-litre tank, and 7 BHP. In the last five years, Bajaj Auto had launched at least ten different models of the Pulsar, Discover, and Boxer motorcycles, and of its three-wheelers. Each had to go through the test of Bajaj's new realizations: Is it differentiated? Specialized? Unique? Sharp? Is it just better, or different? If the answer to all the questions is yes, Bajaj knew he was on track to create a market and not merely serve an existing one. Rajiv echoed his view, "If you are trying to ape someone, you would only endorse that someone. Every time I made a mileage bike like Hero, people said Hero was right because Bajaj was doing the same thing."[26]

Flanking with the Product

The challenge for Rajiv and his team was how to create the new category. The competition used all possible features to carve their categories in the scooter market, leaving hardly any option for Bajaj. The electric scooter was the only option left to create and dominate the category. It was almost the '*first mover*' like situation for Rajiv. 'Hero' was the only two-wheeler manufacturer that entered that segment but it was not standing on the firm foot. Their product was yet to be developed to suit the palate of Indian customers. Hero's electric scooter was struggling with many technical and non-technical issues. They did not enter with the required funfair. They could hardly sell 25,000 electric scooters, in a year.

The product didn't get the required management attention and starved for resources. It didn't get the customer's attention either. Other scooter manufacturers were keeping their fingers crossed and waiting for the market to develop and the right demand to emerge. They would jump when they smell the scale. The demand wasn't coming because good models were not available from reputed manufacturers. It became the 'chicken and egg story', requiring the major players to enter and set the product right. Most importantly, Bajaj was not carrying any baggage in the electric scooter market. They were free from prejudices and not the prisoners of history. Their slate was clear and they wanted to write a fresh brand success story on it. The beauty of this strategy was that it was a *flanking attack*on Honda, using a product from a radically different category. But Rajiv had to catch Honda napping. He had to launch an electric motor before Honda. It created a sense of urgency.

The Decision

Rajiv was not prepared to launch 'another electric scooter'. His research told him that electric scooters have come a long way in the last couple of years. Honda launched portable Li-ion batteries. These batteries could be easily carried to home or office for recharging if you do not have the infrastructure to charge them while they were fitted in a scooter. Refer to **Appendix 6** for details. BMW developed scooters, in Germany which could run about 150 km between two charges. Refer to **Appendix 7** for details. They also achieved a top speed of 130 km per hour. The longest range electric scooter, the ZEV 10 LRC, traveled 220 km at 89 km/h, or about 129 km at 112 km/h. An Austrian bike, the Johammer J1, is capable of traveling 200 km on a single charge. European electric two-wheeler company Zero developed a model, Zero S ZF6, in 2012 which could run at a maximum speed of 161 km/h.[27] With present-day technology, it was possible to work on the limitations of electric scooters in the Indian market. All that Rajiv was required to do was technological tie-ups and transfers. The best part was that the strategic partners of Bajaj Auto had developed state-of-the-art electric scooter technology. KTM was the largest motorcycle company in Europe. Bajaj had bought a 48% equity share in KTM. Rahul Bajaj was also the Dy. Managing Director of this Austrian company. KTM had developed a few of the best electric bikes in Europe. Refer to **Appendix 8** for the details.

Kawasaki Japan, the technological partner of Bajaj since the 1980s, also developed an electric scooter. The news that Kawasaki applied for the major innovations in electric bikes was making circles in the market.[28] Bajaj could develop access to electric scooter technology of KTM and Kawasaki using its deep relationships with these companies.

Rajiv felt Bajaj should enter the scooter market with a big bang, by creating state of art electric scooter which uses all the latest available technologies. Most importantly, he wanted it to be superior to existing scooters on all other sub-systems like suspensions, brakes, wheelbase, tires, storage space, seating, lighting, ignition, etc. He wanted his team to design the best scooter and power it with the best electric system. Rahul Bajaj could see the enthusiasm of a brilliant engineer. He saw the same Rajiv in the 1990s when he developed 'Pulsar' with great passion.

Rajiv argued with his father that he was just changing the source of power used in the scooter, from a petrol engine to an electric motor operating on a battery. He was not going away from their business model. He maintained the strategy of '*stick to knitting*. He was just changing the product form, changing to modern technological solutions to serve customers better and creating better value for them by saving their money. The definition of the business, laid down by his predecessors was too narrow and restricted the company from getting into technological advancements. In Rajiv's opinion, it was *marketing myopia*. He just re-defined, rather than re-worded the business definition to allow him to explore better solutions to the customers' problems.

Rahul Bajaj saw a point in Rajiv's argument. But he still felt that the move to enter the market with electric scooters was too early, very costly, and overly risky. He thought it would be early because the market size was too less for a two-wheeler manufacturer to shift the focus and commit to production capacities. Converting non-users to users was a costly proposition. It would need fat advertising budgets and mega promotional efforts. When the product is in the introduction stage, like electric scooters, the marketer has to sell the product category rather than his brand.

Customers go through *Attention-Interest-Desire* and *Action* cycle. Initially only '*innovators*' buy, in the next phase the '*early adopters*' will buy. In phase three '*early majority*' customers will buy and then the majority of customers start using the product. The brand has to spend a lot at every stage which might last for a few years. Such pioneering efforts need deep pockets. Rahul Bajaj reminded Rajiv of the fact that Coke in India took almost a decade to see profits, after investing $ 700 million. Above all, there was no guarantee that after convincing, the non-users would buy electric scooters of the brand Bajaj. There was a risk that the competitors might get benefited more and Bajaj would land up incurring customer education expenses. He wanted to enter the market with petrol engine scooters. He thought Bajaj could leverage the goodwill they created earlier. In his opinion, the consumer franchise could not be extended to the electric scooters since it was being looked at as a radically new product line.

He asked Rajiv not to jump to conclusions and prepare detailed proposals for both options, keeping aside the bias for electric scooters. Rahul Bajaj wanted to discuss the dilemma in the board meeting. He wanted the board to decide whether to re-enter the scooter market. If yes, then whether to launch petrol or electric scooter? He wanted to do it before September 2017 so that he could announce the final decision to the press, in Oct 2017 along with the half-yearly results.

Appendix 1: The Two-wheeler Sales in India

Two-Wheeler sales in India in 2015			Difference	
Company	CY 2015	CY 2014	Units	Growth (%)
Hero MotoCorp	62,96,920	64,44,542	-1,47,622	-2.29%
Honda Motorcycle & Scooter India	43,14,558	41,72,717	1,41,841	3.40%
TVS Motor Company	21,48,025	20,82,676	65,349	3.14%
Bajaj Auto	18,09,612	18,85,263	-75,651	-4.01%
India Yamaha Motor	5,94,608	5,66,749	27,859	4.92%
Royal Enfield	4,44,527	2,96,380	1,48,147	49.98%
Suzuki Motorcycle India	3,28,423	3,37,620	-9,197	-2.72%
Mahindra Two Wheelers	1,50,927	1,94,516	-43,589	-22.41%
Piaggio Vehicles	27,830	26,998	832	3.08%
Harley-Davidson Motor Company India	4,445	4,080	365	8.95%
India Kawasaki Motors	1,312	851	461	54.17%
Triumph Motorcycles India	1,135	1,055	80	7.58%
TOTAL	1,61,22,322	1,60,13,447	1,08,875	0.68%

Source:http://www.autocarpro.in/analysis-sales/indian-scooter-segment-million-unit-market-11161

Appendix 2: Market Leader V/s Bajaj Auto: Production Capacities and Utilization

The installed capacity of Hero was 7.8 million units per annum. Against which Hero sold 6.63 million two-wheelers. Honda had ten assembly lines in India with an installed capacity of 5.8 million per annum.[29] Honda commissioned an exclusive scooter plant in 2016, at Vithalapur in Gujarat which produced 1.2 million scooters annually and is the largest in the world. In FY 2016-17, Honda sold 5 million two-wheelers. Bajaj Auto had three manufacturing plants with a total installed capacity of about 6 million units. The plant at Waluj, Aurangabad in Maharashtra was the biggest, with a capacity of 3 million vehicles. Pantnagar plant in North India had a production capacity of 1.8 million. The Chakan plant near Pune had a 1.2 million capacity. In FY 2016-17, Bajaj sold 3.21 million two-wheelers against 3.35 million sold in FY 2015-16, losing 4% sales.[30] Honda was operating at nearly full production capacity and planned to add the eleventh assembly line in Karnataka, the southern state. The company invested $ 15 million to add 0.6 million production capacity. That addition of the capacity would take Honda's installed capacity to 6.4 million, making it the second largest, in the two-wheeler industry, ahead of Bajaj Auto, by production capacity. Bajaj was operating almost at half the production capacity creating pressure on the total overheads. They were required to increase volumes.

Appendix 3: Scooters in India

In April 2017, the scooter market stood at 32% of the Indian two-wheeler market and the rest was motorcycles. The scooter market grew from a share of about 13% in 2005. Scooter sales in 2016-17 were at 5.6 million units in comparison to 5.03 in the previous fiscal, up 11.39 percent. The market leader HMSI, posted 3.35 million units during the year as against 2.8 million in 2015-16, up 14.32%. Chennai-based TVS Motor posted a growth of 6.81% in its domestic scooter sales at 826,291 units becoming the number two player in the category. Hero MotoCorp dropped to the third position with its scooter sales last fiscal at 789,974 units. The scooter segment was an umbrella to 100cc, 110cc, 125cc, and 150cc scooter classes but dominated by 110cc models, which was estimated to record growth in the 125cc and 150cc scooter categories shortly. HMSI almost tripled sales, from 1.6 million a year in 2010-11 to 4.45 million in 2014-15. Honda sold 2.27 million units of Honda-Activa, the flagship model.[31] TVS Scooters was the second largest scooter company in India with a 14.75% market share. Their popular model was Jupiter which had sales of 0.6 million units in FY 2016-17.[32] Hero and Suzuki occupied the third and fourth positions respectively, and Yamaha stood in the 5th position.

Source:http://www.autocarpro.in/analysis-sales/indian-scooter

Appendix 4: The Market Leader V/s The Challenger in the Indian two-

wheeler market

Hero MotoCorp Ltd., (formerly Hero Honda), was an Indian motorcycle and scooter manufacturer. The company was the largest two-wheeler manufacturer in the world. The company was based in the Indian capital city, Delhi. The market capitalization of Hero was $ 4.8 billion. The company operated five manufacturing plants and controlled over half the motorcycle sales, in India.[33] However, the share in the overall two-wheeler industry came down to 37.5%, in FY 2016-17, due to booming scooter sales and Honda's splendid performance in scooters. The company had about 6000 dealers and service centers in India. The joint venture with Honda was terminated in December 2010. Honda sold their 26% share to promoters at a discounted price of $ 1 billion. The rising differences between the two partners gradually emerged as an irritant.[34] Differences had been brewing over three main issues. First, is Honda's reluctance to fully and freely share technology with Hero (despite a 10-year technology tie-up that expired in 2014). Second, the Indian partner's uneasiness over high royalty payouts to the Japanese company, and lastly, the refusal of Hero Honda to merge the company's spare parts business with Honda's new fully owned subsidiary Honda Motorcycle and Scooter India (HMSI).[35] The company was selling popular motorcycle models in India but its ability to develop new technologies got severely damaged due to the end of the technology tie-up with Honda. The company launched an electric scooter, Hero Flash, powered by a 250-watt electric motor coupled with a 48-volt 20 Ah VRLA battery. The Flash electric scooter has a claimed range of 65 km per single charge, while it weighs just 87 kg, much lighter than most scooters conventional entry-level scooters on sale at present. Unlike conventional scooters, the Hero Flash does not need a driving license or vehicle registration[36]. Hero had been maintaining the leadership position on account of its strong position in the domestic motorcycle market. However, Honda, the challenger was closing in rapidly. After the grand success in the scooter industry, Honda was closing the gap in the market. With the increase in capacity, Honda was expected to get much more aggressive.

HONDA Motors and Scooters India (HMSI) Honda was the global leader in the two-wheelers. They started Indian operations through two joint venture projects (JV), separately for motorcycles and scooters. The JV in scooters, Kinetic-Honda, ended in the year 2000. The company launched its scooter,

Activa, in the Indian market in the year 2001, through the Indian arm, HMSI. Activa became the first Indian two-wheeler brand to cross the annual sales mark of $1 billion. In April 2017 Honda released a press note informing that Activa's population in India crossed the mark of 15 million scooters. Honda leveraged the success of Activa and grew its market share above 50% in the Indian scooter market. In FY 2016-17, 'Activa' contributed to two third of Honda's two-wheeler sales in India (67%). Incidentally, another Japanese company, Suzuki was holding the same position in the Indian car market (more than 50% market share). But Honda did it in just 17 years, half the time compared to Suzuki. Honda started accelerating only after 2010 when it concluded the alliance with the Hero group. HMSI became the largest division of Honda International, in the two-wheeler segment. Honda had developed an electric scooter but it didn't launch in India.

Appendix 5: Top 10 two-wheeler brands in India (basis-Sales Volume)

How India's scooter market fared in FY2015-16	Domestic Maket			Exports		
Companies (75cc - 90cc	2015-16	2014-15	Growth	2015-16	2014-15	Growth
TVS Motor Company	85,610	1,34,767	-36.48%	1,208	5,186	-76.71%
TOTAL	85,610	1,34,767	-36.48%	1,208	5,186	-76.71%
Companies (90 - 125cc models)						
Honda Motorcycle & Scooter India	27,89,537	25,02,347	11.48%	1,03,242	77,814	32.68%
Hero MotoCorp	8,18,777	7,52,052	8.87%	77,521	79,956	-3.04%
TVS Motor Company	6,87,987	5,45,173	26.20%	37,722	16,543	128.02%
India Yamaha Motor	3,18,450	2,16,960	46.78%	22,263	6,271	255.00%
Suzuki Motorcycle India	2,20,388	2,75,190	-19.91%	8,510	5,712	48.98%
Mahindra Two Wheelers	84,061	46,261	81.71%	6,149	3,915	57.06%
Piaggio Vehicles (Vespa)	22,266	28,062	-20.65%	866	10	8560.00%
TOTAL	49,41,466	43,66,045	13.18%	2,56,273	1,90,221	34.72%
Companies (125 - 150cc models)						
Piaggio Vehicles (Vespa 150)	4,599	0	NA	0	0	NA
TOTAL	4,599	0	NA	0	0	NA
GRAND TOTAL (Scooters, Scooterettees)	50,31,675	45,00,812	11.80%	2,57,481	1,95,407	31.77%

Source: Society for Indian Automobile Manufacturers (SIAM)

Appendix 6: Li-ion Batteries

Traditional Car Batteries: Each cell of a lead storage battery consists of alternate plates of lead (cathode) and lead coated with lead dioxide (anode) immersed in an electrolyte of sulfuric acid solution. ... This causes a chemical reaction that releases electrons, allowing them to flow through conductors to produce electricity. (https://en.wikipedia.org/wiki/Automotive_battery). During the battery recharge cycle lead sulfate (sulfation) begins to reconvert to lead and sulfuric acid. During the recharging process as electricity flows through the water portion of the electrolyte water, (H2O) is converted into its original elements, hydrogen, and oxygen. (www.progressivedyn.com/battery_basics.html)
Li-ion Batteries: Although slightly lower in energy density than lithium metal, lithium-ion is safe, provided certain precautions are met when charging and discharging. In 1991, the Sony Corporation commercialized the first lithium-ion battery. The energy density of lithium-ion is typically twice that of the standard nickel-cadmium. (batteryuniversity.com/learn/archive/is_lithium_ion_the_ideal_battery) Lithium-ion batteries are great because they are rechargeable. When the battery is connected to a charger, the lithium ions move in the opposite direction as before. As they move from the cathode to the anode, the battery is restored for another use (sustainable-nano.com/2013/10/15/how-do-lithium-ion-batteries-work/) NMC 3.6 / 3.85 V, LiFePO4 3.2 V. A lithium-ion battery or Li-ion battery (abbreviated as LIB) is a type of rechargeable battery in which lithium ions move from the negative electrode to the positive electrode during discharge and back when charging. ... Lithium-ion batteries are common in-home electronics. (https://e Refer to **Appendix 8** for the details. n.wikipedia.org/wiki/Lithium-ion_battery)

Appendix 7: Highlights of the BMW Electric Bike

An overview of the highlights: The new e-scooter is offered in two versions: the ‘Long Range’ version and the ‘European version’. The ‘Long range’ is capable of up to 100 miles (160 km) on a single charge, while the ‘European version’ is restricted to meet the requirements for the A1 driving license. It gets up to 62 miles (100 km) of range on a charge.

- Innovative electric drive via drivetrain swing arm with liquid-cooled e-motor, tooth belt, and planetary gear.

- Significantly increased range due to enlarged battery cell capacity of 94 Ah (previously 60 Ah).
- Long Range version: 19 kW (26 HP) continuous output and 35 kW (48 hp) peak output. Top speed 129 km/h, range approx. 160 km.
- A1 driving license version (Europe only): 11 kW (15 HP) continuous output and 35 kW/48HP peak output. Top speed 120 km/h, range approx. 100 km.
- Intelligent recuperation in coasting mode and when braking.
- Standard charge cable with a smaller diameter.
- Short charging times are possible.
- Synergy effects with BMW automobiles and electrical safety according to car standards.
- Hybrid chassis with agile handling due to low center of gravity.
- The powerful braking system with ABS.

Appendix 8: The KTM Electric Bike

The KTM E-Speed employed -ion batteries with a capacity of 4.36kWh that used to get fully charged within two hours via a regular power socket. KTM claimed that the E-SPEED had a range of 64km on a full charge. KTM has announced plans to produce the Speed scooter concept it showed in Tokyo this year as the E-SPEED. Based on the FREERIDE E electric drivetrain, the production version of the E-SPEED is expected to deliver a performance profile similar to a 125cc gas-powered scooter. At nearly 15 HP, the output of the E-SPEED should be well suited to urban riding, especially given its top speed of just under 55 mph. That puts it in Stella or Symba territory performance-wise. Take a close look at the front rotor and you'll see an ABS ring. Will this make it to production? While no mention of the range was given, the 4.36kWh battery is said to charge in as little as two hours on 220v of wall power. Most larger electrics perform a 150cc gas-powered scooter in the form factor of a 650. Meanwhile, the electric scooters sized like 150s give a performance output that's shamed by many 50cc gas-powered bikes.

Foot Notes: -

[1] It was based on the technology of Piaggio of Italy (the 1960s). The brands were Chetak, Super, and Cub.

[2] The financial year in India is from April to March. It is written as FW 2015-16 meaning from April 2015 till March 2016.

[3] a variator is a mechanical power transmission device that can change its gear ratio continuously (rather than in steps).

[4] All the quotes are taken verbatim from the interview of Rajiv Bajaj given to Forbes magazine. It was published in Forbes magazine on 4th Nov. 2011. The quotes are selectively taken to put forward the case of Electric scooters. However, Rajiv did not say anything about launching electric scooters, in the interview.

References:

[1]http://www.businesstoday.in/magazine/cover-story/rajiv-bajaj-bajaj-group-plan-and-future/story/198329.html

[2] "The Quadricycle Diaries", Suveen Sinha, Business Today, Sept 2013.

[3] "India overtakes China to become the ... - The Economic Times. 02 Jul. 2017

[4] "India overtakes China to become the ... - The Economic Times02 Jul. 2017

[5]https://www.technologicvehicles.com/en/page/1/electric-vehicles-history-ev

[6]https://www.gminsights.com/pressrelease/electric-motorcycles-and-scooters-market

[7]http://docplayer.net/18943099-The-role-of-electric-two-wheelers-in-sustainable-u...

[8]https://www.gminsights.com/pressrelease/electric-motorcycles-and-scooters-market

[9]http://docplayer.net/18943099-The-role-of-electric-two-wheelers-in-sustainable-u...

[10] Global Market Insights, NASDAQ Globe News Wire, 10 April 2017

[11]http://www.forbesindia.com/article/leaderhip-awards/rajiv-bajaj-being-original-t...

[12]http://www.futuremarketinsights.com/reports/electric-scooters-market

[13]http://docplayer.net/18943099-The-role-of-electric-two-wheelers-in-sustainable-u...

[14]http://docplayer.net/18943099-The-role-of-electric-two-wheelers-in-sustainable-u...

[15]https://sustainabledevelopment.un.org/content/documents/3792fu2.pdf

[16]https://en.wikipedia.org/wiki/Electric_vehicle_industry_in_China

[17]http://docplayer.net/18943099-The-role-of-electric-two-wheelers-in-sustainable-u...

[18]https://globenewswire.com/news-release/2017/04/10/958180/0/en/Electric-Motorcycles-Scooters- Market-to-hit-55bn-by-2024-Global-Market-Insights-Inc.html

[19] Company website: http://yobykes.in/about/#about_ul

[20] https://auto.ndtv.com/news/hero-flash-electric-scooter-launched-in-india-at-rs-19-990-1655698

[21]http://www.autocarpro.in/news-national/hero-electric-launches-flash-scooter-roll-products-fy2018-23508

[22] Rajiv Bajaj: Being Original to Succeed | Forbes India02 Jul. 2017

[23]http://www.forbesindia.com/article/leaderhip-awards/rajiv-bajaj-being-original-t...

[24] Rajiv Bajaj: Being Original to Succeed | Forbes India02 Jul. 2017

[25] "Rajiv Bajaj: Being Original to Succeed Forbes India 02 Jul 2017<http://www.forbesindia.com/article/leaderhip-awards/rajiv-bajaj-being-original-t>.

[26] “The Quadricycle Diaries”, Suveen Sinha, Business Today, Sept 2013.

[27]https://en.wikipedia.org/wiki/Electric_motorcycles_and_scooters

[28] https://motorbikewriter.com/kawasaki-plans-electric-motorcycle/

[29] “India is now the world’s biggest two-wheeler market”, Pankaj Doval, Times of India, May 7, 2017.

[30] “Hero, HMSI post record annual two-wheeler sales in 2016-17 despite note ban”, PTI, Business Standard, April 3, 2017.

[31] “The New Number one”, Chanchal Chauhan, Business Today, 5 August 2016

[32] http://www.autocarpro.in/analysis-sales/india-sales-scooters-2016-24426

[33] Annual Report FY 2012-13, Hero MotoCorp.

[34] Hero MotoCorp - Wikipedia.". 02 Jul. 2017

[35] "Hero Honda (Joint Venture) by Tushar Jain on Prezi. 02 Jul. 2017

[36] Hero Flash Electric Scooter Launched in India At... NDTV India, 02 Jul. 2017

CHAPTER TEN

How Can Cottonking Expand the Kingdom?

It was the end of July 2016. Pradip Marathe, the founder, and CEO of 'Cottonking', a men's readymade garments manufacturer, was sitting in his Pune office, in western India. He was analyzing the sales figures of his franchisees for the discount period which was just concluded. Some of the key shops reported a major drop in the sales compared to the sales during the same scheme period last year. The franchisees were blaming it on the competition. He wanted to know whether the better sales promotion scheme by the market leader was the only reason behind the poor sales performance or were there other reasons too. The majority of the franchisees were struggling to make profits. Out of the 104 Cottonking franchisees, hardly one-third achieved breakeven sales by 2015.

Just a year back, Mr. Marathe had started another venture, LinenKing. It was a chain of stores selling exclusively the LinenKing range of men's wear. By July 2016, they could expand to 11 franchise stores in Maharashtra. The LinenKing brand was not offered to Cottonking franchises. This decision of not offering LinenKing range to them was not received well by most of the franchisees. The management thought selling the linen range would dilute the '100% cotton' brand position of Cottonking. The challenge was how to improve the profitability of Cottonking franchises. Should the margins be increased? Should the LinenKing range be offered to them? Should the 'CottonQueen' brand be launched exclusively for women's formalwear? Mr. Marathe was to decide before the franchisee meet, scheduled in August 2016.

Men's wear Market in 2012-13

Indian apparel market size was INR 875 billion (USD 16 billion). Men's wear was the largest segment accounting for 42% of the overall market. It was divided into different categories like Shirts, trousers, denim, winter wear, innerwear, T-shirts, suits, activewear, ethnic wear, and daily wear. Shirts were the single largest category within the menswear market, followed by trousers and denim. The men's wear market was growing at a CAGR of 8.5% and was to reach INR 1310 billion (USD 24 billion) by 2017. Denim, T-shirts, and activewear were high-growth categories within the menswear segment with CAGRs of 16%, 12%, and 14% respectively. The demand for denim was growing with the younger generation. The men's denim segment contributed 80% to the denim market. The rising trend for casual or 'Friday' dressing in metros and 'A' category cities, and the penetration of denim into Tier II, Tier III cities, and rural India were contributing to the growth of men's denim in India. The shift from formal attire to comfort-oriented casual attire was driving the market for men's T-shirts. This segment was also witnessing an increase in the demand for colored trousers. In addition to the traditional colors like black, blue, brown, and grey, Indian men started experimenting with newer colors like red, green, orange, etc. Almost all major brands were offering newer colors as they were optimistic about the growth. The women's wear market contributed 38% of the total apparel market in India. The total market size stood at INR 785 billion (USD 14.4 billion). The growth of this market was faster than the menswear market. There was a relatively lower penetration of brands. The income of modern Indian women was growing rapidly. As a result, this segment became the focus of many Indian and international brands. With increasing women in the workforce and the growing economic independence of women, the demand for women's western wear was at an all-time high. Women's western wear was emerging as a clear winner in the women's wear market. This trend was expected to continue as more women enter the workforce. In addition to traditional sarees and salwar kameez, the working women were moving towards dresses, formal suits, and business attire. Though these markets were relatively small, they were expected to grow rapidly.

Company

Mr. Marathe was an Engineer-MBA and worked as General Manager-Marketing with a Kirloskar group of companies, a reputed engineering business house, based in Pune city, in India. In 1996 he founded a company with his wife Shubhada. They sensed the potential market for 100% cotton garments and started manufacturing menswear under the brand name 'Cottonking'. The state-of-art ultra-modern manufacturing plant was situated at Hi-tech Textile Park in Baramati; near Pune. It had an integrated manufacturing facility spread over 84,000 sq. ft. which ensured that all garments were made under one roof - right from cutting of the fabric to finishing with a state of the art machinery. In 2014, the company invested over Rs 30 million in the existing factory, on the latest imported machinery, to double production to meet the growing demand for its range of apparel. The factory produced 1,500 ready-to-wear garments per day and had a capacity to produce 6000 garments a day.

Product

Cottonking became known for the 100% cotton, value-for-money shirts. Mr. Marathe was successful in developing a quality product at a fairly good price. But the product line length and depth were a problem. There were a lot of scopes to improve the consistency of the product mix. Only one category, shirts contributed to two-thirds of the sales. Hardly a third of the revenue came from other product lines. In shirts, the company sold subcategories like formal, semi-formal, slim fit, and casuals. More than half the sale was of formal shirts 20% was of slim-fit and the rest was casuals and semi-formals. The popular shirt sizes were 39, 40, 42 & 44. The customers also demanded 36 and 38 sizes which were not sold by 'Cottonking'. The company sold both full and half sleeve shirts. The product range involved plain, striped, checks, lined, wrinkle-free, and printed shirts. (See Exhibit 1). T-shirts were all half sleeves, in plain colors, striped, with and without pockets, with collar and round neck. The limited choice restricted the sales of trousers. The Jeans sale was very poor with hardly any promotional support and with a lack of required variety. The company launched limited accessories like handkerchiefs and socks. The conversion rate in the stores is high. Almost 80% of the footfalls get converted. It was an indication of customer satisfaction with the quality of the product.

'Cottonking' believed in innovation and gave its customers a completely new product every season like the launch of Cool Slubz, Aerosoft, and Easy2Iron shirts.

Price

The price range of shirts was Rs 714 to 995. The average MRP for Shirts was Rs 800. It was estimated based on the sales mix of the stores. For T-shirts average, MRP was Rs 500. The price range for T-shirts was Rs 280 to 795. For trousers, MRP was Rs 1195. The selling prices were tightly controlled by the 'Cottonking' management and franchisees were expected to adhere to that. The selling price of every Stock Keeping Unit (SKU) was displayed on the tag as Maximum Retail Price (MRP). The gross profit margin (GP) for the retailers was guessed to be around 22 %. The average retail margin prevailing in the Indian garment industry was around 30%. The promotional, branding, replacement, and other marketing expenses were borne by the manufacturer. The 'value for money pricing strategy required that all channel partners focus on the sales volume rather than the margins. The MRP in the Indian garment industry was 350% to 400% of the ex-factory price against a global average of 500%.

Promotion

Cottonking was also one of the visible brands in terms of its Marketing Campaigns in Print, Radio, or TV. Cottonking hired famous Marathi star, Milind Gunaji as a brand ambassador. He hosted a popular Marathi TV show, 'Bharari'. The company developed a brand through TV commercials on the regional channels, in the local language. Hoardings at critical locations in the target cities were rented and newsprint advertisements in the local media were released. As a result of the successful promotional strategy mostly pre-sold customers visit stores. Cottonking offered an off-season scheme of 'flat 20% off' whereas Peter England, the national leader in the category, offered a better scheme 'buy 2- get 1 free', during the same period. In July 2016, Peter England franchises in Maharashtra reported healthy sales growth while Cottonking was losing battle to them.

Place

The first and flagship showroom of Cottonking was at 'Nal-Stop', which was a thickly populated residential area in Pune. The company decided to appoint exclusive franchise stores for their brand rather than selling the brand to regular garment wholesalers and retailers. By 2011, 'Cottonking' reached a tally of over 50 exclusive brand outlets spread across Maharashtra. By July 2016, the company appointed 104 retail outlets, mostly in Maharashtra, and crossed a mark of Rs 1 billion in annual sales. Most of the 'Cottonking' franchisees were doing business in the state of Maharashtra. Out of the total of 104 retailers about 15 were having an annual turnover of around Rs 20 million. Another 15 stores were having an annual turnover of around Rs 10 million. During the last couple of years, about 10% of stores were closed due to a lack of commercial viability. The average sales turnover per store per year was about Rs 10 Million which was barely about the required breakeven sales. The top 15 franchises were earning good money on account of their higher sales volume. Franchisees developed survival power by different measures. Some franchisees had deep pockets due to other businesses and hence they could sustain the Cottonking franchise business, hoping to improve it in the future. Some franchisees-owned stores hence did not consider the rent as an element of the cost. Some used their own savings as capital and saved interest component in the costing. Family members of some franchisees worked in their stores saving the cost of employees. The franchisees who could cut corners by one or more of the above methods could survive in spite of the sales being less than the theoretical breakeven sales volume. The challenge to the 'Cottonking' management was to increase the per-store sales to the level of at least Rs 20 million a year and the net profit margin to 3% to ensure a win-win situation with franchises in the long term. (See Exhibit 2)

Customers

'Cottonking' customers were men in the age group of 30 to 50. They were from the middle class. They spoke 'Marathi', the local language of the state of Maharashtra, read local and regional vernacular newspapers, and watched local and regional vernacular TV channels. They came to the store with a predetermined intention of buying. The average quantity per bill was 2 and the average value per bill was about Rs 2000.

The brand had poor awareness and acceptance among non-Marathi customers in Mumbai, Navi Mumbai, Thane, and Pune. A promotion team was required to address this issue to improve market penetration.

Competition

The industry was dominated, nationally, by large business houses and locally by the unorganized sector. Peter England was the major national brand with which Cottonking competed. Both the brands were in the same strategic group. Peter England was the largest menswear brand in India with over 5 million garments sold every year. First launched by Madura Fashion & Lifestyle (then known as Madura Garments) in the mid-price shirt segment in 1997, the company acquired the world rights for the brand in the year 2000. Peter England had a strong national presence with 643 exclusive stores and over 1600 multi-brand outlets in more than 300 towns. Madura Fashion and Lifestyle reached its discerning customers through an extensive network comprising more than 1,000 exclusive and franchise stores, and over 2,000 premium multi-brand trade outlets, both within and outside India. Madura Fashion and Lifestyle is defined by its brands — Louis Philippe, Van Heusen, Allen Solly, Peter England, and People — that personify style, attitude, luxury, and comfort. Aditya Birla Nuvo (ABNL) continued to be the market leader with a retail value share of 5% in 2015. Madura Fashion and Lifestyle is a Division of Aditya Birla Fashion & Retail Limited, a US$ 4.5 billion conglomerate by revenue size (FY12). It was formally known as Pantaloons Fashion and Retail Limited. ABNL is present across financial services, telecom, fashion and lifestyle, IT, and manufacturing businesses. It is part of the Aditya Birla Group, a US$ 40 billion (FY12) Indian multinational. Anchored by over 60,000 employees, ABNL touches the lives of more than 100 million Indians. To meet consumers' aspirations, MF&L created a complete end-to-end, demand-driven, manufacturing-to-retail ecosystem in India. It owns a vast retail network comprising exclusive outlets, premium multi-brand, and department stores. Four of its brands are among India's top fashion names, with MRP sales in excess of INR 10 billion each. Louis Philippe leads the aspiration for fashion excellence, giving its customers access to the finest in global fashion. Van Heusen focuses on empowering fashion-conscious professionals, and partnering career ambitions with power dressing.

Allen Solly is for those looking for a smart fashion alternative. It came out with the concept of Friday Dressing. Peter England with its promise of honest-to-goodness prices emerged as the favorite for a large mass of first jobbers. See Exhibit 6 for the top Men's ware brands in India.

Linen

Linen emerged as an alternative to cotton in garment manufacturing. Linen is the strongest of the vegetable fibers with 2 to 3 times the strength of cotton. It is smooth, making the finished fabric lint-free, and gets softer the more it is washed. Both cotton and Linen are natural plant fibers (cellulose), but there are many differences between them. (See Exhibit 3)

Linen King

In early 2013, after Kunal (son of Mr. Marathe) came back from the USA, the company launched the 'Limelight' brand, offering exclusively a linen range of ready-mades for men, a separate brand of the company. In the market, they did not associate both the brands, keeping them distinctly different.

In 2015, the company operated 11 Limelight stores through a franchise route in Maharashtra, selling trendy apparel of linen with starting price tags of Rs 795, Rs 995, and Rs 1,295. More than half the stores were in and around Pune city and the rest were in Western Maharashtra. Limelight brand had crossed Rs 250 million in 2014 and the company was eying 100 percent growth next year. Mr. Marathe was, probably, doing succession planning wherein he wanted both the sons to look after different brands and chain stores but still connected strongly through the factory which was shared between both the brands.

He was a successful and seasoned first-generation businessman who wouldn't give up easily. He took more than 20 years to develop Cottonking as a powerful brand in Maharashtra and was prepared to wait and experiment with the Linen range of Men's garments. Over the years Mr. Marathe developed deep pockets and business acumen.

Can Cottonking be a LinenKing too?

After the initial success of Limelight stores and Linen shirts, Cottonking started feeling the competitive pressures. A few of the Limelight stores had to be closed down on the account of poor performance. The franchisees complained about the commercial viability. Some argued that 'Linen doesn't have a power and popularity, in India; to match the commercial performance of the 'Cotton' range hence exclusive stores for linen was a bad idea'. There was also a feeling that the image created by the Cottonking brand was not leveraged properly while launching 'Limelight'. Rather than going for a multiple brand strategy, some seniors wanted to go for the brand extension. They thought might be 'LinenKing' could be a better name for the linen chain store. In 2015, Mr. Marathe launched another Exclusive Brand Outlet (EBO) chain, LinenKing. All limelight stores were merged and renamed 'LinenKing'. For the LinenKing brand, the company hired another Marathi actor, Ritesh Deshmukh who mostly acted in Hindi films as a supporting actor. He was cast as a hero in the Marathi movie 'Lai Bhari' which was released in 2014. (See Exhibit 4). The brand position created was 'Love for Linen'. In addition to Pune city, the stores were started in 6 other cities in Western Maharashtra. The product range included Linen Shirts (Linen Look, Linen Rich, and Linen Pure), Trousers, Jacket, and Kurtas. (See Exhibit5)

Bringing Commercial Viability for the Franchises

Mr. Marathe had to make a choice. He had to work on the channel conflict before it could take a wrong turn. The franchisees of Cottonking were not happy with the decision to open an exclusive store for the Linen range. They felt Cottonking management could have helped the existing franchises to achieve commercial viability by offering a Linen range of products in the Cottonking chain. They wondered why the management was after opening another chain of stores in their catchment area when more than 70% of the franchises of the existing chain were struggling for a breakeven. Franchisees felt both the EBOs, Cottonking, and LinenKing, were competing for the same consumer basket and the market segments were not separate. The company felt that the strong brand position created on the '100% cotton' fabric would be diluted if the linen range was to be offered to the existing Cottonking franchises.

According to franchisees, many actions were overdue in Cottonking. They wanted a more consistent product mix which should include a range of trousers and jeans. Certain gaps in terms of sizes of the shirts were required to be filled immediately. Due to missing inventory, some customers were going back without any purchases. The demand was also to raise the retailer margin to the industry level. Franchisees were very well aware of the cost of the manufacturer and felt that there was enough cushion to increase the retail margins to bring commercial viability for them. One view was to adopt the marketing strategy used by the brands like Van Heusen and Allen Solly. They wanted Cottonking to launch 'Cottonqueen', an exclusive brand for ladies' wear. The suggestion was to launch '100% cotton', a formal ware for ladies with a separate section in the Cottonking stores rather than opening a separate EBO chain. Mr. Marathe was required to act swiftly and come out with the appropriate solution before the forthcoming franchisee meeting.[1]

Exhibit 1: Product range

Shirts:

T Shirts:

Trousers:

Exhibit 2: Economics of a retail store

- An investment of Rs 6 million ($90,000) was required to run a franchise readymade garment shop, in an 'A' or 'B' category city, excluding the investment in buying a shop.
- The interest on the investment was around 11.5% to 15% per annum.
- The rent was about Rs 60 to 120 per square foot (sq. ft.)
- The required area: For Cottonking franchise shop: 700 to 1000 sq. ft.
- Manpower: 4 to 5 sales persons were required to run the shop.
- Average salary: Rs 5000 to 7000 per month.
- The power cost: For the air-conditioned stores was about Rs 18000 to Rs 20000.
- Other related expenses: Around Rs 10,000 per month.

Note: The retailers in 'C' category towns could save money on rent, salaries, etc but they were lagging far behind the average sales.

Exhibit 3: Linen

Linen is known to be the world's strongest natural fiber. Linen is from the flax plant. It is durable and even used in paper money to increase strength. It is thicker than cotton and linen fiber has variable lengths, most of which are very long. This contributes to strength, which contributes to longevity. Linen lasts a very long time. Linen is known to gain strength when wet. It has the natural ability to prevent bacterial growth. For towels, this is very important as hand and bath towels tend to be the perfect home for microbes. The affinity of cotton and linen to moisture is one reason why natural fibers are most comfortable to wear and to have in our bedrooms. They interact well with our bodies and contribute to our comfort. Over time linen becomes softer and even more comfortable. However, if you are not fond of wrinkles, linen may not be best for you. Linen fibers are hollow, moving air and moisture naturally. During the colder months, layer linen blankets or a throw to retain heat and warmth from your body. Linen reacts to the season and the body in contact with the cloth to give the best of all circumstances. Linen is a natural insulator. It is valued for its ability to keep cool in the summer months and trap warmth in colder weather. This is all achieved through the natural properties of the fiber itself.

Exhibit 4: LinenKing Brand Ambassador- Ritesh Deshmukh

Exhibit 5: LinenKing Collection

Linen Shirts (Linen Look)

Linen Shirts (Linen Rich)

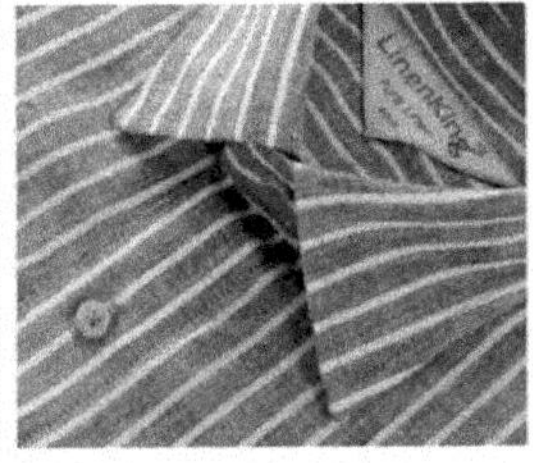

Linen Shirts (Pure Linen)

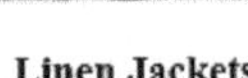

Linen Jackets

Linen Kurtas

Linen Trousers

Exhibit 6: Top Men's ware brands in India

(Source: http://business.mapsofindia.com/top-brands-india/top-men-clothing-brands-in-india.html)

Top Men's Clothing Brands in India

- Madura Garments (Louis Philip, Van Heusen, Peter England)
- Arvind Brands (Allen Solly, Arrow)
- Raymond Apparel Ltd (Park Avenue)
- Wrangler
- Provogue
- Killer
- Pantaloon Retail (India) Ltd
- Levi Strauss & Co. Etc.

References:

1. https://www.zaubacorp.com/company/COTTON-KING-PRIVATE-LIMITED/U29309PN1995PTC084413

1. http://punestartups.org/events/tie-pune-my-story-people-behind-puneri-brands-pradip-marathe-of

3. http://www.mydigitalfc.com/companies/cotton-king-eyes-rs-100-cr-revenue-next-1-year-549

4. http://www.brahmsmount.com/blog/cotton-vs-linen-whats-the-difference/

5. http://www.mydigitalfc.com/companies/cotton-king-eyes-rs-100-cr-revenue-next-1-year-549

6. https://en.wikipedia.org/wiki/Peter_England_(brand)

7. http://www.adityabirla.com/businesses/Profile/madura-fashion-and-lifestyle

8. http://www.abfrl.com/

9. http://www.technopak.com/Files/indian-apparel-market.pdf

10. http://www.cottonking.in/12-buy-formal-cotton-shirts-online-for-office-use

11. http://linenking.in/

[1] Disclaimer: This case study is prepared on the basis of informal academic research and the intellectual creation of the case writer with the intention to impart management decision-making skills to the student. It is not based on any company reports. It is purely designed for academic learning. The figures related to the company are either taken from published sources available in the public domain or by the professional guestimate of the case writer. The intention behind writing the case is purely academic and not to harm the commercial interest of the organization. The case author did not gain any financial benefit. The research and the case were not sponsored by any organization or individual.

CHAPTER ELEVEN

Maruti Suzuki: Marketing Plan in Turbulent Times

In October 2015 Mr. Bhargava, the Chairman of Maruti Suzuki Motors Ltd. who was associated with the company since its inception, was exploring options for the growth of the company in the next 5 years. The mission was set to achieve the landmark of selling 2 million cars a year, by the year 2020. The company already bought 600 acres of land in the state of Gujarat for increasing production capacity since both the plants in north India reached saturation in capacity utilization. The challenge was to achieve a growth of more than 50% in the next 5 years. The Indian car market was heated up. Most of the global players were getting aggressive. Maruti Suzuki's options were defined and limited. Preparing a sound Marketing Plan was never so challenging for Mr. Bhargava.

Maruti Suzuki: Leading the Indian Car Market

Indian car market which was estimated to be around 2.5 million cars a year was dominated by Maruti Suzuki Motors Ltd. In just over 30 years it reached the mark of $ 8 Billion, in sales. Maruti Suzuki acquired almost half of the Indian car market. It was the market leader holding almost 3 times the market share that of the number two in the industry, Hyundai motors. Managing the environment, en-cashing on the support of the parent company (Suzuki motors of Japan), focusing on the fastest-growing mass markets (the small and compact cars), creating a 'value for money' proposition for the customers, and the best service network in the country were the reasons behind Maruti Suzuki success in India. The company reached optimum market share in the small and compact petrol cars leaving hardly any room for further growth.

However, the company could not create the required impact in the SUV, Van, Sedan, and semi-luxury segments. Electric cars remained an unexplored market.

How did Maruti Suzuki reach the leadership position in India?

Maruti Suzuki forged many competitive advantages in the Indian market.

- **Strong support of the Government of India due to its equity and political stake.** A Political party supported the venture due to the strong interest of their leadership in it. With the change in political equations, Maruti Suzuki offered to open up a plant in the home state of the prime minister. Took support of the new government in acquiring 600 acres of land in Western India. This is the first time they have moved out of North India to remain politically correct.
- **Early mover advantage** Suzuki got into the Indian markets when other global giants ignored it as a small and restricted market, spread across a wider geography. With almost no resistance offered by ailing car manufacturers like Premier and Hindustan Motors, Maruti had a cakewalk. It took a strong grip within a few years blocking other potential entrants with government support. The Maruti 800 was released in 1983; This 796 cc hatchback was based on the SS80 Suzuki Alto and was India's first affordable car. The initial product plan was 40% saloons, and 60% Maruti Van. Local production commenced in December 1983. In 1984, the Maruti Van with the same three-cylinder engine as the 800 was released and the installed capacity of the plant in Gurgaon reached 40,000 units.
- **Leveraging Suzuki's core competency for competitive advantage.** Suzuki, the principal company, from Japan, had been known for its small and compact petrol cars. Maruti rode on their success to earn a competitive advantage over domestic players like Tata and Mahindra. In India's closed market, Maruti received the right to import 40,000 fully built-up Suzukis in the first two years, and the early goal was to use only 33% indigenous parts. In 1985, the Suzuki SJ410-based Gypsy, a 970 cc 4WD off-road vehicle, was launched. In 1989, the Maruti 1000 was introduced as India's first three-box sedan. By 1991, 65% components, were local.[i]

- **Focusing on small and compact car market segments** Maruti understood the pulse of the Indian customers and focused on the small and compact, hatchback, fuel-efficient cars and constantly kept launching such models to expand the market. In 1993, the Zen, a 993 cc, hatchback was launched and in 1994 the 1298 cc Esteem was introduced. Maruti produced its 1 millionth vehicle since the commencement of production in 1994. Maruti's second plant was opened with an annual capacity reaching 200,000 units. Maruti launched a 24-hour emergency on-road vehicle service. In 1998, the new Maruti 800 was released, the first change in design since 1986. Zen D, a 1527 cc diesel hatchback Maruti's first diesel vehicle, and a redesigned Omni were introduced.[ii]
- **Value for money proposition** Maruti Suzuki always maintained scale. They understood prudent Indian masses that always look for 'Value for Money. They maintained prices on the lower side of the price band, launched fuel-efficient models, and kept after-sales service and spare parts affordable. Maruti also ensured better resale value for the pre-owned Maruti cars.
- **Blocking strong competitive moves** Maruti always knew their weaknesses and focused on blocking any strong move by a competitor. Tata could not get a license for their small diesel car project on time, Toyota did not launch Daihatsu cars in India, and Honda focused on Sedans.

Indian Car Market in the year 2015

Maruti Suzuki posted its highest market share in more than a decade in July 2015, when almost one in every two passenger vehicles rolled out of the country's manufacturing plants had a Maruti badge on it. In July 2015 it produced more vehicles than ever before in its history, posting growth of over 15%. The undisputed leader of the Indian market manufactured 133000 cars in that month, as it aimed for an output of 1.39 million to 1.44 million cars in the fiscal year 2016.

From 2012 till 2015 Maruti had grown its market share by over 8 percentage points, and that of Hyundai Motor had expanded more than 3% to 17%. For Honda Cars India, the market share almost tripled to 7.2%. These three companies grew at the cost of two-vehicle makers, Mahindra & Mahindra and Tata Motors.[iii]

Maruti's top gear drive has been led by three best-selling models - Alto, Dzire, and Swift. Alto sold 232000 units in the April-February period, nearly double that of its closest competitor. Dzire sold 180000 units and Swift 179000 units. Together these models also made up the top three sellers in the Indian car market.[iv] From 2001-02 Maruti saw the same level of market share as in 2015. But the market size in 2001-02 was just over 670000 against 2.6 million in 2015. In the last 14 years, the Indian car market grew almost 4 times.[v] Maruti was aiming at selling 2 million cars by 2020.[vi]

The government-subsidized diesel fuel, which had been sold for 30% less than petrol. This led to the dieselization of the Indian car market: the share of diesel cars in new car sales had risen from 23 percent in 2002 to 40 percent in 2010. Finally, passenger cars with diesel engines use to make up as high as 52% of the Indian market. Diesel cars were driven almost twice as far as gasoline vehicles and, given, current emissions standards, were far more polluting.

Maruti's parent Suzuki Motor Corp. took 31 years to introduce its first diesel engine in India. Since 2008, the company sourced its 1.3-liter diesel engine from Fiat SpA under a licensing agreement. The engine powers its top-selling models such as the Swift, the Dzire, the Ertiga, and the Ciaz. The new S-Cross crossover has a 1.6-liter diesel engine, also sourced from Fiat.[vii]

There was a time when the market demand for diesel vehicles was almost at par with petrol vehicles in India. In 2012-13, the ratio of diesel to petrol was 47:53. With the news of diesel prices being deregulated, in 2013-14, the ratio of diesel to petrol cars widened to 42:58. Finally, in October 2014, the government removed the subsidy from diesel and deregulated its prices. This meant that the price of diesel would be directly related to the global crude oil prices. This diesel deregulation resulted in the ratio reducing further to 37:63 (in favor of petrol) in 2014-15. According to the Society of Indian Automobile Manufacturers (SIAM), the ratio as of April 2015 was 34:66. After this move, the gap between the price of diesel and petrol reduced considerably, and no longer do buyers find any real monetary benefit to sway in favor of a diesel vehicle. Where diesel vehicles truly shine, was their outstanding fuel economy when compared to petrol.

However, these vehicles were more expensive to purchase (in comparison) and buyers need to do some serious mile-crunching to justify the premium over petrol vehicles.[viii]

The move from Euro 4 to Euro 5 and beyond would require significant investment in technologies like Diesel Particle Filter (PDF) and Selective Catalytic Reduction (SCR) which would increase the cost of small diesel cars and also of SUVs by Rs 65,000-100000. Petrol engines on the other hand would require simpler technology tweaks and would only see a mark-up of Rs 7000-11,000 max. Because of the sophistication of the technology involved, small diesel vehicles would become "prohibitively expensive when they are Euro 6-compliant in India.[ix] The major players and their approximate market shares in the Indian car market was as follows: Maruti Suzuki: 50%, Hyundai Motors: 18%, Mahindra and Mahindra: 9%, Honda Motors: 8%, Tata Motors: 7%, Toyota Motors: 6%. General Motors, Ford Motors, Nissan, and Volkswagen had market shares equal to or below 2% each despite mass marketing efforts.[x]

Industry Structure

As per the latest sales figures of the Indian car manufacturers, the following industry structure emerged; the leader: Maruti Suzuki, Challenger: Hyundai motors, Followers: Honda, Tata, and Mahindra. Global leaders like General Motors, Ford, Nissan, Renault, and VW were reduced to Niche players because of only one or two successful models in a specific market segment, even though they claimed a presence in many market segments.

Market Segments

- Maruti Suzuki was dominating the ‘Small Car’ segment with ‘Alto’ and ‘WagonR’ with hardly any challenge of ‘Hyundai eon’. ‘Tata Nano’ failed to create any dent.
- ‘Compact Car’ market segment was also dominated by Maruti with models like Swift, Celerio, and Ritz. Hyundai was competing with the ‘i10’ and ‘i20’ models. Almost all manufacturers were trying their luck with hatchback models.
- Maruti Suzuki also ruled in the ‘Small Utility van’ segment with models like ‘Omni Van’ and ‘EECO’.

- 'Compact Sedan' market was served by Maruti (Dzire), Hyundai, Tata, and Honda.
- 'Sedan' market was focused on Hyundai and Honda and VW.
- 'Van' and 'SUV' market segments in India were not demarcated. Models in these segments competed with each other. Customers preferred diesel models with a larger capacity to carry a number of passengers. Toyota Motors dominated it with its models like 'INNOVA' and 'Fortuner'. Mahindra served with models like XUV, Scorpio, and Xylo. Tata Motor was a loser with an initially successful model, 'Sumo'. Honda, Nissan, Renault, and GM also jumped into it. Maruti Suzuki created a ripple with the launching of the model 'Ertiga', with diesel and CNG versions.
- The 'Luxury' segment was dominated by German brands, Mercedes, BMW, and Audi.
- 'Semi Luxury' market was en-carved by Toyota (Camry and Corolla), VW(Passat, Jetta, Skoda)
- Mahindra was trying its luck in the 'Electric Car' market. The market size was very tiny.

Maruti Suzuki: Product Mix

Out of the 9 market segments of the Indian car market, Maruti Suzuki was leading in 4 segments. As of March 2015, small cars contribute 40% of the sales volume of Maruti Suzuki. 'Compact cars' and 'Compact Sedan' market contributed to 38% and Small Utility vehicles 11% of the sales. Thus almost 90% of the market leader's sales came from the 4 market segments where it was in the leadership position. Of the rest, 10% comes from 2 more segments 'Van /SUV' and 'Sedan'. Maruti Suzuki never attempted the 'Luxury' segment and failed in the 'Semi-Luxury' segment where it launched 'Kizashi'. The electric car segment was not yet touched.

Challenges in maintaining the leadership position

Small is beautiful. Compact cars were core to the success of Suzuki globally. Kei was a Japanese category of small vehicles, including passenger cars, micro-vans, and pickup trucks. Even in India, their compact theme worked. Not only the compact hatchbacks but also compact sedans, compact vans, and compact SUVs. Every time they introduced a compact version in any market segment, it worked for them.

How to maintain this core brand value while preparing a marketing plan, to fulfill its mission, was the major challenge for Maruti Suzuki. Maruti Suzuki stuck to their core technology, petrol engines even in tough times. Their diesel engines were sourced from Fiat, for all the models. They had a conviction for petrol engines and they never departed from that conviction. Maintaining this conviction in petrol engines was another challenge faced by Mr. Bhargava. Developing a new car on a new platform and commercializing it would certainly take more than 5 years. Maruti Suzuki was therefore likely to continue its practice of launching existing models of Suzuki Japan in India.

Exhibit 1

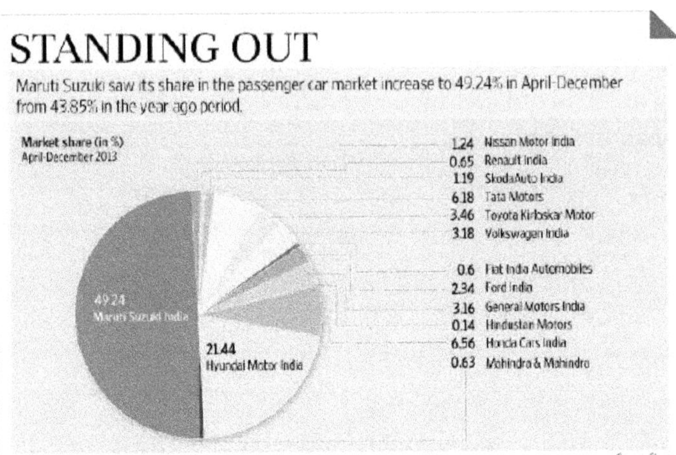

Exhibit 2

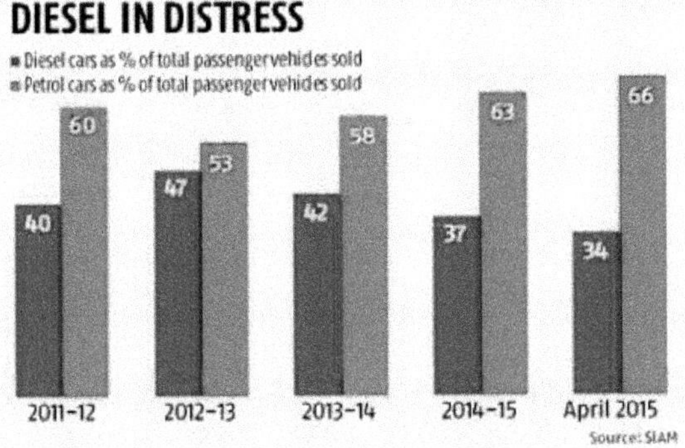

Exhibit 3

New models

In Auto China 2014 in Beijing Suzuki revealed two models Alivio, a sedan and iV4, a compact SUV. They also have other models like the new Vitara, Air Triser, a compact mini-van, Mighty Deck, a new concept mini car, APV, a compact minivan and Jimny another mini SUV, Solio, a compact hybrid car.

Vitara **Solio** **Mighty Deck**

APV **Jimny**

References:

[i] https://en.wikipedia.org/wiki/Maruti_Suzuki

[ii] https://en.wikipedia.org/wiki/Maruti_Suzuki

[iii] 'Maruti Suzuki posts highest market share in more than a decade in July',

Ketan Thakkar, ET Bureau, Economic Times, 12th Aug 2015.
http://economictimes.indiatimes.com/articleshow/48445994.cms?utm_source=contentofinterest&utm_medium=text&utm_campaign=cppst

[iv] 'Maruti gains 50% market share', Nandini Sen Gupta, Times

of India 24 March 2014
http://timesofindia.indiatimes.com/business/

india-business/

Maruti-regains-50-market-share/articleshow/32577532.cms

[v] 'After 14 years Maruti regained…', Mint 12th Aug 2015,
http://www.livemint.com/Companies/tHt4EcYdIBIKqAjgi7VhoL/

After-14-years-Maruti-regains-50-share-of-domestic-market.html

[vi] 'Maruti LaunchesBaleno…', Mint, 26th Oct 2015,

http://www.livemint.com/Consumer/fCakNLJBD8Xv2QWjjFRjyI/

Maruti-launches-its-first-madeinIndia-car-Baleno-at-Rs499.html

[vii] 'After 14 years Maruti regained…', Mint 12th Aug 2015, http://www.livemint.com/Companies/tHt4EcYdIBIKqAjgi7VhoL/

After-14-years-Maruti-regains-50-share-of-domestic-market.html

[viii] http://www.team-bhp.com/forum/indian-car-scene/

165156-diesel-cars-down-down-down-market-share-34-a.html

[ix] 'Small diesel cars, SUV set to cost more', Economic Times, 3 Oct 2015, http://economictimes.indiatimes.com/industry/auto/news/

passenger-vehicle/cars/Small-diesel-cars-SUVs-set-to-cost-more/

articleshow/49203655.cms

[x] Based on the figures given by the Society of Indian Automotive

Manufactures (SIAM) for the financial year 2014-2015

CHAPTER TWELVE

Maruti Suzuki: Defending the Market Leadership

It was June 2017, R. C. Bhargava, the Chairman and past CEO of Maruti Suzuki India Ltd., was pondering in his office, situated in the company's headquarters in Delhi, India. He was going through the proposal provided by the marketing team on the aligning of the product strategy with the distribution strategy. The parent company, Suzuki Japan, would be celebrating its 100th year of inception in 2020. Mr. Bhargava wanted to celebrate that occasion by achieving the annual sales of 2 million cars, in India. The company owned many assets in India in terms of brands, brand equity, consumer franchise, plants, market share, distribution network, clout with the government and other regulating agencies, and much more. Bhargava's challenge was how to align these assets to create a synergy that would block the major global car manufacturers from expanding in India. The competitors like Hyundai were finding the weakness in the strength of Maruti Suzuki. As a market leader, Maruti was selling more of the fast-moving brands with value-for-money propositions. The dealers wouldn't travel the extra mile to push certain slow-moving niche brands. The company became the leader of the masses, the competitors were pampering and targeting the classes. The dealers were complaining about overlaps between the regular dealerships and the new premium dealerships, Nexa. The new distribution network was being viewed as a parallel network rather than the network for premium cars. The hardware was very much in place but the software was not bug-free. The sales persons at the dealerships were not courteous enough like their counterparts in the competitors' showrooms. The market was going to grow multi-fold in the coming decade.

There was a prediction that India would be the third largest car market in the world by 2030. Maruti Suzuki wanted to be a leader of the future and maintain half of the pie of the Indian car market which they were holding in 2017. But it was getting more and more difficult with the global car warfare reaching the Indian shores. Maruti Suzuki so far won the Indian battle. But soon the global giants were likely to get into action and try hard to snatch the crown. Mr. Bhargava and his team had to create a well-entrenched strategy to defend the market leadership position. The marketing strategy was required to sell premium cars to existing customers and existing cars to premium customers. Maruti Suzuki created a separate network, Nexa, for premium cars-premium customers but it was creating a dilemma. The management was not sure whether to keep the old and new network as mutually complementary, as it was decided earlier, or make it mutually competing. Both options had strong pros and cons. The decision could be defined by aligning the product strategy with the distribution strategy. The marketing team provided their inputs and recommendations. Mr. Bhargava was to make the decision. In the following month, the Gujrat factory of Suzuki Japan was scheduled to start the commercial deliveries and Mr. Bhargava was required to address the press. He knew the press would pester him over many strategic issues. He had to make the decision and keep his strategy ready.

The Car Market: Global Perspective

The global market stood at around 88 million cars in 2016. It showed an annual growth of 4.6% in 2016. In terms of growth, China ranked first with a 13% increase in sales. In 2016, it added 3.2 million more cars compared to its annual sales in 2015[i], the annual car sales in China were 28 million cars followed by the USA at 17.5 million, Japan at 5 million, Germany at 3.5 million, and the UK at 3 million.[ii]

India was the sixth largest car market in the world but it was poised to become the 4th largest market by 2020. India's car sales growth rate was second only to China. The USA car market grew only by 0.4%, European Union by 7% whereas Brazil, Russia, and Japan's car markets declined by 20%, 11%, and 2% respectively.

Indian Car Market and the Industry Structure (as of May 2017)

Indian car industry created history by crossing the 3 million units of sales, in domestic sales. It grew annually by almost 10%, during 2016-17. Maruti Suzuki was the clear market leader with a 47.38% market share. Hyundai (from South Korea) was the challenger with a 16.72% market share. All other players were having a market share in the single digit. Tata Motors, Honda, and Toyota were the followers. Mahindra, Skoda, VW, Renault, Nissan, and Ford were successful only in certain niches with specific models. Fiat was not even on the map and was struggling hard for survival. GM left the heated market. See the market shares of the Indian car manufacturers in **Appendix 1**. Some larger cities have multiple dealers. See **Appendix 2** for the number of cities with the market presence of the car dealers of the respective car manufacturers.

Maruti Suzuki: Wearing the Crown

Maruti Suzuki India Limited (MSIL), formerly known as Maruti Udyog Limited, a subsidiary of Suzuki Motor Corporation of Japan, was India's largest passenger car company. The company offered a full range of car brands from entry-level Maruti Alto to stylish hatchback A star, Swift, Baleno, Celerio, Wagon R, Ritz, Estillo, and sedans DZire, SX4, Ciaz, and Sports Utility Vehicle Grand Vitara. Along with new categories S Cross, Ignis, and Ertiga. The company was born as a government company, with Suzuki as a minor partner, to make a people's car for middle-class India. Over the years, the product range had widened, ownership had changed hands and the customer evolved. The parent company, Suzuki Motor Corporation, had been a global leader in mini and compact cars for three decades. Suzuki's technical superiority lay in its ability to pack power and performance into a compact, lightweight engine that was clean and fuel efficient.[iii] It owned two manufacturing plants in the North Indian state of Haryana, Near Delhi with an installed capacity of just over 1.6 million units. Both the plants were operating with almost full capacity utilization, as a result, there was a waiting period for customer deliveries on a few popular models. Suzuki Japan was aiming at global volumes of 5 million by 2020.

Maruti was a key to reaching that target which was estimated to account for 40% of Suzuki's revenue and 25% of profits, by 2020.[iv] In June 2017, Maruti Suzuki was holding a market share of about 50% in the Indian car industry. It was owning a product portfolio of 15 brands and 150 variants. They had a few successful launches in the premium category, Baleno and Vitara Brezza models. Domestic sales grew by 10.7% to the total sales at 15.68 million units, in the year 2016-17. Maruti Suzuki occupied the top 5 slots in the top 10 most sold car brands (models) in India (Alto, Swift, Desire, WagonR, and Celerio). Followed by Hyundai with three slots (i10, i20, and Eon) and Honda with 2 (City and Amaze). See **Appendix 3** for the most sold car models in India in FY 2015-16. Maruti Suzuki Alto had emerged as the best-selling car in India for the 13th consecutive year. In 2016-17 fiscal, more than 2.41 lakh Altos were sold, which was close to 17% of Maruti Suzuki's total domestic sales.[v]

The Competition

The challenger, Hyundai Motors, was way behind. Maruti Suzuki was holding almost three times the market share than that of Hyundai, the number two player, But Hyundai was the only competitor who stood firm with a decent overall market share and also in the relevant segments. Maruti Suzuki was holding the nearly equal market share to the following six car manufacturers put together. Other than these two players only three more manufacturers, Mahindra, Tata, and Honda, were having a market share of more than 5%. Even the major globally leading players like VW, GM, Ford, and Toyota were marginalized and could not show their magic to the Indian masses. The major competition for Maruti Suzuki continued from Hyundai Motor India (HMIL). Hyundai also recorded a record-breaking sale in FY2016-17. Hyundai reported a 5.2 percent increase in sales, from 484,324 units in the previous fiscal to 509,707 units in FY2016-17. Hyundai was able to close the financial year with the highest-ever sales creating strong momentum for the next year. They decided that the company would launch ten products over the next four years. Eight would be new models and the remaining upgrades of the existing models. Hyundai planned to invest $2 billion in India over the next five years to develop and upgrade products. It also aimed to expand its market share.[vi] Hyundai could stand against Maruti by its strengths. While Suzuki entered India from the North, Hyundai preferred entry from the South.

Hyundai competed by aesthetics, product features, and competitive service matched by value for money pricing like Maruti Suzuki. The other competitors were holding marginal market shares. Most of them were focusing on specific market segments. Honda was strong in Sedan. Toyota sold Innova (MPV), and Fortuner (SUV), and though it sold large and small sedans (Corolla-Altis, Camry, and Etios) it lacked the required numbers to challenge Maruti Suzuki. Mahindra was also focusing on SUVs. Both of them were betting on the diesel engines. Tata Motors was trying its luck with diesel cars, small hatchbacks, and sedans along with a minor presence in the MPV market. Renault also sold Nissan cars through a separate distribution network but it was still too small to compete with Maruti Suzuki. Other global players like Ford and VW could not impress Indian customers and barely existed in the market with respective market shares of 3% and 1.6%. General Motors decided to get out of the Indian market and use its manufacturing plant exclusively for export markets.

Global Car Wars on Indian Battlefield

The 'car wars' was being played at the global level. The major battlefields were China, the USA, Japan, Germany, the UK, and many other countries in Europe, Asia, and South America. Suzuki successfully handled the battle in India by forging the first mover advantage. They consolidated their position by containing the global giants. Suzuki transformed itself by indigenizing as 'Maruti'[1]. In India, it wore a new identity, 'Maruti Suzuki'. It was no longer considered as a foreign company, to the extent that it became a national icon. Maruti Suzuki's challenge was to maintain market leadership in such a dynamic and growing market. Suzuki and Maruti collectively occupied 9th rank in the list of global car manufacturers. Most of the competitors of Maruti Suzuki were divisions of the globally leading car manufacturers. Their global power was more than Suzuki and they were ranked higher on the list of global car manufacturers. See **Appendix 4** for the ranks of the global automobile (not just cars) manufacturers. There was a high probability that they may get extremely attacking when the market heats up. Maruti Suzuki was gearing itself to encash the mega opportunity in the market penetration. They were creating the infrastructure to cater to the demand which would grow four times in the next 12 to 13 years.

Losing out in the entry-level market: The major concern for the company was its declining supremacy in the mass volume generating, entry-level segment. The company had been reporting degrowth for quite some months in the segment. In March 2017 sales of mini segment cars, including Alto and WagonR, declined 15.6 percent to 30,973 units from 36,678 units in the year-ago month. Maruti's small cars were facing tough competition from Renault 'Kwid' and Tata 'Tiago'. Both the companies clocked a strong double-digit growth in FY2016-17. Maruti was struggling with the production capacity for the small cars. They were hoping that once the Gujrat plants start operations then the issue will be resolved. Meanwhile, Kwid was exploiting the opportunity. Renault Kwid sold about 1.09 lakh units in FY2017. Toyota motors were planning to launch the 'Daihatsu' small cars in the Indian market to justify their existence in India.[vii] Daihatsu was one of the most successful small car companies owned by Toyota. It dominated small car markets in many countries with petrol and diesel small cars. Introducing Daihatsu cars may take at least 3-4 years, said N. Raja, director (sales and marketing) at Toyota Kirloskar Motor, in an interview to Live mint daily. Toyota's move to acquire Daihatsu had Suzuki president Toshihiro Suzuki worried. "This will be a threat for SMC (Suzuki Motor Corp.) not only in India but also for other markets," Suzuki said in February 2016. [viii]

Other Threats: Hyundai was challenging Maruti on the 'Product' front. They introduced fluidic design in 2010. Hyundai designers stated that the "Fluidic Sculpture" was the inspiration behind their design, both inside and outside their vehicles. The Fluidic aspect of this design was drawn from nature, and since nature is made from curves and not sharp angles, the emphasis was on organic shapes and flowing lines. This design made the vehicles more aerodynamic, more beautiful, and graceful. The Sculpture aspect evoked ideas such as craftsmanship and the bespoke attention to detail. Hyundai engineers and designers wanted their vehicles to be more than simple pieces of metal rolling off assembly lines, they wanted them to look and feel like something crafted and graceful: a sculpture. Hyundai increased its sales in America by 20% after it introduced fluidic design. In India, they launched fluidic models, in 2012.

The fluidic design improved product looks getting admiration from women and youngsters in the family who had a major influence on the family car buying decision. The aesthetics were supported by product features. Hyundai started including many optional features as built-in features increasing the value of the customers' money. On account of these strategies, Hyundai cars were creating a luxury image in the minds of customers. They were the image made for 'classes' when Maruti Suzuki was ruling the masses. Honda was doing good in the sedan segment with its model, 'City'. For many years it remained the most sold premium sedan. For many years Maruti left the SUV market segment vacant. Hyundai's Creta and Ford's Ecosports started gripping the market. Both brands were good-looking urban compact SUVs designed for emerging nuclear families. Maruti's entry in the segment was overdue.

Market Penetration Strategy: The marketing objective of Maruti Suzuki was to maximize the market share. They dominated almost half of the Indian car market, the highest market share held by any car company in the major global market. The next best was Toyota holding about 30% of the car market in Japan. In all other major countries, the market leaders were holding less than 20% market share. The research conducted by various international management consulting firms, on the Indian car industry indicated a lot of untapped potential for cars. A PWC-Booz and Company report predicted that India would be the third largest car market in the world by 2030 with market size of about 11.7 million units.[ix] The Euromonitor predicted that the major portion of the growth would come from small cars and SUV segments whereas the second tire cities would be the growth centers.[x] These predictions were triggering the war. The global car giants were hungry for volumes. They had a presence in the Indian market which could be scaled up by investments. Maruti Suzuki was the market leader hence any major development would harm their position. They were required to be pre-emptive and block any strong competitive move to maintain their market share. If they couldn't block then they had to respond swiftly to nullify the competitive advantages of others. Maruti Suzuki identified the criticality of the production capacity and reach in terms of width and depth of the distribution channel. Normally it would need at least 4 to 5 years to identify the plant location, install the factory and start commercial production.

Maruti Suzuki was starving for production capacity. They had customers waiting for a few brands on account of constraints on production capacity.

The Parental Support:

Suzuki Japan, the parent company of Maruti Suzuki was very supportive. In 2015, Suzuki Motors, Japan invested $ 1.3 billion in the 600-acre plant at Hansalpur, on the outskirts of Ahmedabad, in Western India. As per the understanding, Suzuki Japan would do 100% investment in the Gujarat plant and machinery, whereas, Maruti Suzuki, the Indian subsidiary, would buy the entire production of the Gujrat plant. The deal was a win-win situation for both. Maruti Suzuki was not investing any money while doubling the manufacturing capacity, by adding the estimated capacity of 1.5 million units a year. It was at least 50% more than their sales target of 2 million vehicles by fiscal 2020. The plant was expected to deliver vehicles by July-August 2017; They could sell more cars to retain their higher market share and reduce the customer waiting time. Additionally, Maruti Suzuki could increase the investments in marketing rather than production capacities. Such major support was critical for Maruti Suzuki to maintain its massive market share in the rapidly growing Indian market.

Success in Product Development Strategy by penetrating the premium market: One of the most important things that happened to Maruti Suzuki was its growing dominance in the premium segment. After missing making a big impact in the premium category in the past, Maruti Suzuki cemented its position in the three top premium categories- premium hatchback, compact SUV, and mid-level sedan. Honda Cars India earlier dominated the premium mid-size sedan market with a model Honda-City. Hyundai Motors India had a stronghold in a premium hatchback with the i20 model and the compact SUV with the model 'Creta'. In 2016-17 Maruti Suzuki's compact SUV, Vitara Brezza, had clocked over 110,000 units in the first year of its launch while the premium hatchback Baleno still commanded a waiting period of 5-6 months and was not expected to ease in FY2018. Baleno had driven past the 150,000-unit sales in 18 months.[xi] In the months from April to February 2017, Maruti sold 59,530 units of the Ciaz, as against 51,713 City units sold by Honda Cars India Ltd.

Thus Maruti dislodged Honda City as India's largest-selling premium sedan, according to the Society of Indian Automobile Manufacturers (Siam). Multi-Purpose Vehicle, MPV, segment Maruti Suzuki Ertiga was fighting with Toyota Innova. It also competed with the Mahindra Xylo, Tata Sumo Grande, Toyota Avanza, Honda Mobilio, Renault Lodgy, and Nissan Grand Livina. It was holding an almost equal share to Toyota Innova, of the MPV market, leaving hardly any room for expansion. Maruti Suzuki dominated the Hatchback and compact sedan segments with models like Swift, and Swift Desire. Maruti Suzuki already reached the optimum market share in the Indian market however, they were still hungry for growth. In 2020 Suzuki International would celebrate its 100 years of inception. The Indian division wanted to celebrate it by crossing the landmark sales of 2 million cars a year. Maruti was hunting for growth. They were trying penetration and product development strategies for business expansion. The company decided to resort to database marketing.

Database Marketing: Maruti Suzuki had a database of 15 million customers out of which 12 million were identified as unique customers. The company ran about 2000 customer relationship campaigns on this database. Five percent of the total sales were done through database marketing initiatives, the company sold over 100,000 cars under this initiative. Almost 28% of the Maruti customers were upgrading, repeat customers whereas 27% were buying a second car. In Pune, a campaign to generate sales of Ciaz, Maruti Suzuki found that customers between the ages of 26-75 years who owned either an SX4, Dzire, or a Swift for over 5.5 years were more likely to upgrade to a higher-end sedan. This outreach yielded about 100 prospects out of which about 50% of customers purchased the Ciaz.[xii] Maruti Suzuki saw a very different trend in their sales figures. Repeat customers were the ones who were increasingly adding to the sales numbers. A Maruti official in a press conference said, "We have observed that the percentage of first-time buyers has come down marginally. So, additional cars in the family and repeat buyers or exchange buyers have taken some more percentage. In the last four years, the first-time buyer percentage has come down from 52 percent to 45 percent (of the total sales)"[xiii]

Car Distribution in India

The Indian car industry used the 'Exclusive Distribution Strategy'. The exclusive distribution agreement bound the dealer and the manufacturer. The manufacturer provided exclusive distribution rights to the dealer while the dealer stocked and sold only the Maruti Suzuki brands. The market leader Maruti Suzuki had a bigger dealership footprint than that of its top six competitors put together. Maruti's network tally as of FY 2017 was 1800 outlets across 1450 cities in India. It was larger than that of the distribution network of the next top 6 competitors put together. The combined market presence of Hyundai, Mahindra & Mahindra, Honda, Tata, Toyota, and Ford was less than Maruti Suzuki. See the number of car dealers of the Indian car manufacturers in **Appendix 5**. Maruti's network got even bigger if the Nexa dealerships were added to that list.[xiv] Maruti was also the most aggressive regarding outlet expansion. They added 201 outlets and another 127 Nexa showrooms till March 2016. It was planning to add around 325 outlets in the following financial year. The company could add so many dealerships on account of the profitability it offered to its dealers along with the volume of sales. See **Appendix 6** for dealer profitability among Indian automobile companies. Maruti Suzuki created a strong network of 3213 service centers all over India.

Maruti Suzuki Opened Nexa, the Branded Showrooms for Premium Cars

In July 2015 Maruti Suzuki launched branded showrooms, Nexa for their premium cars. They had some products in the pipeline. Some would go to the regular channel and some would go to Nexa. The company was also planning for separate service centers for the Nexa customers however as an interim arrangement their regular dealers would service the cars. There was a plan to hire around 2500 relationship managers for Nexa outlets. At the launch, the company expected to have around 30 Nexa outlets operational in the initial stage, and for that over 1,000 relationship managers were already hired. Maruti Suzuki was hiring people from sectors such as hospitality, aviation, and financial services to offer a differentiated luxury car buying experience for its "discerning customers".[xv] Premium cross-over S-Cross, premium hatchback Baleno, and premium urban compact IGNIS were sold through NEXA. Maruti declared that it would sell Ciaz, the midsize premium sedan, through Nexa showrooms from April 2017.[xvi]

Rationale Behind Nexa

Competitors were trying to catch Maruti Suzuki on the wrong foot. The leader develops certain weaknesses only because of the leadership position. At that scale of operations, certain services couldn't be given. Personalized service, luxury products, and attending to premium customers were a few areas where Maruti was being outfoxed by the competitors. They were encashing on the weaknesses in the strength of the leader. Maruti Suzuki wanted to change the way in which the cars were sold in India. To tap buyers who were upgrading from Maruti's small cars to premium cars and create a differentiated identity for themselves, Maruti launched the Nexa outlets. "Through NEXA, we offer a unique car buying experience, built on pampering, innovation, and technology. With all these initiatives, we are able to attract new categories of customers who were earlier not considering us. We have taken the challenge to create newer segments to fulfill the wishes of our customers," Mr. Kalsi, the Marketing head at Maruti Suzuki, said while inaugurating the 200th NEXA showroom in Hyderabad.[xvii] The Ciaz would be the fifth model to be sold through Nexa. In June 2017, Maruti Suzuki also sold the S-Cross (cross-over), Baleno and Baleno RS hatchbacks, and Ignis through Nexa.[xviii] A substantial difference is noted regarding safety features, as vehicles sold from Nexa outlets come standard with dual front airbags, along with ABS (Anti-Lock Braking System). Another noticeable difference is in the variant nomenclature. Nexa cars acquire variant names such as Sigma, Delta, Alpha, and Zeta, while the rest receive regular tags such as LX/Di, VX/Di, and ZX/Di, depending on whether they are petrol or diesel variants. Regarding features, Vitara Brezza was the latest entrant from the regular dealerships and boasts of features similar to the ones offered to Nexa vehicles. The Ignis micro SUV, which was retailed from Nexa, featured dual front airbags with ABS and EBD.[xix]

Nexa: Sales Performance

With Ciaz joining the Nexa line-up, the contribution of the premium retail chain is expected to top 15% of total sales by end of 2017-18. In Jan 2017, Maruti Suzuki reported that its premium automotive retail channel, NEXA, had sold over 185,000 vehicles since its inception in July 2015.

"Since its launch, NEXA has received an overwhelming response from customers and has done extremely well in its objective of changing the way cars are sold in India," R.S. Kalsi, Executive Director (Marketing and Sales), Maruti Suzuki India was quoted as saying in a statement. The passenger car major planned to expand the number of NEXA outlets to 250 by end of 2016-17. By March 2017, when NEXA completed 20 months of its launch, it sold 200,000 units. According to the company, the premium automotive retail channel was an important initiative in its journey of achieving a 2 million sales target by 2020.[xx]

Two Channels: Two Product Strategies

Some dealers thought Maruti Suzuki was playing with fire. It was using multiple distribution strategies in the industry which was operating on the exclusive distribution system. Such an exclusive distribution system required a trust-based relationship between the dealer and the principal. Both were required to maintain each other's exclusivity. However, the regular dealers felt Maruti Suzuki was violating the agreement and stepping over their feet. Maruti was operating two showrooms in the same geography, regular Maruti Suzuki showrooms, and the 'premium' Nexa outlets. They were required to differentiate the products, brands, customers, services, and prices. Any ambiguity would develop contempt which would lead to major channel conflict and a lose-lose situation for both, the dealer and the company. The company sometimes took decisions keeping in mind the competition and ignored the dealers. They launched a premium brand, Vitara Brezza, through the traditional distribution channel rather than the Nexa channel. It was done to restrict the rapid advance of Hyundai 'Creta'. Giving the brand to Nexa could have restricted the reach of the brand. The company added salt to the injury when they asked the traditional dealers to service Nexa vehicles because Nexa showrooms were not yet provided with the service centers. On the flip side, cars retailed from existing showrooms offer optional dual front airbags, while a few also get ABS with EBD (Electronic Brakeforce Distribution). In 2016, the company launched the S-Cross and Baleno from Nexa, and also offered optional safety features in its existing products – the Alto 800 and the K10 (driver airbag) – that were being sold through its regular dealerships. Similarly, the Vitara Brezza received optional dual front airbags along with ABS and EBD, as it was sold through regular dealerships.

On the other hand, the Nexa dealers also complained about the restrictions. Their volumes were not in the line with their investments and expenses. Maruti Suzuki was selling only one variant per brand in Nexa which had fully loaded features. This is not the way the cars were purchased. Customers wanted the freedom to choose features if they had to pay for them. Ciaz was a premium mid-size sedan but sold through traditional channels. When it was pointed out to the Maruti management they launched the Ciaz Hybrid model exclusively through Nexa. But the customers had strong reservations about the new hybrid technology. Such customers were directed by Nexa to the traditional channel for other models. In the bargain, Nexa lost customers to Honda City and Hyundai Verna. The dealers felt that the company was acting on adhocism rather than a well-crafted strategy. They were keeping a low profile because of the fear to lose the dealership.

Hyundai removed a few dealers, with which they had conflicts accusing them of poor sales and service to customers. Many Maruti Suzuki dealers preferred to invest in Nexa dealerships. They thought it was a better way of managing the channel conflict. It looked like Maruti itself was in dilemma as to which product they sell through Nexa and which product through Maruti Suzuki. For aligning the product strategy with the distribution strategy Maruti Suzuki was required to make decisions on products, product range, product line decisions like length, width, depth, etc., brands and branding, warranty, and service policy. The pre-and post-sales services were also required to be defined clearly.

Customer Responses to Nexa

The research done through the secondary data from auto magazines and auto blogs indicated the following reactions from customers about Nexa, their experience, and their opinion.[xxi]One customer wrote in a blog that instead of S-Cross Maruti should have started selling Kizashi and Ciaz through Nexa. The Nexa was a good concept by Maruti but the way they were handling was not clear. See **Appendix 7** for more reactions of customers to the Nexa experiment by Maruti.

The Dilemma

Mr. Bhargava had to decide about the future of the Nexa. There were a few options available. One view was that both Nexa and the regular channel should be clearly separated by distributing the existing product line rationally. Nexa should be given all premium brands, from all segments and other brands should be given to the regular dealers. But Nexa must sell all brands at prices higher than the highest price of the brands in the regular dealership. The Baleno should not undercut the prices of Swift's high-end model. In such a case, Ciaz should be given to the regular dealership and Nexa should focus on Kizashi as a premium sedan. Alternatively, if Ciaz was to be given to Nexa then the company should upgrade and re-launch SX4 and sell it as a mid-size sedan through the regular dealership. The dispute would also occur about Vitara Brezza. The company needed to identify and launch one more brand in that segment. Ignis, Baleno, Ciaz, Kizashi, Vitara Brezza, and S Cross would form a premium band whereas the rest of the brands to be given to the regular channel. Another argument was that 15 brands and 150 variants were difficult to handle for any dealership in any territory. Ultimately, every dealer was displaying and pushing only certain fast-moving brands and achieving targets. Nexa should also be made like a regular dealership and all products should be given to all the dealers. It would increase the business potential for every dealer on account of the availability of all products, at the same time, the competition among dealers would benefit the customers. The complacent regular dealer would be alert on account of the competition from Nexa dealers. On the other hand, the Nexa dealers would also contribute higher sales and would become commercially viable. The customer would get a choice of the dealership and the monopoly of the dealers in their geographies would be broken. Mr. Bhargava was thinking hard about how to align the product and pricing strategy with the distribution strategy and support it with the required promotional strategy. He knew the importance of the apt marketing mix to fight the Indian car wars which were soon to become part of the Global car wars. He was the first CEO of the company that established Maruti Suzuki in India. Now, the company needed to leverage its wisdom to maintain its dominance even in 2030 and beyond.

Appendix 1: The Market Shares of the top car manufacturers in India

Source: Society of Indian Automobile Manufacturers (SIAM) April 2016 to March 2017

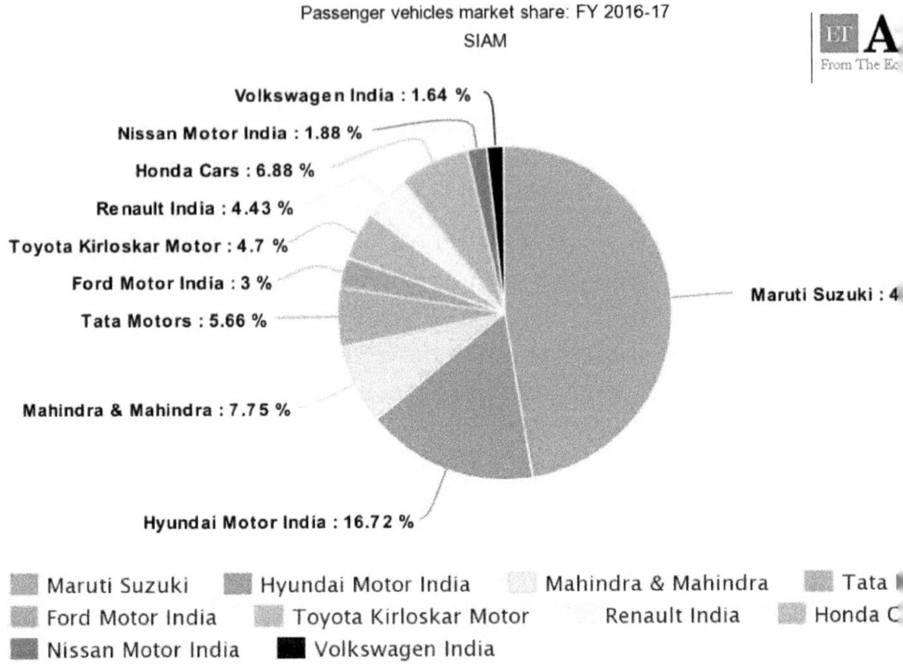

Source: Times of India/Auto/Cars May,18.2016

Appendix 2: The number of cities with the market presence of the car dealers of the respective car manufacturers

The Indian Car Manufacturer	Number of Cities with Car Dealers (April 2015 to March 2016)
Maruti Suzuki	1450
Hyundai	276
Mahindra & Mahindra	212
Honda	170
Tata Motors	200
Toyota	140
Ford	209

Source: Times of India/Auto/Cars May,18.2016

Appendix 3: The top selling car brands (models) in India, in FY 2015-16

Top 10 selling passenger cars in fiscal 2016					
Fiscal 2015	Model	Rank	Model	Fiscal 2016	% Change
264492	Alto	1	Alto	263422	-0.4%
201338	Swift	2	Dzire	199100	4%
192010	Dzire	3	Swift	195043	-3%
161250	WagonR	4	WagonR	169555	5%
99088	Grand i10	5	Grand i10	126181	27%
78334	Eon	6	Elite i20	126028	62%
77747	Elite i20	7	Celerio	87428	28%
77384	City	8	City	77548	0.2%
68143	Celerio	9	Eon	68199	-13%
66703	Amaze	10	Amaze	54594	-18%

Source: Economics Times, ET Auto, April 8, 2016

Appendix 4: Ranks of the global Vehicle Manufacturers (all vehicles, not just cars)

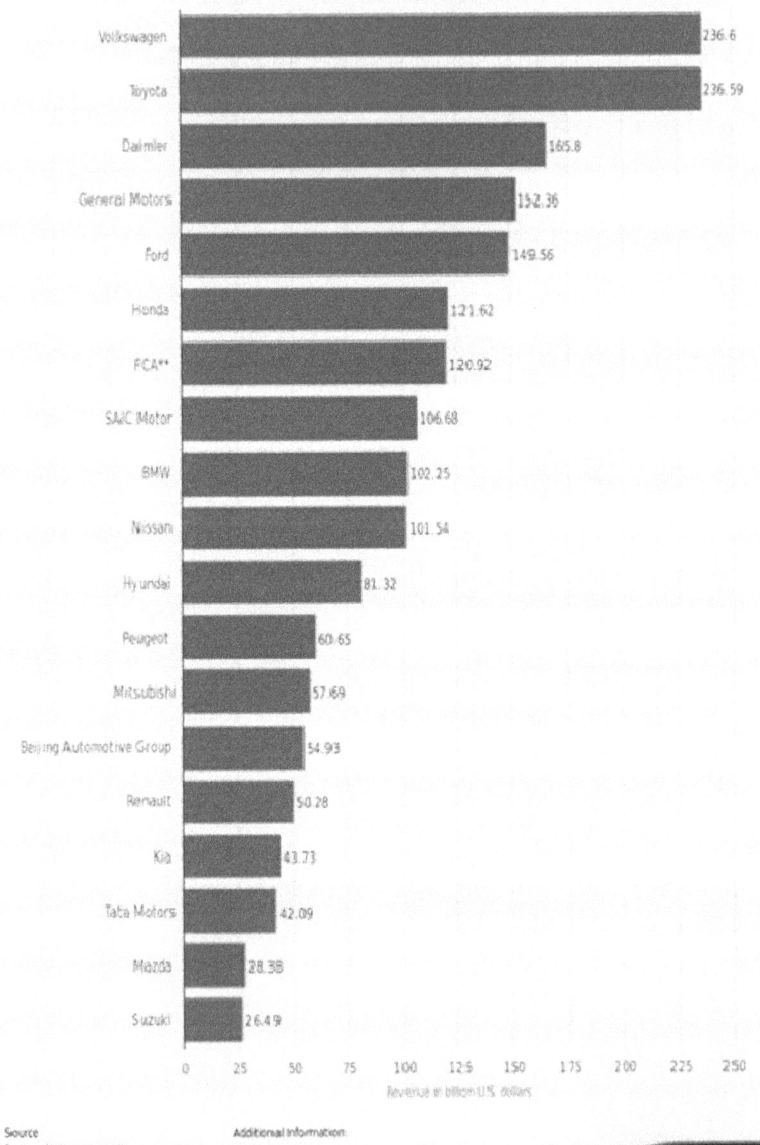
Revenue* of the leading automotive manufacturers worldwide in FY 2015 (in billion U.S. dollars)
Volkswagen
236.6
Toyota
236.59
Daimler
165.8
General Motors
152.36
Ford
149.56
Honda
121.62
FCA**
120.92
SAIC Motor
106.68
BMW
102.25
Nissan
101.54
Hyundai
81.32
Peugeot
60.65
Mitsubishi
57.69
Beijing Automotive Group
54.93
Renault
50.28
Kia
43.73
Tata Motors
42.09
Mazda
28.38
Suzuki
26.49
0
25
50
75
100
125
150
175
200
225
250
Source
Additional Information:
statista

Appendix 5: Number of dealers of various Indian car manufacturers

The Indian Car Manufacturer	Number of Car Dealers (April 2015 to March 2016)
Maruti Suzuki	1950
Hyundai	512
Mahindra & Mahindra	291
Honda	265
Tata Motors	311
Toyota	213
Ford	376

Source: Times of India/Auto/Cars May,18.2016

Appendix 6: The comparative profitability of the Indian car dealers:

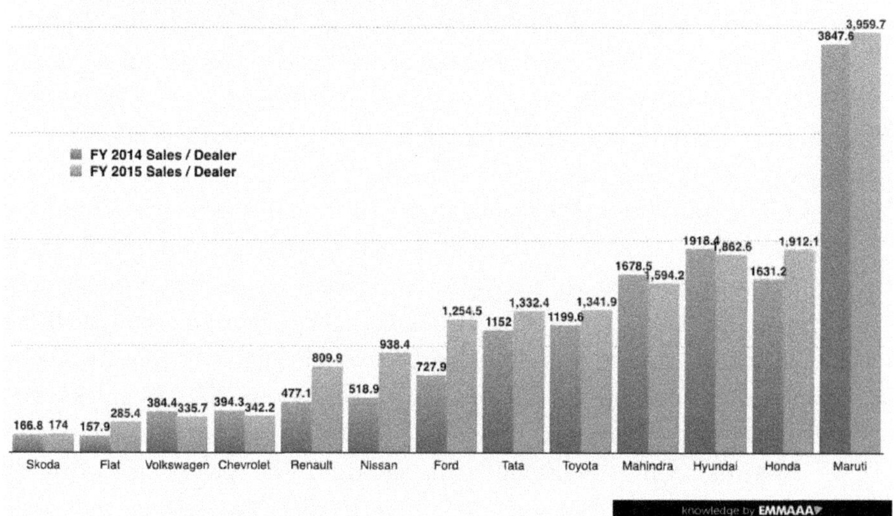

Appendix 7: The Customer reactions to the concept of Nexa:

- "When S-Cross was launched via Nexa, the salesperson was very humble as the product was not selling. Now it's just the opposite due to the success of Baleno, just try to visit any Nexa showroom and you will find the same set of people as one of the most arrogant you can come across."
- "Dealership experience is just a one-time affair for a person buying a car, the product and service experience is the one he/she goes through every time. Sadly Nexa doesn't address these 2 critical parameters."
- "Right from the beginning, I am against Nexa. The simple reason is that a car buyer today is more informed about the product, the features, and the drawbacks of each and every competing car. The buyer is more informed in the case of high-value model buys. All special TV programs, special magazines, net savvy data sites, etc., are helping the prospective buyers to be more informed about the products on offer. More often than not, the sellers - the salesmen, the counter staff, the front desk - is NOT competent to answer all the questions asked by such informed buyers. In such a scenario, I wonder whether NEXA's staff are well equipped?"
- "Anyway, just because you have a NEXA showroom, will a BMW or an MB customer will come to it and buy a Maruti?"
- "NEXA can only survive if it has the entire range of products for those select few who crave the shopping experience more than the product being shopped. A fine dining restaurant so to speak, where people go to get served the EXPERIENCE and the actual meal is so small in portion"
- "Who would like to buy a higher-end product from a regular showroom if Maruti itself is indicating that it is not a premium product? Poor strategy. It is high time that NEXA branding must be abolished. Nowadays, even the entry-level cars are turning out to be premium."
- "NEXA is a good channel through which Maruti can differentiate and identify products that fall into different categories. Instead of being very selective, Maruti should define products that can be sold through NEXA and the same products should also be made available at Maruti Suzuki Dealership so that buyers who do not have access to NEXA can also buy high-end products from Maruti."
- "Is Maruti selling high-end cars at different prices in ordinary showrooms and in Nexa showrooms? If they are selling the same product, at different rates, in the same city, it becomes a problem. No

one would buy in the Nexa showrooms. Same product - why would any sane fellow will pay more? If they are selling at the same price, then, why would a dealer invest so much money in the up-scale showroom, in having better-informed staff, and in giving extremely personalized service to only a handful of customers? Are the margins given to the Nexa dealers different? If not, why would anyone open a Nexa showroom in the same city which almost certainly would have had more than one or two Maruti showrooms? What about the service charges and the service setups at these Nexa showrooms? Do they have different service standards and procedures at these high-end showrooms? What if a customer bought a high car from a Nexa showroom and approaches a regular showroom for either regular service or breakdown service, will he be treated differently? Only because, he bought his car from a Nexa showroom? What if on the same day, two customers get similar high-end cars to the regular showroom for service - one bought from Nexa and another from the same regular showroom - will they be charged differently? If these financial issues are not clear, both for the customer and the dealer, they are dealing in doubt and ambiguity"

Foot Note:

[1] 'Maruti' was a Hindu god, worshiped in India. He served his master, Rama, another Hindu god. Maruti was an icon for strength/power and modesty. He served his master well and carried him on his own shoulders. In a way, Maruti was a vehicle for this master.

References:

[1] http://www.businessinsider.com/2016-was-a-record-breaking-year-for-global-car-sales-and-it-was-almost-entirely-driven-by-china-2017-1?IR=T

[2] http://focus2move.com/world-car-market/

[3] http://www.indiainfoline.com/article/research-leader-speak/mr-rc-bhargava-chairman-maruti-suzuki-india-ltd-113111400653_1.html

[4] "Suzuki plans Rs 8500 cr investment in Gujrat", Economic Times, Jan 29, 2015 http://economictimes.indiatimes.com/articleshow/46048616.cms?utm_source=contentofinterest&utm_medium=text&utm_campaign=cppst

[5] "Maruti Alto Best Selling…", Hindustan Times April 10, 2017 http://www.hindustantimes.com/autos/maruti-suzuki-alto-best-selling-car-for-13-consecutive-years-sells-2-41-lakh-cars-in-fy-2016-17/story-ox6SKAbrj18wraLEPCtUMP.html

[6] http://businessworld.in/article/Maruti-Suzuki-Posts-Record-Sales-Gains-Market-Share-In-2016-17/05-04-2017-115734/

[7] "Toyota Targets Indian Small Car Market", Business Standard, Feb 16. 2016 http://www.business-standard.com/article/companies/toyota-targets-indian-small-car-market-116021500764_1.html

[8] http://www.livemint.com/Companies/BLQUZzzVNNkexyvnvaXVOI/Toyota-setting-up-the-ramp-for-Daihatsus-India-entry.html

[9] https://www.strategyand.pwc.com/media/file/Strategyand-India-Automotive-Market-2020.pdf

[10] http://blog.euromonitor.com/2015/05/indias-car-market-returns-to-growth-potential-to-be-the-worlds-third-largest-market-by-2030.html

[11] "Maruti Suzuki posts record sales Gains market share in 2016-17", Business World April 5, 2017

[12] "Change of Marketing Gear Maruti using analytics to reach 2020 sales tagets", Hindu Businessline, Jan 7, 2016. http://www.thehindubusinessline.com/companies/in-change-of-marketing-gear-maruti-using-analytics-to-reach-2020-sales-target/article8077955.ece

[13] http://indianautosblog.com/2011/01/repeat-customers-driving-sales-of-maruti-suzuki

[14] Maruti tops dealership charts with 1,800 outlets across 1,450 cities Nandini Sen Gupta| TNN | May 18, 2016. http://timesofindia.indiatimes.com/auto/cars/Maruti-tops-dealership-charts-with-1800-outlets-across-1450-cities/articleshow/52316309.cms

[15] Maruti Suzuki launches Nexa brand outlets for premium products, The Hindu, JULY 23, 2015 http://www.thehindu.com/business/Industry/maruti-suzuki-launches-nexa-outlets/article7456265.ece

[16] "Maruti Suzuki Ciaz will now be sold through Nexa showrooms", Mint, March 31, 2017 http://www.livemint.com/Companies/Cs5MXWcAxfi8sThROQR79J/Maruti-Suzuki-Ciaz-will-now-be-sold-through-Nexa-showrooms.html

[17] "Maruti Suzuki Starts Its 200th Nexa Showroom", Business Today Jan 30th 2017 http://www.businesstoday.in/sectors/auto/maruti-suzuki-starts-its-200th-nexa-showroom/story/245228.html

[18] http://www.livemint.com/Companies/Cs5MXWcAxfi8sThROQR79J/Maruti-Suzuki-Ciaz-will-now-be-sold-through-Nexa-showrooms.html

[19] http://www.business-standard.com/article/news-cd/the-difference-between-cars-retailed-from-maruti-suzuki-and-nexa-outlets-116031401259_1.html

[20] "Maruti Suzuki's NEXA outlets sell over 185,000 vehicles" IANS | Jan 31, 2017, http://timesofindia.indiatimes.com/auto/miscellaneous/maruti-suzukis-nexa-outlets-sell-over-185000-vehicles/articleshow/56886082.cms

[21] http://forum.autocarindia.com/index.php?/topic/11073-the-dealership-dilemma-nexa-and-maruti-suzuki/

Enter Caption

CHAPTER THIRTEEN

Branding Smart City: Solapur

It was August 2015. Supriya[1], the Principal Secretary in the Maharashtra state Chief Minister's office[2], was sitting in her office in 'Mantralaya,' the main administrative building, in South Mumbai. She was thinking hard about his hometown, Solapur which was situated about 400 kilometers south of Mumbai. How to bring back the lost glory of the city, was her concern. She wanted to re-create an identity for her birthplace. In mid-2015, the Government of India announced the project of 'Smart City,' as a major initiative to modernize Indian cities. The project ensured the necessary funding for urban development. In the first round, the government wanted to select only 20 cities from all over India, based on the competition involving a project proposal on their vision and the implementation plan. Supriya was to play a pivotal role in preparing the plan to be submitted to the government of India. The Chief Minister appointed her as the 'caretaker bureaucrat' who was required to facilitate the coordination and co-operation between the local governing body (Solapur Municipal Corporation, SMC) and the state government. Supriya was to work in close collaboration with the Municipal Commissioner of SMC and his team for formulating the vision of the city. It would be closely related to the image of the city. Supriya wanted to use this opportunity to develop her hometown. She wanted to re-position Solapur city and create a brand. Branding Solapur was important to provide an identity to the ailing city and attract investments to create jobs. Such employment would bring back economic prosperity resulting from better living conditions and an increased standard of living for the citizens. Radical rethinking was required to develop the 'Brand Solapur' by re-positioning it in the light of the emerging opportunities in the macro-environment. Through a massive campaign, citizens were asked to provide suggestions on their perspectives and how they visualize Solapur in the future.

They suggested looking into rejuvenating textiles, developing the city as a pilgrimage destination, creating a hub for healthcare and education, etc. Citizens desperately wanted economic development through job creation, clean and green Solapur with better water supply & roads along with uninterrupted power supply. Residents felt that the city lost its shin and required the government to bring back the lost glory. Supriya and her team at SMC had to finalize the strategy for Solapur and submit the detailed proposal for the Smart City to the government of India by mid-Oct 2015.

India: A Change Lead by the Hope

India, the largest and youngest democracy in the world, had a population of over a billion people. In 2014, after a decade of Indian National Congress rule, the Bhartiya Janata Party (BJP) came to power. People voted for the change. The election was driven by the hopes created by the leadership of Mr. Narendra Modi. The campaign focused on his vision for his home state, Gujarat, and how he, as the head of that state, transformed it within 15 years, by successfully implementing his vision. His leadership caliber and reputation raised hope in the minds of young Indians. The youngest nation in the world and the largest democracy was expecting Mr. Modi to recreate the environment, which he did in Gujarat, on a larger scale, at the national level. The election campaign was all about raising hopes with slogans like *'Achhe din aane wale hai'* (Good days are coming).After assuming office, the Prime Minister declared certain campaigns and projects to initiate the change. The 'Digital India' campaign, the *'Swatch Bharat'* (Clean India)campaign,the 'Startup India' campaign, the 'Make in India' campaign, and the Smart City project. The 'Smart City' was an urban development program that focused on better public service delivery and good governance. The objective was to promote cities that provided core infrastructure and a decent quality of life to their citizens through the application of 'Smart' Solutions. The focus was on sustainable and inclusive development. According to the Government of India, the Smart City offered sustainability regarding economic activities and employment opportunities to a broad section of its residents, regardless of their level of education, skills, or income levels.[i] In June 2015, the Ministry of Urban Development (MoUD) of the government of India shortlisted 100 cities from all over India, on the recommendations of respective state government committees.

It was meant to set examples that could be replicated both within and outside the Smart City, catalyzing the creation of similar Smart Cities in various regions. Solapur was recommended by the state government committee and was shortlisted by the MoUD of the government of India among 100 cities. These shortlisted cities were now required to compete by their proposal for 'Smart City,' for inclusion in the first round of implementation of the project. Only 20 cities were to be selected in this 'Challenge round' of the smart city project. The idea was to create a replicable model which would act as a lighthouse to other aspiring cities. It was expected that the Smart City project proposal should contain a wish list of infrastructure and services that describe the needs and aspirations of citizens. Urban planners were required to develop the entire urban ecosystem around the expectations of people. The SMC carried out a mass campaign and awarded prizes for the best suggestions. The scheme was named '*Maze Swapna,*' (My Dream). There were four cash prizes for the best ideas.[ii] The SMC website was flooded with suggestions from citizens of Solapur. The suggestions could be categorized into three major areas. Those were job creation, better public service delivery, and good governance.

Solapur: A City Profile

Solapur was located 397 kilometers (km) south of Mumbai, 236 km south of Pune, 309 km north of Hyderabad, and about 600 km north of Bangalore. "(see Exhibit 1)" for the location of Solapur on the map. It is situated in Western India in the important state, of Maharashtra. In 2013-14 the GDP of Maharashtra was more than many countries in the world including Pakistan (about $150 billion). Solapur is a part of the sub-region, 'Western Maharashtra' which is considered one of the affluent areas of India. Western Maharashtra is known for its balanced economic growth with strong agriculture and manufacturing base. Solapur is bordering two major states/ provinces of South India, Andhra Pradesh, and Karnataka. According to the Köppen climate classification, Solapur is in the category of dry (arid and semiarid) climate with three distinct seasons: summer, monsoon, and winter. The summer months are from March to May, with maximum temperatures ranging from 30 to 40 °C (86 to 104 °F). In the month of May occasionally mercury can hit 43°C. In May 1988, the highest temperature ever was recorded, 46°C. The population of the city, as per the 2011 census, was about 1 million "(see Exhibit 2)".

The city had 188,503 households with an average size of 5 persons/ household. One-fourth of the population stayed in a slum. The literacy rate was 75%. Though '*Marathi*' was the common language of the city, a high percentage of the population could also speak Kannada, Telugu, Hindi, and Urdu. About 40% of the population could speak at least three languages. Solapur was the most cosmopolitan city in Maharashtra, after Mumbai. For religious community break up "(see Exhibit 3)".

Branding a City

Supriya recognized that there was a direct link between the image and reputation of Solapur and its attractiveness as a place to visit, live, and invest. In her opinion, if Solapur weren't attracting more income, talented people, new residents, and investment then it would slowly vanish. A strong identity for the city was vital when it was vying with other cities in Maharashtra for attention in tourism and business. They wanted to turn a location into a destination by branding. They wanted to reverse the trend and create an inward migration and make people want to live, work and visit Solapur. In the era of super brands, Solapur city was considering becoming a brand. The hallmark of the brand Solapur was to be determined by the value of the promises it made and the promises it kept. Through branding exercise, Supriya's team wanted to add value, meaning, and aura to Solapur city. Supriya knew she could create the brand through a collection of associations and thoughts that were stored in the minds of people. Brand Solapur must make a clear, single-minded promise and consistently keep it. Supriya told her team, "Effective brands make customers' choices easier. They directly aim at their heart because emotions drive most of the decisions, but brands also provide logic to rationalize the decisions." However, Supriya was aware that branding was not a magic wand to solve the city's problems. "The brand has to be based on what is already there in a city, or else it is just like giving someone a nice haircut — it might look good for a while, but it doesn't give you a new personality," says Marcus Mitchell, strategist at branding agency Corporate Edge.

City Branding: The Process

Supriya and her team decided to start by working on reality, not image — do the regeneration, the investment, and the transformation first, and only when change is visible should they start to "brand" it. Supriya told her team, "Branding a city is not just about the logo or a strap line but the intricate details — as small as clean streets and as deep as getting a city's residents to feel proud to be brand ambassadors. When citizens are proud, visitors are encouraged to find out what the fuss is all about and then tell the world. It is easy for residents to overlook the appearance of their streets, the absence of trees, the poor lighting, trash, and bad signage that may have evolved over the years. Visitors, however, are much less forgiving." [3]She insisted that attention had been paid to the aesthetics of a city, including preserving and enhancing its natural qualities and environment. In her opinion the city must earn the reputation as a "special place" or a "fun place to hang out," and that would go a long way toward supporting its brand identity. Supriya was looking at the critical assets of the city with the view to create a magic formula to make something about the city tangible and make people switch on to that — location, for example. She wanted coordinated activity and a joined-up approach to attract all the city's audiences. Brand Solapur needed to address the tourist, investors, new businesses, and students who would migrate for education and inward migration for doing businesses and employment. Just publicity with photography was also difficult because it's hard to capture the spirit of a place. The city branding experts who were approached for advice on the city branding suggested that the planning team had to answer the following questions: What does Solapur want to be known for? How could Solapur stand out from the crowd and be more competitive? What thoughts and feelings did they want to come to mind when people were exposed to the name, Solapur? How could they build and preserve their heritage and authenticity? How could they gain improved results from limited resources? They also suggested focusing on interactions with residents and businesses, the journey to Solapur from other cities by rail and road, the sense of arrival in the city, and time spent in the city as a visitor or resident. It's not enough to only say Solapur was different and unique in some way, or that it's the perfect choice for a visit. The reality must match the promise made in brochures and advertising while trying to attract visitors, new residents, or investors. If the place isn't distinctive or doesn't measure up, they would quickly tell the world via social media.

Benchmarking Other Cities in the World

Recommending practices of Las Vegas, Melbourne, and London to Solapur was hardly appropriate. Studying American cities through literature, Supriya identified that many cities had no control over their image and reputation. Some cities had a blank slate, 80% of the American cities did not have any dominant image in the minds of people. Small cities like Oshkosh WI (USA), Todmorden (England), and Wollongong (Australia) were doing a great job in city branding in spite of limited recourses. These cities had to project that they were distinctive, relevant, and meaningful constantly. Such winning cities break through the clutter to become well known and easily stand out because of something special. They projected compelling reasons to think of them as being different and representing greater value than other choices. They were able to stand the test of time, public debate, political scrutiny, and media questions. Repositioning a city and changing what it means in the customers' minds could be challenging and expensive. In the 1970s a small city, Chemainus, on Victoria Island (Canada) was facing a tough time due to a decline in the timber and mining industries. Many thought the town was finished. A revitalization program was undertaken. The city was transformed into an outdoor art gallery featuring Murals on many of its buildings, most of them portraying the history of the city.[4] Chemainus is a famous tourist center today. It is the world's preeminent mural city. The Israeli city of Eilat repositioned itself to be seen not just as a port city but as a city of diverse attractions and shopping. The objective was to become the only western tourism city on the Red Sea. Eilat (population of 85,000) is the southernmost town in Israel, isolated from the rest of the country by the Negev desert. It is sprawled along 7 kilometers of the Red Sea coastline, between the borders of Egypt and Jordan, and offers spectacular views of the Gulf of Aqaba. Originally a strategic military outpost, Eilat's first incarnation was as a port, used for importing goods from Asia, such as oil and vehicles. In the 1970s, tourists began visiting Eilat. They were attracted by the coral reefs, sandy beaches, and the dry and sunny desert climate. Eilat is an oddity in Israel because it has so many tourists (many of the tourists are still Israelis). Located at the southernmost tip of the country, within its small "window on the Red Sea," Eilat is first and foremost a resort town these days, devoted to sun, fun, diving, partying, and desert-based activities. 320 km (200 miles) away from the tension often felt in Tel Aviv or Jerusalem, Eilat is a convenient escape for Israelis on vacation, but during the mild winter months also attracts thousands of European sun-seekers. Being a resort driven it is sometimes called the Ibiza or Las Vegas of Israel.[5] These place brands were a total of thoughts, feelings, and expectations that people hold about a location. It was the reputation and enduring essence of the site. Place branding provided a framework and toolkit for differentiating, focusing, and organizing around these areas' competitive and distinctive identities. It was grounded in truth and reality.

Solapur: A City with Strong and Unique Identity

Manchester of the East Like Mumbai, Solapur was developed during the British Raj in India and was a well-known textile manufacturing center. The first textile mill was started in Mumbai in 1854. Solapur was among the first Indian cities to join the textile revolution in India. 'Solapur Spinning and Weaving Mill' was the first textile mill started by the British in 1887. There were four major textile mills Laxmi Mill, Vishnu Mill, Narsingh Girji Mill, and Jam Mill. These mills used to process raw cotton collected from farms to the final printed cloth. All manufacturing processes were done inside these plants. Besides selling in the local markets, their cloth was exported to Russia, CIS, and other countries. Solapur got its identity as the textile hub. It was branded as the 'Manchester of the East' since the British era.

City of Martyrs During the Indian independence movement, 17 years before India became free, Solapur enjoyed full freedom on 9, 10, and 11 May 1930. All the British officers were driven out of the city. However, this resulted in the British declaring Martial Law, crushing the freedom moment with military power and executions of 4 citizens *Mallappa Dhanshetti, Kurban Hussein, Jagannath Shinde,* and *Kisan Sarda* who were hanged on 12 January 1931, in prison in Pune. This resulted in a new identity for the city. Solapur got recognition as "The City of *Hutatmas*" (Martyrs).[6]

Generic Name for Bed-sheets Post-independence the migrated population from Andhra Pradesh started manufacturing towels, bed sheets, and similar textile products on the handlooms. Those hand-looms were upgraded to power looms. Solapur got branded as 'City of *Chaddars*' (city of bed sheets). In India, bed sheets are called '*Solapuri Chaddars.*'

Smoker's Paradise The migrated population also started a business of manufacturing *'Bidi'* (Indian cigar for the poor). Bidi manufacturers employed women on a large scale. They trained women to make *'Bidi,'* at home, using the material supplied by the *Bidi* manufacturers. By the 1970s many households had men working in either textile mills or power looms and their women making *Bidis* at home while taking care of the family responsibilities. Such double-income families contributed to the prosperity of the city.

The Vatican of Maharashtra Solapur got prominence as it was a religious and trade center. Three famous (Hindu religion) pilgrimage destinations, *Pandharpur (70 km), Tuljapur* (45 km), *Akkalkot (40km),* and *Gangapur* (2 *hours by train)* were in proximity. Thousands of pilgrims traveled to these holy places. They preferred to stay in Solapur and commute to these rural pilgrim locations because of the connectivity, convenience, and infrastructure. Every village/town/city in India has its main God/Goddess and his/her temple. It is called *'Gram Daivat,'* in the local language. There is an annual festival/pilgrimage called *'Yatra'* which is celebrated by citizens on a big scale. Those who migrated to other towns travel to the village/town for the Yatra every year. Migrated population from nearing Karnataka state worshiped the great saint, *Siddheshwar* whose Temple in Solapur became the main holy temple for the Hindu population. It became the *Gram Daivat* of Solapur. The entire city celebrated the holy festive season for a week, in mid-January. It is called *'Gaddyachi Yatra.'*

Boston of Maharashtra Solapur was a known education center. It had Medical, Engineering, Law, and Pharmacy colleges in addition to quality primary and secondary schools. Strong academic culture prevailed among the working middle class. Their kids secured ranks and scholarships at the regional and state levels. Bright students from Solapur went to many institutions of global repute for higher education. Supriya was one good example herself who never stood second during her schooling, secured admission into IIT Mumbai[7], and then joined public administration after getting into IAS[8]. Year after year, dozens of students went to IIT, top medical schools, and other quality educational institutes including Ivey League universities in America.

Medical Centre Solapur was well known for reputed doctors and quality medical treatment at affordable prices. Western Maharashtra had only two medical colleges, and one of them was in Solapur. The Government Civil Hospital was big with a capacity of almost 1000 beds and facilities to conduct most of the modern surgeries. The medical treatment was provided almost free in the government hospital with quality pre-surgery diagnosis and post-surgery patient care. There were a few good hospitals run by charitable institutions which offered excellent medical treatment. Many doctors started their private hospitals after graduating from medical school. Solapur became a known medical center. Patients from all over the district, nearby district of Marathwada, and also from Karnataka came to Solapur for medical treatment. Many doctors could speak 4 to 5 languages and strike a chord with their patients, in their mother tongue. Solapur always had a robust and unique identity. It created a strong position in the minds of the Indian masses using different memory hooks and attracted investments and migration. When Maharashtra state was formed in the 1960s, there were only 3 Municipal Corporations in the state other than Mumbai. Those were Nagpur, Pune, and Solapur. It was the 4th largest city in the state (province) of Maharashtra. The brand personality of Solapur was cosmopolitan, multi-lingual, and friendly. It was known pilgrimage center, textile, medical, and education hub. It became a generic brand in *Chaddar, Bidi,* and *peanut chutney.*

Solapur: Balanced Economy

Solapur always had balanced growth. Its economy struck a delicate balance between industry, agriculture, and the service sector. Also in manufacturing and trading. The manufacturing industry included foundries, chemical plants, and small engineering units. The government of Maharashtra completed the construction of the *Ujjani* dam in 1980. The dam was constructed in the Solapur district. It was situated between Pune and Solapur. Due to the *Ujjani* Dam, its canals, and other related irrigation projects, the agricultural sector also made a significant contribution to the economy of the city. Solapur district had a maximum number of cooperative sugar factories in the sugar manufacturing hub of India, Western Maharashtra. Indian Railways had a strong base in Solapur. It was the major junction of the central railway. It had a major divisional railway office headed by very senior railway officers.

It also had a locomotive car-shed workshop. Indian Railways was one of the major employers for the white collared and blue collared jobs. Other major employers were Municipal Corporation, Indian Postal Services, banks, and insurance companies, and educational institutions. Due to the significant portion of the employment for the blue-collared people, Solapur was associated more with a 'labor class.' The immigrant from Karnataka, Gujarat, Rajasthan, and Sindh (in Pakistan) was controlling the trading activity. Solapur was the shopping destination for small towns and villages in the district. Shoppers also use to come from other backward districts of the Marathwada region of Maharashtra and the neighboring Karnataka state.

Solapur: A Cultural Centre

Solapur shared a strong bond with Bollywood and Hindi movies. Solapur had a concept of multiplex cinema since the early part of this century, decades before it came even to Bollywood itself. Bhagwat Cinema Hall had four big movie theatres, in the same complex, ever since it was constructed in the early part of the 1900s. Almost a dozen cinema halls were situated at a distance of just a few hundred meters. The area was called theatre chowk. Movies were always crowded and it is hard to get tickets at the eleventh hour. The labor class saw their aspirations getting fulfilled by the hero in the Hindi movies. Every Bollywood star had a fan following in Solapur. Fans would see movies of their favorite start multiple times, mug up their dialogs, and the songs in the film. Fans had a craze to see the newly released movies of their Bollywood stars on the first day, the first show. They would pay more than double the amount of the official ticket just to see the movie on day one. There was an exclusive cinema hall for South Indian movies (Kannada, Telugu, Malayali, and Tamil). The cinema hall owners were among the wealthy people in the city on account of their cash-rich business and also got celebrity status. Other passions of people were Hindi songs, Marathi drama, paintings, etc. Solapur Municipal Corporation (SMC) built an auditorium, '*Hutatma Smruti Mandir*' with a capacity of 1000 spectators. Marathi stage had been well known for its talent. Many celebrated actors and actresses performed on stage show at this auditorium. The Marathi-speaking middle class was the typical audience for such shows. Many dramas and music clubs were pursuing that as their hobby. A film club showed international movies to members regularly.

Another passion of Solapurkars was food. They were foodies and enjoyed it with family and friends. Due to the cosmopolitan face of the city, there was a lot of variety in vegetarian and non-vegetarian food. Karnataka preparations are based on groundnut gravy. Andhra food has a variety of pickles and Muslims specialized in non-vegetarian food. Solapur had a unique way of socializing. It was known for '*Hurda Parties.*' *Hurda* was the local name for the roasted green millet. *Hurda* was a super, healthy seasonal cereal grain that was served astender, moist, green, farm fresh, aromatic, and wholesome green millet. Usually, December to February was the only particular period during which delicacies were available to tantalize your taste buds. The *Jawar* chaffs were freshly plucked and roasted on coal or dried cow dung in the mud ovens. After slow backing, a crackling sound could be heard indicating that the delicate seeds were ready to serve. The *hurda* was then served hot, with peanut- garlic chutney. *Hurda* was accompanied by *Jaggary*, dry coconut, and well-cooked eggplant (Brinjal).

Contemporary Governance Challenges in Solapur

Though Solapur was called the 'Manchester of the East,' all textile mills had to face closure. It no longer remained a textile city. Thousands of families dependent on textile mills had to face poverty. Some of the prominent players in the textile industry like Vishnu Textile and Laxmi Textile wound up their operations because of the financial crisis; this resulted in the closing down of ancillary units and increased unemployment. The city was also known for the production of bed sheets and towels, but those units had also closed down. Due to the reduction in government subsidies and lack of up-gradation, these textile units in Solapur were lagging behind. New legislation for the beedi industry and mandatory minimum labor standards resulted in the migration of beedi industry workers to other states, adversely affecting the beedi industry in Solapur. The decline of the dominant industries in Solapur had a great impact on the vibrancy and growth of the city. The population growth stagnated. There were out-migration and a lack of a new labor force. The economic crisis made the living conditions of the workers pathetic and reduced the purchasing power of the citizens which affected the local businesses adversely. Solapur had been a feeding market for other small cities, towns, and talukas like Akluj, Pandharpur, Barshi, Usmanabad, Tuljapur, Vijapur, Gulbarga, etc.

The customers from these towns would come to Solapur for shopping but over a period the supply chain and distribution improved. Companies appointed local dealers/retailers. People in these towns started to prefer buying goods locally and this reduced customers for the businesses in Solapur. The overall financial position of Solapur Municipal Corporation (SMC) was precarious. Octroi, which was the primary source of income for SMC (55% of the total revenue), was abolished by the State Government in 2010. Local Body Tax (LBT), which replaced Octroi, was resisted by the industry and traders for a couple of years. SMC could collect hardly 20% to 30% of the revenue. The grants from the state government were irregular. A collection of the municipal charges was also reduced. [iii] Solapur Municipal Corporation had limited financial strength and capacity to leverage resources on account of its small budget. SMC would require substantial grants to fund its capital investment. To sustain its investment requirements, SMC would need to embark on a reform program to support the necessary cash flows and improve its credit worthiness. The future development of Solapur was dependent on the ability of SMC to be innovative in resource generation and its efficient management.[iv] The administration and finances of Solapur were small and would not be able to support the required developments under the Smart City initiative. The lack of Sewage treatment facilities was a major problem in Solapur. The wastewater treatment plant was non-functional since the year 2000, and the non-treated sewage was disposed of off without any treatment, causing significant environmental threats and contamination of the groundwater.[v] National Thermal Power Corporation (NTPC) started the project work for a thermal power generation plant in Solapur which was scheduled to commence production by 2018-19. The large-scale burning of coal would pose a major problem of air pollution. Although Solapur district had the highest number of sugar factories in Maharashtra, the cooperative sugar industry had not created a significant impact on the economy of the city as it did in other affluent areas in western Maharashtra. Agriculture was also poor due to the draught-prone area and acute water shortage. Religion and castes played a major role in local politics. The city was prone to riots based on religion and castes. The proportion of minorities was higher than the national average, 21% Muslims, and 15% STSC. "(see Exhibit 4)".

Branding Options for Solapur: (As Suggested by Citizens)

The required approach for branding a city like Solapur was more conciliatory and inclusive than that found in consumer products. Primarily because the city was not owned by anyone. Developing a place brand was challenging for the city because it took passion, commitment, innovation, and collective efforts. To resolve the identity crisis, four strong branding options could be adopted, by the suggestions given by the citizens "(refer to Exhibit 7)". The advice provided by the management consulting firm which had exposure to international urban development was very useful. These options were articulated by Supriya as follows:

A. **Boston of Maharashtra**Solapur was known for its talented students. Those who did their schooling here got into the institutions of excellence, for their higher education, in the USA, India, and other parts of the world. Three out of the top five bureaucrats in the Maharashtra State Government, in 2015-16, were educated in Solapur. Brilliant Solapurkars bagged places in Indian Administrative Services (IAS and IPS), Indian Institute of Technology (IIT), and also got into the Ivy League universities in the USA. Many were working in Mumbai, Pune, and Bangalore in top positions in the Government and the corporate sector. Information Technology (IT) was the most favored profession here. But the city faced a brain drain due to a lack of career opportunities. Poor agriculture, industry, and service sector development resulted in an exodus of talent from the city. The middle class was more vulnerable to such migration. Solapur was an educational hub. Solapur University, a public university, was relatively new, started in 2004 with an objective to focus on higher education. There were 119 colleges affiliated with the university having more than 75,000 students in 7 faculties.[vi] But the university could not generate courses focusing on skills, employment, and entrepreneurship. Medical education, however, was an exception. In addition to two medical colleges, there were Ayurveda Medical College and Pharmacy Institutes offering bachelor's and master's education in Solapur. The doctors opened hospitals and clinics after completing their studies.

B. **Medical Tourism Centre**Solapur became the center for healthcare. Patients from the district, nearby districts of Marathwada, and the bordering states of Karnataka and Andhra Pradesh traveled to Solapur for quality healthcare at competitive rates. But due to the lack of vision on the part of the government and the leadership, there was no organized effort to make Solapur a destination for medical tourism. Hospitals in Pune had been observing a surge in foreign patients who came from the UK, Nigeria, Kenya, Iraq, and the Gulf countries for knee, spine, kidney, Cardiac, Urology, cosmetic, and obesity surgeries.[vii] Apollo hospital in Chennai treated 70,000 foreign patients in the year 2015. They had a separate section for foreign patients, in their hospital.[viii] Solapur could leverage the reputation it earned in the region, in healthcare. In addition to international patients, it could also target patients from Indian metropolitan cities where healthcare expenses were going beyond the reach of even the higher middle class. The major cost component for patients in the metro cities was hospitalization due to the high real estate rates and labor charges. The following steps could facilitate medical tourism:

- Providing land to corporate houses that run chains of the hospital at the subsidized rate on a long-term lease.
- Facilitating the faster movement of patients and specialists from Mumbai, Pune, Hyderabad, and Bangalore.
- Creating an infrastructure of reputed budget hotels near the hospitals for relatives of patients, with a shuttle service to the hospitals and the bus/train station. There should also be restaurants that can provide breakfast and box lunch/dinner.
- Developing tie-ups with hospitals and super specialty doctors in Mumbai, Bangalore, Hyderabad, and Pune for complex medical problems.
- Facilitating smooth functioning of cashless medical insurance

Creating separate zones along the lines of SEZs to provide a one-stop shop for all healthcare needs along with convenience and value for money. It could be the first medical tourism center of its kind in India.

C.The Vatican of Maharashtra, Many Hindu devotees in Maharashtra travel to Pandharpur, Akkalkot, Tuljapur, and Gandgapur for the annual pilgrimage. But they had poor infrastructure and connectivity. Due to excellent rail and road connectivity, they preferred to stay at Solapur. These sacred sites surround Solapur, with Pandharpur at 73 kilometers and Tuljapur and Akkalkot at 40 km each. The city could explore this business opportunity and create a hub for religious tourism.

D. The Rotterdam of India The port of Rotterdam, in the Netherlands, was the largest cargo port in Europe. Rotterdam's success in logistics was based on its strategic location.[ix] Solapur also has a strategic location for logistics. In the era of online retailing, the supply chain is very critical. Solapur could focus on allocating its huge pieces of land for warehousing and offer logistics and warehousing solutions by leveraging its strategic advantages. Solapur, as a location, offered comparative advantages. Solapur had been an important railway station since the British days. It was an important junction on the Mumbai/Pune rail link to Hyderabad, Bangalore, and Chennai. Every day more than 30 trains passed through Solapur. Solapur had two National Highways (NH-9 and NH-13) passing through it. The strategic advantages of Solapur in the field of warehousing and logistics were many. Solapur was situated strategically on some major consuming markets in India. "(See Exhibit 5)". Though not a port city, it was just a seven-hour drive from Mumbai, by road. This highway was of high quality, which is rare in India.

Real estate in and around Mumbai reached to point where getting a large piece of land for warehousing, at a competitive rate, became impossible. The property rates in Solapur were relatively much cheaper than in other cities in India, and it was abundantly available. It was connected by National Highways to the main cities in the region.

The climate was dry, and the rainfall was scanty. The connectivity through railways was also excellent. Semi-skilled and unskilled labor required for packing and loading/unloading was cheaply available.

Creating a Brand for Solapur: The Decision

Identifying and targeting the right audiences and positioning the 'Brand Solapur' in their minds was a must. Supriya was thinking hard on different aspects of brand re-positioning and then branding Solapur. There was consensus, in her team, on developing the city and its brand image as a pilgrimage destination, education, and healthcare hub. The differences were regarding the industries to be attracted for the employment generation. Some thought textiles was not a sunrise industry, and Solapur had lost its attractiveness for it. It was also too competitive. The modern textile industry was using automation and barely any labor. For software and call center industries, Solapur would be a late entrant. The growth in these industries was tapering off. It required specialized and detailed study to identify the sunrise industries suitable for Solapur. Formulating the branding strategy based on past laurels was pointless. A distinct brand position in the minds of investors, tourists, students, and patients was required to be created. Infrastructure and support systems were to be developed for the sun-rise industries. It could be done through the Smart City project. Pre-2000 Solapur city had an identity. By 2016, most of the identities were washed out. The city faced an identity crisis. Solapur was known for nothing. It just remained a railway station on the Mumbai to Chennai/Bangalore/Hyderabad route.' The assistance received under the two major initiatives of the Government of India, 'Make in India' and 'Startup India', was to be leveraged for Solapur. Efforts were required to educate youngsters about entrepreneurship. Citizens sought reasons to be proud of their city. They wanted the 'Brand Solapur' to be created. Smart Solapurkars needed a smart Solapur. They were not fond of migrating for jobs. They wanted to stop the brain drain. They desired a prosperous Solapur. Supriya was thinking about the principles to follow while branding the city, the target groups and their preferences, the brand architecture in case of multiple facets of branding, the brand personality, Logo, slogan, etc. She was also thinking about how to reposition the brand Solapur and how to launch the new brand once the concept gets ready.

Exhibit 1: MAPs - Map of India showing Solapur

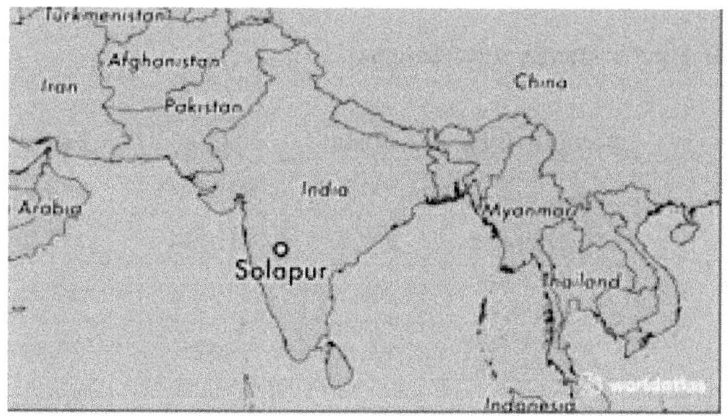

Solapur Shown in the Indian Map

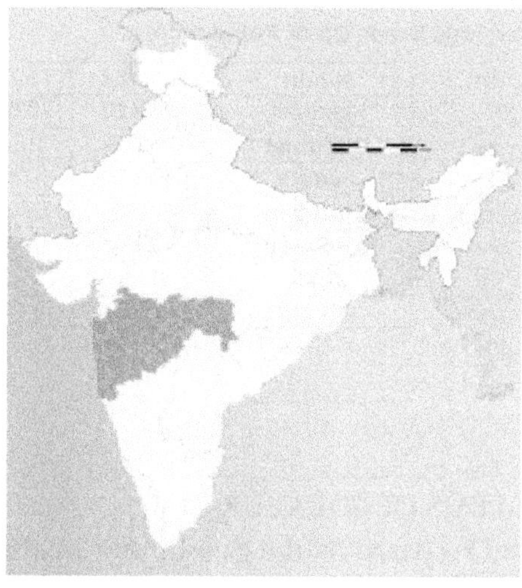

Maharashtra Highlighted in the Indian Map

Exhibit 2: Solapur Population (2011 Census)

Solapur City	Total	Male	Female
City Population	951,558	481,064	470,494
Literates	697,327	380,064	317,263
Children (0-6)	109,360	57,001	52,359
Average Literacy (%)	82.80%	89.62%	75.88%

Source: http://www.census2011.co.in/census/city/383-solapur.html

Exhibit 3: Solapur Religious Break-Up of Population

Exhibit 3: Solapur Religious Break Up of Population

Hindu	720,582	75.73%
Muslims	196,425	20.64%
Buddhist	15,378	1.62%
Jain	9,489	1.00%
Christian	6,993	0.73%
Not Stated	1,830	0.19%
Sikh	613	0.06%
Others	248	0.03%

Source: http://www.census2011.co.in/census/city/383-solapur.html

Exhibit 4: PROBLEMS OF SOLAPUR CITY

Water Shortage: (Prepared by the case author by the information taken from various sources like a research report, Dr. Wadakbalkar, "Drinking water supply schemes for Solapur, Development Problems and Future," newspaper reports, and SMC officials). Up to 1980, Solapur city was supplied water through Ekrukh Lake which was built in 1869 with a capacity of 61.61cubic mm. In 1980, the Ujani dam was constructed to the North West of Solapur city at the distance of 103 km, with a capacity of 332,000 cubic mm. 46% of the water in it is usable through force of gravity, 54% is dead stock, and almost 25% is evaporation loss. This loss was more than the water requirement of Mumbai. Water was supplied to Solapur from 3 main sources Ekrukh dam (20 MLD), Bhima River (70 MLD), and Ujani dam reservoir through a 103 km long pipeline (60 MLD). The total capacity of the water supply was 150 MLD, and it was just enough for the daily consumption of the city.[x] But Ekrukh and Bhima sources dried up in 2015-16 due to a shortfall of rains. The lake is full of mud; the estimated mud there is 2.6 million truck loads. It had accumulated over 90 years. It is being removed to increase the water carrying capacity of the lake. Mud is being given to the farmers as it is a good fertilizer for farms. As of March 2016, the water scarcity of Solapur city had become acute. The Municipal Corporation was supplying water every fifth day. In reality, the citizens were getting 130 MLD of water every day which was good enough for the city for a day. As per the water audit conducted by Smith and Co Bangalore, the water leakages in Solapur were about 30%. This was mainly because of the leakages of underground GI pipes which were laid decades back and required immediate replacement. The capacity of overhead water tanks and other tanks used for storage of water pumped through the Ujani dam pipeline was limited.

Unemployment: (Prepared by the case author by the information taken from various sources like Solapur University, TISS research report, and census data) Getting employment was a problem in Solapur at all levels. Skilled, semi-skilled, and unskilled laborer's lost their jobs because of the crises in textiles, handlooms, power-looms, and bidi industries. There were about 15 engineerings, and architecture colleges in Solapur offering degree and diploma courses and producing 15,000 students a year but no jobs for engineers. They had to either migrate to Pune (the engineering industry hub) or get into the trading business. Those who had family businesses preferred to join them though they were never given an opportunity to apply their engineering knowledge. For 60,000 students graduating out of other courses too, education had no role to play in earning a livelihood. About 150-year-old *beedi* industry, which employed 70,000 home-based women workers, was under threat from imported mini-cigarettes as well as the Anti-Tobacco Law, 2004. The government figures showed a misleading picture. It claimed the unemployment rate as 1.65%, 45% as self-employed, 28% regular salaried, and 27% casual labors (as on 2011-2012). It showed that 28% of people were either in managerial positions or professionals, hardly 2.5% were clerks, 14% worked on farms, 22% were artisans, 13% had primary occupations, 7% sales persons, and 11% plant and machinery operators.

Exhibit 5: Distances of Solapur from Important Markets (Cities) in India

Exhibit 5: Distances of Solapur from Important Markets (Cities) in India

City	Distance from Solapur in Kilometers	City	Distance from Solapur in Kilometers
Pune	236	Surat	675
Hyderabad	309	Indore	700
Nasik	375	Baroda	800
Mumbai	397	Ahmadabad	900
Goa	410	Bhopal	900
Bangalore	620	Chennai	900
Nagpur	630	Raipur	900

(Extracted from Google maps)

Maps showing the connectivity of Solapur with prominent cities in India

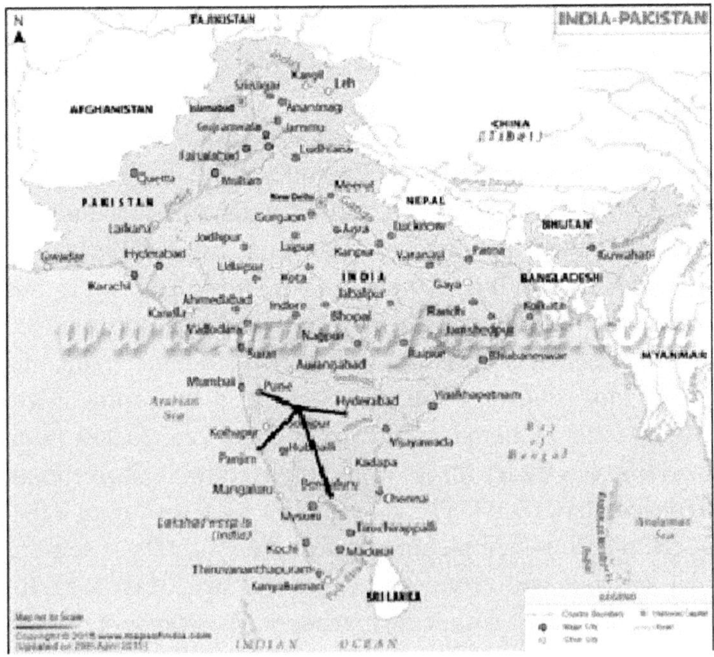

Maps show how Solapur is connected to Mumbai, Bangalore, Hyderabad, Pune, and Goa (Panjim)

References:

[1] https://en.wikipedia.org/wiki/Smart_city
[2] http://www.solapursmartcity.com/
[3] Lalitha Kamath et al, "Uneven Development and Weak Governance…a Case Study of Solapur", Tata Institute of Social Science, Mumbai, May 2013, http://urk.tiss.edu/images/pdf/Case-study-of-Solapur- publication.pdf
[4] A report by reputed consulting firm CRISIL http://jnnurm.nic.in/wp-content/uploads/2014/03/26-Solapur-Draft-Report.pdf
[5] http://urk.tiss.edu/images/pdf/Case-study-of-Solapur-publication.pdf
[6] http://su.digitaluniversity.ac/
[7]http://timesofindia.indiatimes.com/city/pune/Pune-is-sunshine-city-for-medical tourism/articleshow/6966128.cms
[8] http://www.businessinsider.com/india-is-becoming-a-hub-for-medical-tourists-2014-6?IR=T
[9] https://en.wikipedia.org/wiki/Rotterdam
[10] Dr Wadakbalkar, "Drinking water supply schemes for Solapur, Development Problems and Future", http://www.slideshare.net/vadagbalkar/water-supply-of-solapurdrinking-water-supply-schemes-for-solapur-town-development-problems-future-a-review-for-last-125-years-by-dr-vadagbalkar-sk-head-geology-department-dayanand-institutions-solapur-413002-maharashtra-state-india

CHAPTER FOURTEEN

Implementing Smart City Vision: Solapur

It was 28th Jan. 2016. Supriya[1], the Deputy Commissioner of Solapur Municipal Corporation, was waiting in the lobby of Mantralaya, the secretariat of the Maharashtra State Government, situated in the posh South Mumbai area in India, for her seniors. She just got the information that their proposal for 'Smart City' was accepted by the Govt. of India. Solapur became one among just 20 cities in India that got selected in the 'Challenge round' of the smart city project. The entire Solapur city was celebrating the news. Supriya was staring at the vision statement of Solapur city, on her iPhone. "Develop Solapur as a religious center, textile, medical and education hub and improving quality of life for citizens of Solapur by improving public service delivery and governance through smart and sustainable solutions"[1] She used this vision statement during the presentation to the Ministry of Urban Development (MoUD) of the Govt. of India, the previous month. Supriya's worry was how effectively would the great vision be implemented. Was the strategy to implement the smart city project through a quasi-corporate institution, Special Purpose Vehicle (SPV), which was answerable to investors, right? Or should it be implemented through Solapur Municipal Corporation (SMC), which was represented by democratically elected representatives and which was accountable to the citizens who voted for the local governance? She was also not sure whether to opt for the Private Public Partnership (PPP) or to go for soft loans. The implementation of the smart city project was scheduled to start by mid-2016.

Smart Cities Project in India

India is the largest democracy in the world with the youngest population. More than two-thirds of its one billion population was below 35. Young Indians had high aspirations. They wanted a change in the way the government worked. After a decade of rule by the Congress Party, Indians voted them out to bring the change. The world was looking at India to lead in creating economic stability and investing in infrastructure development projects was the right step in that direction. Prime Minister Narendra Modi's election campaign in 2014 focused on creating hope in the minds of young Indians. In 2015, immediately after the change in the Central Government, India started working on the 'Smart City' project. The smart city council of India defines a smart city as one that uses information and communication technologies (ICT) to enhance its liveability, workability, and sustainability. Enhanced liveability means a better quality of life for city residents on a day-to-day basis and during major events or crises. In the smart city, people have access to a comfortable, clean, engaged, interconnected, healthy, and safe lifestyle. Some of the most highly valued aspects include inexpensive energy, convenient mass transit, good schools, faster emergency responses, clean water and air, low crime, and access to quality green spaces, entertainment, and cultural options. Smart cities improve the lives of people today and in the future. Enhanced workability means accelerated economic development. Put another way, it means more jobs and better jobs, and increased local GDP. In the smart city, people have access to the foundations of prosperity — the fundamental infrastructure services that let them compete in the world economy. Those services include clean, reliable, inexpensive energy; broadband connectivity; educational Enhanced sustainability means giving people access to the resources they need without compromising the ability of future generations to meet their own needs. Managing a resource so that it is not depleted or permanently damaged. It refers not only to the environment but also to economic realities.[2] It was a smart way of handling large-scale urbanization and improving the quality of life by meeting the increased needs and expectations of residents with the use of technology. Additionally, local bodies can use Smart City development to increase the efficiency of services offered and reduce their expenses. The focus of the Indian smart city project would be on Liveability, Workability & Sustainability.

Frost & Sullivan's study scanned through Smart City projects globally and found some key parallels. They identified the eight key aspects that define a 'Smart City' as follows: - smart governance, smart energy, smart building, smart mobility, smart infrastructure, smart technology, smart healthcare, and smart citizen. The agency further drew a conclusion, that 'Smart Cities' are those that have at least five out of the eight 'Smart' parameters listed above. Those cities that are only implementing a couple of these are what they define as eco-friendly cities, like Nice in France and Masdar in the UAE. Supriya and her team went through the suggestions provided by citizens in response to a massive campaign for Solapur's vision statement. They formulated a vision statement that was liked by the Govt. of India. Solapur was shortlisted among the 20 cities to be considered for the Smart City Development Project, in the first round.

Implementing the Vision – Developing Appropriate Governance Model

The Government of India wanted to execute the project through a quassi-government body, called 'Special Purpose Vehicle' (SPV). Modi's Government wanted SPV to function like a corporate body rather than a democratically elected local body, with a Chief Executive Officer (CEO) heading the team. They also wanted certain bureaucrats to be on the board of directors whereby ensuring their access to critical information, control, and influence on the key decisions. The State Government and the Municipal Corporation were to contribute equity in SPV. Although the funds provided by the Central Government gave a boost to the Smart City project, options for long-term financing were to be developed.

Understanding the Vision and the difficulties in implementation

A lot of effort had gone into formulating the vision statement for Solapur. It was done in the most democratic way. Time was also a limiting factor due to the deadline of the competition organized by the Government of India. With the given time and resources, Team Solapur did a really good job. However, developing consensus always involves some trade-offs and costs. These compromised areas become problematic during implementation. Generally, such areas were not defined clearly in the vision statement due to paucity of time and lack of clarity of thoughts.

They were subjected to multiple interpretations. It could be done intentionally to facilitate implementation. Vision statement, once formulated and adopted, becomes decree, the bible to swear by. It can't be challenged. There could hardly be any vision statement that did not include a part difficult to implement, particularly when the sentiments and aspirations of the majority of the citizens were given their due share. The analysis of such a grey area in the vision statement and a clear action plan for it were critical for the development of a smart city.

Challenges in Implementation of the Smart City Project in Solapur

There were many challenges in the implementation of the Smart City project in Solapur. The problems were institutional, political, financial, administrative, managerial, and behavioral. Some problems could arise in the short term while others could affect in the long term.

Some felt that the Municipal Corporation went overboard while defining the vision. They encroached on areas where they did not have legitimate governing powers. Certain subjects were beyond the scope of local bodies. It required coordination with Central and State Governments. One such example was working towards economic prosperity. The financial sops were controlled mostly by Central Government and partly by the State Government. Many were not convinced about developing textiles in Solapur. According to their view, certain business cycles were irreversible. Handloom, for example, was a sunset industry. The textile machinery and the processes which were used by mills in Solapur were long due for upgradation. Citizens thought after a long time the government was doing something for their city. They knew many of the promises were difficult to keep but they were certain about improvement in their standard of living.

In short term, they wanted regular water and power supply, a clean/ green city, good roads, and other public amenities. They knew it was not easy to bring back the lost economic glory. It would take quite some time and needed a broader plan with higher resources. (The views expressed here were taken from the suggested documents collected by Solapur Municipal Corporation and available on the website).

Supriya identified some areas which would create friction.

- Accelerated implementation of the Smart City project would be a real challenge in the democratic setup where litigations and local politics could slow down the pace of work.
- The legal, political, and bureaucratic structures in democratic India tend to escalate the total project cost.
- It was important to redefine the role of Solapur Municipal Corporation (SMC). How to take care of the overlaps in the authorities and responsibilities of the SPV and the SMC was the primary issue.

- The Central Government wanted to keep Municipal corporations away to avoid local politics and corruption. They felt the local body was responsible for the misery of Municipal Corporation.

- Corporators of Solapur Municipal Corporation would not agree to share funds without exercising any control on the execution. How to convince the corporators, the elected members who manage SMC, to support the funding to SPV, the body which was not under their clutches was a problem.
- The problem got worse because different political parties were ruling in the state/province (BJP) and in the Solapur Municipal Corporation (INC and NCP coalition). Developing consensus and a 'political will' was a challenge.

- Solapur was very cosmopolitan. Many citizens could speak multiple languages like Marathi, Telugu, Kannada, Urdu, Hindi, and English. More than half of the population spoke a minimum of 3 languages. The city was also known traditionally for communal riots. It was sensitive to rioting between Hindus- Muslim and between high caste- low caste Hindus. People from different communities preferred staying in clusters. This gave them a sense of security. During the elections, many preferred to vote for the candidate from their community and also the political party which had a soft corner for their religion/community/caste. Political parties would field candidates by carefully working out the caste politics. They ensured that they would be politically correct.

Newly developing areas were free of religious clusters. These were dominated by a white collared middle class. Certain professions, businesses, institutions, and even jobs were dominated by certain communities. ***Annexure 1*** gives details.

- The funding would come from different sources like Central Government, State Government, international loans from World Bank/ UN, etc., local bodies, NGOs and charity, taxpayers, government bonds, and many other sources. The implementation team had to take care of all the stakeholders. Managing reporting formats, deadlines, and standards of different agencies and keeping them in good humor needed a high level of managerial skills. Sometimes different stakeholders could have a conflicting interests. Hence, the striking golden mean was a challenge.
- The leader of the team should be acceptable to the politicians, bureaucrats, corporates, and citizens, which demanded good leadership skills. He was required to be young enough to catch up with modern management practices and technology but old enough to demonstrate the maturity required for handling discretionary decisions.
- Maharashtra State Government was burdened with heavy debt and their financial support was critical in the implementation of the smart city project.
- The money to be provided by the Central Government was to be used as seed capital and the real challenge of the project was to raise the funds required. The market forces would determine the merits of the project. Hence, the managing team had to go through the toughest managerial assessment. They would be required to maintain transparency in decision-making.
- The available timeframe and budget were tight. The performance and productivity norms were also challenging. ***Annexure 2*** explains some of the parameters for the performance measurement of Smart Cities.

Given the challenges involved in the execution of the Smart City project, Supriya started looking at the mega projects which had been carried out successfully in India. She was studying the challenges they faced and how they overcame the critical ones. Supriya came across the story of E Sreedharan, the 'Railway Man'. In spite of tough terrain, political hurdles, and limited resources; he constructed 'The Kokan railway' which was not dared even by the British rulers who laid the entire railway system in India.

(***Annexure 3*** covers the story of this successful project of Indian railways.) E Sreedharan also completed Delhi Metro with similar efficiency. These two projects became landmark projects in the history of Indian project management providing a case study. Another project which was carried out effectively in Maharashtra was the 'Mumbai-Pune Express highway' (***Annexure 4*** provides details of this project) Supriya was also looking at how some projects failed and why they failed. A project which failed badly in the 1990s in Maharashtra due to political, economic, ecological, legal, and other problems was 'Dabhol Power Co.' owned by a Fortune 500 American multinational company, Enron. (***Annexure 5***)

Developing Appropriate Financing Model for the Smart City Project

How long does it take? Hong Kong, Singapore, and Chicago took about 50 to 75 years to reach a large and diverse world population. In the modern era, a city can develop a little faster, in 25 to 50 years. UAE government took 25 years to construct a city, like Dubai. By a pure population definition, you could call this a metropolis, but people are mostly immigrants, they aren't really being "of the place" they are occupying. To achieve a unique, metropolitan political and cultural identity, you'll need time for people to be born and raised in the city. People whose only home is the city in question.

How much does it cost to build a smart city?

New cities like Songdo, Dubai, Guangzhou, King Abdullah Economic City (CAEK), and other Asian and Middle Eastern boomtowns have had price tags of roughly $40 billion. Masdar City in Abu Dhabi UAE is being constructed for 45,000 to 50,000 people and is projected to cost almost 20 billion USD by the time of expected completion in 2020-2025. Masdar City will be one of the most sustainable cities in the world.[3] The Government of India has allocated INR 70.6 billion (USD 1.2 billion) for Smart Cities in Budget 2014-15 for developing 100 smart cities over a period of 5 years. The Smart City Mission will be operated as a Centrally Sponsored Scheme (CSS) and the Central Government proposes to give financial support to the mission of INR 480 Billion over five years i.e. on an average of INR 1 Billion per city per year. An equal amount, on a matching basis, will have to be contributed by the State/ULB; therefore, nearly INR 100 billion of Government/ULB funds will be available for Smart Cities development.[4]

The Urban development ministry of India has estimated a cost of approx. $105 billion to develop '100 Smart Cities' over the next 20 years. The ministry thought the cost of building a Smart City is quite high and can be done only through public-private models. The major challenge was financing the project. The state government and SMC could hardly provide budgetary support. The SPV was to take up a fundraising activity. Supriya actively searched for the financing options explored by other Smart cities in the world. Through their management consulting firm, they got information and reports on Chinese, Dutch, and American methods of financing Smart city projects.

Chinese Model[5]

Financing the urbanization in China was worth a study. The funding for urbanization was arranged by local government bodies rather than the central government. The funding was done in the following ways:

- The selling land by local bodies.
- The local governments were allowed to issue public bonds for 3, 5, and 10 years.
- Raising funding through banks
- Public-private partnership (PPP). Laibin Power Plant in Guangxi Province, the first major State-approved BOT in the mid-1990s. It was awarded through international competitive bidding and was a platform for other BOT launches in China. The PPP model was used extensively in the water and wastewater treatment sector.

Amsterdam Model

Among the 26 Smart Cities in the world, Amsterdam had been one of the most forthcoming in the implementation of projects. The projects were in energy, mobility, governance, and so forth. Amsterdam had created a formal channel and mechanism through which such projects could be catalyzed, funded, and implemented. It evolved into a 50:50 public-private model. The model was funded by the EU, city government, and private participants.

American Model

In the US, where municipal bonds have been in the market for the past 120 years, and for Urban Local Bodies (ULBs), the usual accepted method of raising funds was by the way of entering the debt market by the issuance of municipal bonds. In 2009, the US Municipal Bond market was $2.2 trillion. The full potential of the Indian municipal bond market had not been realized. There were a number of constraints like regulatory restrictions on long-term investors such as insurance companies. The market was dominated by banks — who preferred shorter duration assets because of their liability profile. Long-term investors such as pension funds were absent from the bond markets. Since 1947, a mere ? 8.50 billion ($210 million) had been raised through municipal bonds in India. The first municipal bond was issued by Bangalore in 1997. Municipal bonds form nearly 10% of the debt market in the US whereas, in India, Tamil Nadu and Karnataka were the only two states that raised resources through the pooled finance route. The Ahmedabad Municipal Corporation (AMC) had raised ?3.58 billion by 2008 by way of bonds. They raised funds for infrastructure development by the issue of secured redeemable bonds. They issued tax-free bonds worth ?1 billion in the year 2000, ?0.58 billion in the year 2002, and ?1 billion in the year 2005. The AMC instituted many fiscal and management reforms. Improved tax collections, computerization of its accounting system, and strengthening of AMC's workforce were among many. They also worked on financial management and the development of a comprehensive capital improvement program. As a result, by March 1999, the municipal corporation's cash deficit got transformed into a cash surplus of ?2.14 billion.[6] The Indian states in which this model was used showed a greater success rate and a better-organized funding pattern. They had a better success rate in terms of raising timely funds and timely execution of infrastructure projects despite the size of the ULBs balance sheet.

Pooled Financing scheme:In 1996, *the* Tamil Nadu Urban Development Fund was established by the State Government of Tamil Nadu along with Indian financial institutions. A line of credit was provided by the World Bank. It was managed by a private asset management company, Tamil Nadu Urban Infrastructure Financial Services Ltd. They gave in municipal financing in Tamil Nadu without using state government guarantees.

Municipalities, statutory boards, and state-level public sector undertakings were eligible borrowers. The tenor of the loans offered was up to15 years, depending on the nature of the project. Special recovery mechanisms such as escrow accounts of property tax collection, water charges, and hypothecation of movables were used. The debts were blended with the grants to reduce the interest cost. Projects for water supply and sanitation, roads, bridges, streetlights, solid waste plants, bus stations, and shopping complexes were funded. 90 out of 110 municipalities in Tamil Nadu availed finance for about 500 projects.

Global Investment Intentions in the Smart City Project

- Many countries already expressed their intent to invest huge amounts in the smart cities program in India. The UK Government has set a target of 10% for UK ownership of the global Smart Cities market. It was estimated to exceed GBP 900 billion by 2020. The Smart Cities relied on exactly the kind of knowledge-intense, service-oriented sectors that were thriving in the UK.[7]
- Singapore wanted to contribute to the smart city development. They had a strong track record in urban development and infrastructure management.[8] The Singapore minister, while visiting India, offered to help in planning for the Smart City. When they got independence in 1965 from Malaysia, they had to import drinking water. The water management skills of Singapore were worth benchmarking [9]

Lessons from Dholera's Success

Dholera, the first smart city in India was situated 110 kilometers from the Gujarat state capital, Ahmadabad (Prime Minister Modi's home state). There was a focus on attracting foreign direct investment in the Dholera Special Investment Region (SIR). It could generate the funds required for smart city development. This Smart City project was really on the fast track. The project leaders focused on developing and executing a sound marketing strategy for the project which attracted Foreign Direct Investment (FDI). The money which flew in as FDI was boosting the Dholera Smart City project.

Private Investments in Urban Development

Since financing was the major issue, Supriya was also looking for attracting private equity and Foreign Direct Equity (FDI) options. She was impressed with the 'Sarvajal'; a Gujarat-based business that combined old and new technology and financial technologies to provide clean water to people. The model used about 150 franchises. UV purification and reverse-osmosis technologies were used with cloud-based remote monitoring. It provides remotely monitored 'Water ATM". The company spread its operations in 6 states.[10] The ability to use private funds in waste management was very important because it consumed up to 50% of the local body budgets in the developing world. Wen Yibo of Sound Group of China was an Urban Waste entrepreneur. His company operations included the entire supply chain of water treatment, wastewater management, and integrated solid waste capabilities. They managed build-operate-transfer (BOT) and other forms of public-private partnership (PPP). They also created power from the municipal solid waste collected and developed waste to the energy model.

Soft Loans or PPP Which Way to Go?

The financial position of SMC was just next to Detroit Municipal Corporation in the USA. Whether or not they should opt for soft loans was the issue. The majority of citizens were either out of the tax net or were barely paying local taxes. It posed a major challenge in repaying the loans. Supriya was not sure about the repaying capacity of SMC. If the project was to be implemented through a Special Purpose Vehicle (SPV) instead of SMC, they would also not evade the problem. They had to reduce the loan amounts by financing partly through central and state grants. SMC never tried PPP and there were apprehensions because of the recent agitation against toll charges in Maharashtra. PPP would be a cultural shock, particularly to the middle and lower middle class. Citizens expected water, roads, street lights, public health, and waste disposal to be the primary responsibility of the local government and also their lawful right. Those who paid Municipal tax argued against PPP, asking why then the municipal corporation was collecting property tax.

They did not want to pay extra for it. They thought such payment is extra and a penalty charged to them because of the inefficiency of the Municipal Corporation and the political factors behind it. Supriya expected friction to be created in the implementation of PPP where those services would be charged. The vision statement of Solapur Smart City could be analyzed by analyzing its parts and various aspects involved in it. It specified four main areas. The first aspect was economic development for which the areas identified were textiles, religious tourism, healthcare, and education. The other aspects were improving the quality of governance, sustainability, and public service delivery for achieving a better quality of life for the citizens.

- ***Developing textiles:*** The most difficult task was to develop textiles. All the textile mills, having integrated facilities to manufacture fabric from cotton (collected from farms) were closed down. In fact, mega housing project schemes were being developed on the lands on which these mills once stood. Many suppliers and traders who dealt with those mills either closed down those businesses or diversified into related businesses. Hence, there was no question of re-starting those units. Some spinning mills were there and efforts could be made to support them. The ailing handloom and power-loom sectors could also be supported. What could the local body do to support these ailing businesses? The state government had been providing subsidies, tax benefits, and other soaps but it could not be of any help and the businesses met their fate. The relaxation could not be given on rules regarding the treatment of effluents, maintaining the minimum working standards for workers, minimum wages, child labor exploitation, facilities for women employees, etc.

- ***Development of Solapur as a religious center:*** Most of the tourists visited with families for an annual pilgrimage. They preferred to stay at Solapur, travel to Tuljapur, Akkalkot, and Pandharpur in the morning, and come back to Solapur by evening. Covering 3 locations in a weekend was their objective. Long weekends and holidays were preferred. Facilities for travelers who travel from Mumbai and Pune to Solapur were required to be developed. The preferred mode was train travel. It was necessary to increase the capacity and frequency of the trains. The train tickets needed to be booked at least 3 to 4 weeks in advance.

The situation was worse for air-conditioned compartments. Co-ordination with railways was essential to increase the availability of seats. Arranging air-conditioned bus services to Pandharpur, Tuljapur, and Akkalkot was essential. Hotels like bed and breakfast, value motels, and service apartments were simply not there. Travelers did not know what to expect from local hotels since they did not belong to any chain and did not follow standard service practices. Local hotels did not follow the hygiene standards expected by the middle and higher middle class. Smart hotels were badly needed. Travelers reaching Solapur by overnight trains had a tough time getting good transportation from the train station. The auto-rickshaw drivers would exploit the situation and charge high fares. Getting a good breakfast, in the early morning was difficult. Coordination with temple management to provide convenience and hygiene was a priority. The waiting time at temples was too long and people had to stand in queues for long period. No facilities were provided to waiting devotees. Not even clean drinking water and snacks. Those traveling with kids and senior citizens had a tough time. Handicaps were not getting any privileges, even those mandatory by the law. The local tourist attractions were required to be developed. Tourists were worried about how to spend evenings at Solapur after they returned from temples for the night stay. Those who had relatives staying in Solapur hardly realized these problems because of the local support.

- ***Developing Solapur as an Education hub:*** The dream of a local public university was realized in 2004 when the Solapur University was formed under the University Grand Commission (UGC). But the new university was struggling for developing a reputation for excellence in education. It could register around 75,000 students in 119 affiliated colleges but the dream of quality education was a far cry. The problems faced by the university were many lacks of research orientation: Professors became teaching shop. The academic delivery system was unilateral lecturing. Professors questioned the requirement to pursue Ph.D. Those who could complete a Ph.D. considered that as an apex point in their career and did not pursue post-doctoral research. Lack of publications by faculty. In short, there was a lack of scholarship on the part of teachers. There were absolutely no faculty development programs carried out by the colleges.

Students did not see any value in the classroom teaching hence there was poor attendance of students in the classes. Colleges and universities had poor tie-ups with the industry creating a huge gap between education and the industry. There was a lack of life skills training for students in the universities. The university needed the guidance and support of world-class education institutions like American Ivey league Universities like Princeton, Cornell, Columbia, MIT, Wharton, Kellogg, and Booth. Education sector reforms were overdue to achieve excellence.

- ***Developing a Medical Hub:*** This required encouraging corporate hospital chains to open up hospitals in Solapur, inviting foreign direct investment, creating a special 'Medical Zone' by allocating land at competitive prices and creating infrastructure like pure water supply, electricity, and road connectivity. The hospitals in Solapur had to cancel and schedule operations as per the availability of water.
- ***Improving governance through smart and sustainable solutions:*** This part of the vision was comparable with the global definition of a smart city. It was suggested that the use of technology was a must for smart governance. Karnataka state did well in terms of having a progressive MIS system for reforms, projects as well as other initiatives. Annexure 7 gives details of these efforts taken by the state. The vision should also highlight the ecological aspect by asking to develop sustainable solutions for solving the problems of citizens.
- ***Improving the quality of life for citizens of Solapur by improving public service delivery:*** This part of the vision statement clearly highlights the overlap of authority/responsibility of the Solapur Municipal Corporation (SMC) and the Special Purpose Vehicle (SPV), since public service delivery was the function SMC and it was supposed to be committed to it.

The Smart City project was not the first urban development project in India.' Jawaharlal Nehru National Urban Renewal Mission' (JnNURM) was a city-modernization scheme launched by the Government of India under Ministry of Urban Development. It was the first program of its kind and size for urban development. It was launched by the then-Prime Minister, Mr. Manmohan Singh. There were 65 mission cities selected. The central government provided soft loans to Municipal Corporations, on the recommendation of the state government.

A total investment of over $20 billion over seven years was planned. It was started on 3rd December 2005 and was closed in 2014 when the BJP government came to power. ***Annexure 6*** gives some details. Modi's government created a buzz around the Smart city project. The competition among different municipal corporations, a lot of hype created by the media, and active and overwhelming participation by citizens sent it viral. Mr. Narendra Modi kept promising India about '*Ache din aane wale hai*' (good days are coming). He became an icon of hope for young India. Urban India was his main vote bank and he had to return the favor. He did it with great style... Smart Cities. It was too early to comment on the fate of the effort.

Cost of Pace

Formulating the vision was done at a great pace, unusual for the Indian government. The exercise was over within just 100 days. There was a flip side to this commendable achievement. There was a scope for start-ups in tourism, healthcare, and education along with reviving the textiles however the vision statement did not clearly specify the amount and nature of jobs to be created. Where the university graduates would be employed? What will be done to employ engineers who were getting produced in big numbers? What were the steps to curb brain drain? How do develop local trade and businesses? These were the unanswered questions. Agriculture and agro-processing were other areas that remained unaddressed. It was important for those who migrated to Solapur for education and a better standard of living but were still dependent on agriculture in surrounding areas. The development of this sector was important for those who migrated to Solapur for education and a better standard of living but still relied on agriculture in the surrounding areas for their livelihood. The fly ash produced by the thermal power project is used as raw materials in cement manufacturing hence a few cement companies were keen to open factories in Solapur. This opportunity was required to be explored. The British leveraged the location advantage of Solapur for textiles. Other businesses where the location was useful were required to be identified. Developing income of citizens, regular water supply, a clean city, communal harmony, and good governance were the priorities of the citizens of Solapur. They categorically specified these things during the campaign for the defining vision statement. Mr. Modi's dreams for India were on the shoulders of young, bright Indians. Chinese did it during the last two decades with great efforts.

They had their share of problems too. Now, it was the turn of India. If they succeeded they had the potential to take the world out of recession by creating business opportunities worth trillions of dollars. The world was waiting for infrastructure development in India and a consumption wave among the Indian middle class. Meanwhile, in Solapur, the citizens and the planning team were enjoying success. They had reason to celebrate. In spite of all the odds, their city, Solapur, made it to the elite list of the top 20. Supriya, just in her early 30s, had to become a lady who saw the tomorrow. Was she creating history?

Annexure 1: Demographic Details of Solapur

Annexure 1: Demographic Details of Solapur

Religion/Caste	Languages	Areas of the city where clustered residences of this community were found	Businesses/Professions/Jobs dominated traditionally
Muslims	Hindi, Urdu, Marathi	Vijapur Ves, Lashkar	Textile, blue collored/physical labour jobs
Jain, Marwari's	Hindi, Marwari, Gujrathi	Chati Gali, Samrat Chowk, Tilak Chowk	Wholesale, Retail businesses like cloth, garments, building materials, electronics
Ligayats	Kannad, Marathi, Hindi	Bhusar Gali, Tuljapur Ves	Wholesale, Retail businesses of food grains, transport
Padmasalis	Telgu, Marathi, Hindi	Ashok Chowk, Sakhar Peth	Handlooms, Power looms, Bidi
Maratha	Marathi, Hindi	Patra Talim	Agriculture, Politics, government
Lodhis	Lodhi, Hindi, Marathi	Murgi Nala	Construction, Textile
Dalits	Marathi, Hindi	S T Stand, Samarat Chowk, Forest	Blue collored/Physical labour, Construction
Brahmins	Marathi, Hindi, English	Choupad, Vijapur Road	Adademics, Government, Banking
Bhavsar, Kshatriya	kshatriya, Marathi, Hindi	Kanna chowk, Vijapur Ves	Cloth, garment, textiles

(Source: Compiled from various documents)

Annexure 2: *Performance Indicators for Smart City*

The Ministry of Urban Development has adopted National Benchmarks in four key sectors—Water Supply, Sewerage, Solid Waste Management, and Storm Water Drainage. A Handbook was released by the MoUD in 2008-09, the framework of which encompasses the following 28 performance indicators:[11]

WATER SUPPLY

- Coverage of water supply connections
- Per capita supply of water
- The extent of metering of water connections
- The extent of non-revenue water
- Continuity of water supply
- Quality of water supplied
- Cost recovery in water supply services
- Efficiency in the redressal of customer complaints
- Efficiency in the collection of water supply-related charges

WASTEWATER MANAGEMENT

- Coverage of toilets
- Coverage of wastewater network services
- Collection efficiency of wastewater network
- Adequacy of wastewater treatment capacity
- Quality of wastewater treatment
- The extent of reuse and recycling of wastewater
- The extent of cost recovery in wastewater management
- Efficiency in the redressal of customer complaints
- Efficiency in the collection of sewerage-related charges

SOLID WASTE MANAGEMENT

- Household level coverage of SWM services
- The efficiency of collection of municipal solid waste
- The extent of segregation of municipal solid waste
- The extent of municipal solid waste recovered
- The extent of scientific disposal of municipal solid waste

- The extent of cost recovery in SWM services
- Efficiency in the redressal of customer complaints
- Efficiency in the collection of SWM-related user charge

STORMWATER DRAINAGE

- Coverage of stormwater drainage network
- Incidence of water logging/flooding

Annexure 3: Kokan Railway project[12]: It happened in India

The Konkan Railway was the missing link between Maharashtra capital, Mumbai, and Mangalore. The 760-kilometer line connected Maharashtra, Goa, and Karnataka States of India — a region of crisscrossing rivers, plunging valleys, and mountains. E Sreedharan, the project leader, was a retired Indian Railways engineering official. He led a team and constructed a 760 kilometers railway track in the western coastal area of India. Some highlights of this difficult project work:

1. Acquired almost 5000 hectares of land from 43,000 assorted land owners in the 3 different states.
2. Built 2000 Bridges, some major and rest minor, across rivers, backwaters Marshes, and swamps.
3. Dug 92 tunnels, totaling 83 kilometers in length through Basalt, nature's china clay. One would need the power of nuclear weapons to dig basalt while the China clay used to collapse suddenly.
4. Dealt and Negotiated with the Chief Ministers, Home Ministers, Other Ministers of four different states.

And to complete all of the above tasks, Dr. Sreedharan, was given 8 years. He set trend for other infrastructure projects in India, the work provided concrete proof of the skills of Indian engineers, their discipline, team spirit, and courage. It was also a tribute to the unconquerable human spirit. It was a leap of faith that made the long cherished dream of the people of the region possible. The Konkan Railway had also in a way changed the lives of the people associated with the project. Contracts for the Kokan Railway project were awarded to some of the biggest and most reputed construction companies in India, Larsen and Toubro, Gammon India, and AFCONS. Many innovative practices were adopted to enable quicker construction. Piers for major bridges were cast on the riverbanks themselves and launched using cranes. The technique of incremental launching of bridge spans was used for the first time in India. Nine hydraulic tunneling machines were imported from Sweden in order to bore through the hard Basalt rock of the Sahayadris Mountains. The biggest challenge, however, came from the nine tunnels that had to be bored through soft soil. No technology in the world could be of any help for this purpose and the work had to be carried out through a slow manual process which was really painstakingly. Due to the clayey soil that was saturated with water owing to a high water table in the region, excavation was almost impossible. Many times tunnels collapsed immediately after they had been dug requiring work to be redone. Four years were lost while constructing the soft soil tunnels and nineteen lives. Seventy-four people perished during the construction of the Kokan Railway.[13]

Annexure 4: Mumbai – Pune Express Way[14]

The Mumbai Pune Expressway, (Yashwantrao Chavan Mumbai-Pune Expressway) was the first six-lane cement concrete, high-speed, access-controlled expressway in India. There was a toll for using the road. It was 94.5 kilometers (58.7 miles) long and connected Mumbai, the financial capital of India, and the administrative capital of Maharashtra with Pune, an industrial and educational hub.

This six-lane project was completed by the Maharashtra State Road Development Corporation (MSRDC). The cost of the expressway was ₹16.3 billion (US$240 million). The work was over within 4 years. It reduced the travel time between Mumbai-Pune to half, from 4 to 2 hours. From the beginning itself, MSRDC had adopted a very proactive stand towards litigation in the project. There was a realization that litigation could induce substantial delays in the project. The MSRDC could appoint a panel of legal experts for handling cases. Also, there was a policy that the organization would respond to any court order in the fastest possible time. This ensured that the problem of re-seeking appropriate dates was minimized. Political influence was also used to make sure that there would be few legal problems. In addition to this there was a dispute redressal mechanism for contractors, because of which contractors involved themselves in little litigation. During the award of the bid, care had been taken that the contractor did not have a poor history of litigation.[15] The work was divided into 9 parts. Six globally renowned civil engineering consultancy firms along with the best of the construction companies in India (6 of them). The work was accomplished within the given time and budget. It became a hallmark of Indian project management skills along with Kokan Railway and Delhi Metro projects.

Annexure 5: Enron & the Dabhol Power Company

- Thunderbird Case Study
- **Case #:** A07-02-0008
- **Fields:** General Management; Industry and Competitive Strategy
- **Author:** Andrew Inkpen

Abstract:

In September 2001, Houston-based Enron Corporation (Enron) was embroiled in a long-running dispute with various levels of government in India. The dispute involved the Dabhol Power Company (DPC), a 2,184 megawatt (MW) power project in the Indian state of Maharashtra. The dispute began in the mid-1990s. In April 1995, Enron began construction of a $2.8 billion power plant in the state of Maharashtra. In August 1995, the Maharashtrian government announced that the project was canceled based on the recommendations of a committee set up by the government to review the project. After the contract was renegotiated, construction resumed and Phase I was completed in 1999. In 2001, with Phase II of the project 95% complete, Enron announced that it would sell its DPC stake because of payment disputes with its sole buyer, the Maharashtra State Electricity Board (MSEB) and the failure of the Indian central government to honor its counter-guarantee.[16] Critics charged that the power plant threatened the local environment and didn't adhere to government environmental standards. One concern was the safety of importing and storing liquefied natural gas, which is cleaner burning than coal or oil but can emit volatile vapors that can ignite and explode. Other critics said Dabhol could harm local farms and fisheries. Protesters took to the streets to support demands for changes in the plant's design and -- more broadly -- to oppose the Indian government's economic liberalization policies. Social activists, lawyers, villagers, and farmers banded together in groups opposed to the Enron project. The devaluation of India's rupee meant that Dabhol's energy prices would soar to between two and five times the average price.[17]

Annexure 6: Jawaharlal Nehru National Urban Renewal Mission (JnNURM)

The BJP government was planning to continue the scheme but with a few changes and under a different name. It focused on improving the quality of life and infrastructure in Indian cities. JnNURM aimed at creating 'economically productive, efficient, equitable and responsive Cities' by a strategy of upgrading the social and economic infrastructure in cities, provision of Basic Services to Urban Poor (BSUP), and wide-ranging urban sector reforms to strengthen municipal governance. The focus is on serving the urban poor through water supply and sanitation, solid waste management, road network, urban transport, and redevelopment of old city areas. As of 2012, Visakhapatnam, Surat, and Pune had the distinction of having accomplished all 8 city-level reforms. Chennai, Greater Mumbai, and Hyderabad had achieved 7 out of 8 reforms. Out of 67 cities, 30 had achieved the 90% target for property tax collection, 20 had achieved full operation and maintenance cost recovery for water supply and sanitation, and only 8 had achieved cost recovery for solid waste.[18] Under this scheme, 414 projects were given Rs 4.4 Trillion and Maharashtra state got the maximum number of projects. The international consulting firm Grant Thornton audited the mission in 2009.[19]

Annexure 7: MIS Systems in Karnataka – A sample study[20]

A Municipal Reforms Cell (MRC) was created in 2005 under the Directorate of Municipal Administration, Government of Karnataka, exclusively for the implementation of computerization and other reforms in all the Urban Local Bodies (ULBs) of Karnataka. The cell is responsible for the project's complete software development life cycle like understanding requirements, design, development, implementation, verification & maintenance. The task of capacity building and training Municipal staff is also vested with the Cell. The initiative proposes to upgrade all ULBs from the existing manual system to Computer-based systems. This will help ULBs streamline their Municipal systems through process reengineering and the use of IT tools and Technologies, which will bring transparency and ensures smoother delivery of services to the citizens of Karnataka.

It would also bring about better governance in Urban Local Bodies (ULB) through the use of technology and Govt. Process Reengineering. It focuses on creating a robust database of records in various departments like revenue, engineering, accounting, health, etc, and has the day-to-day administration of the ULB based on accurate data, well-defined processes, and more efficient service delivery to citizens by using IT/Communication tools and technologies. A state-level Municipal Data Centre has been established within the Municipal Reforms Cell and a centralized database of all the ULBs is being maintained from it. The ULBs are free from maintaining servers on day to day basis. The Centralized architecture design approach has resulted in easy maintenance of servers. The hub-n-Spoke model allows the scarce few resources to be centralized yet spread the benefits to all cities in the spoke. Centralizing has also allowed for the standardization of formats and processes that automatically drive economies of scale.

Foot Notes: -

[1] The name of the protagonist changed.

2 Indian Administrative Services (IAS), the cadre of top Indian bureaucrats. The best young talent in the country is carefully chosen, after 3 rounds of examination. The selection process is considered one of the toughest in the world. It was developed during the British rule to choose able administrators and was called Indian Civil Services (ICS). Margaret Thatcher mentioned in her autobiography that it was her dream to be an ICS officer but it was too tough for her to clear. Supriya's seniors are IAS officers. They were handpicked by the top leadership and entrusted to the highest power positions to work with the top leadership. Incidentally, they are from Solapur.

References

[1] http://www.solapursmartcity.com/

[2]http://india.smartcitiescouncil.com/article/smart-cities-be-build-substantial-cost

[3]https://www.quora.com/How-much-does-it-cost-to-build-a-small-city-from-scratch

[4] http://www.indjst.org/index.php/indjst/article/download/85418/65635

[5] Thomas Stanley et al, "China's Urbanization: Funding the future", China 360, KPMG report, Dec 2013

[6]http://jnnurm.nic.in/wp-content/uploads/2012/06/Appraisal-of-JnNURM-Final-Report-Volume-I-.pdf

[7] "Business is Great", EY report prepared for UK Trade and Government, Sept 2015

[8] Iswaran, Minister for Industries Singapore, Jan 2015,

http://www.indiantollways.com/category/smart-city/

[9]http://articles.economictimes.indiatimes.com/2014-11-14/news/56093137_1_singapore-model-100-smart-cities-good-decision

[10] https://cb.hbsp.harvard.edu/cbmp/content/sample/R1307B-PDF-ENG

[11] http://jnnurm.nic.in/wp-content/uploads/2012/06/Appraisal-of-JnNURM-Final-Report-Volume-I-.pdf

[12]http://kaipullai.com/2012/02/24/dr-elattuvalapil-sreedharan

[13]https://en.wikipedia.org/wiki/Konkan_Railway

[14]https://en.wikipedia.org/wiki/Mumbai_Pune_Expressway

[15] Amrut Nashikkar et al, "The Mumbai-Pune Expressway- a Case study",

http://www.iitk.ac.in/3inetwork/html/reports/IIMStudReport2000/mpecase1.pdf

[16]http://caseseries.thunderbird.edu/case/enron-dabhol-power-company

[17] Sam Parry, 'Enron's India Disaster', 30 Dec 2001.

https://consortiumnews.com/2001/123001a.html

[18]https://en.wikipedia.org/wiki/Jawaharlal_Nehru_National_Urban_Renewal_Mission

[19]http://jnnurm.nic.in/wp-content/uploads/2012/06/Appraisal-of-JnNURM-Final-Report-Volume-I-.pdf

[20] Final Report for the Appraisal of Jawaharlal Nehru Urban Renewal Mission (JnNURM), Grant Thornton, March 2011, pp170. http://jnnurm.nic.in/wp-content/uploads/2012/06/Appraisal-of-JnNURM-Final-Report-Volume-I-.pdf

www.ingramcontent.com/pod-product-compliance
Ingram Content Group UK Ltd.
Pitfield, Milton Keynes, MK11 3LW, UK
UKHW021905190726
13853UKWH00002B/523

9 798888 051115